CW01521378

The Åland Strait

International Straits of the World

Series Editor

Nilufer Oral

VOLUME 18

The titles published in this series are listed at *brill.com/insw*

The Åland Strait

By

Pirjo Kleemola-Juntunen

BRILL

NIJHOFF

LEIDEN | BOSTON

Library of Congress Cataloging-in-Publication Data

Names: Kleemola-Juntunen, Pirjo, author.
Title: The Aland strait / by Pirjo Kleemola-Juntunen.
Description: Leiden ; Boston : Brill Nijhoff, 2019. | Series: International
   straits of the world ; Volume 18 | Based on author's thesis (doctoral -
   University of Lapland, 2014) issued under title: Passage rights in
   international law : a case study of the territorial waters of the ?Aland
   Islands. | Includes bibliographical references and index.
Identifiers: LCCN 2019010106 (print) | LCCN 2019010679 (ebook) | ISBN
   9789004364189 (ebook) | ISBN 9789004364172 (hardback : alk. paper)
Subjects: LCSH: ?Aland (Finland)--International status. | Bothnia, Gulf
   of--International status. | Innocent passage (Law of the sea) |
   Territorial waters--Finland--?Aland. | ?Aland question.
Classification: LCC KZ4214 (ebook) | LCC KZ4214 .K564 2019 (print) | DDC
   341.4/20948972--dc23
LC record available at http://lccn.loc.gov/2019010106

Typeface for the Latin, Greek, and Cyrillic scripts: 'Brill'. See and download: brill.com/brill-typeface.

ISSN 0924-4867
ISBN 978-90-04-36417-2 (hardback)
ISBN 978-90-04-36418-9 (e-book)

Copyright 2019 by Koninklijke Brill NV, Leiden, The Netherlands.
Koninklijke Brill NV incorporates the imprints Brill, Brill Hes & De Graaf, Brill Nijhoff, Brill Rodopi,
Brill Sense, Hotei Publishing, mentis Verlag, Verlag Ferdinand Schöningh and Wilhelm Fink Verlag.
All rights reserved. No part of this publication may be reproduced, translated, stored in a retrieval system,
or transmitted in any form or by any means, electronic, mechanical, photocopying, recording or otherwise,
without prior written permission from the publisher.
Authorization to photocopy items for internal or personal use is granted by Koninklijke Brill NV provided
that the appropriate fees are paid directly to The Copyright Clearance Center, 222 Rosewood Drive, Suite
910, Danvers, MA 01923, USA. Fees are subject to change.

This book is printed on acid-free paper and produced in a sustainable manner.

Contents

     Appendix 1   157
     Appendix 2   158
     Bibliography   159
     Index   172

Acknowledgements

I have been fortunate to be given a chance to work as a Post-doc researcher on the research project 'Demilitarisation in an increasingly militarised world – International perspective in a multilevel framework: the case of the Åland Islands' led by Director, Jur.dr. Docent Sia Spiliopoulou Åkermark from the Åland Islands Peace Institute. The three-year long research project (April 2015 – March 2018) was funded by the Kone Foundation and also received contributions from the Åland Culture Foundation, *Ålands kulturstiftelse*. The project grant was awarded to the project for being a 'bold' initiative. The research project was a co-operation between the Åland Islands Peace Institute (ÅIPI) and the University of Lapland and its Arctic Center in Rovaniemi (Finland). The present book is a revised and updated version of a part of my doctoral thesis and forms part of the outcomes of the project along with several other books and articles. I also wish to thank my colleagues during various stages of the project; Research Professor Timo Koivurova, Dr. Saila Heinikoski, Reseacher Filip Holiençin and Researcher Yannick Poullie. The Northern Institute for Environmental and Minority Law (NIEM) assisted financially with the publication of this book, particular thanks are due to the Research Professor, Director Kamrul Hossain.

I would also like to thank project's interdisciplinary scientific board: Matthieu Chillaud, Lauri Hannikainen, Kenneth Gustavsson, Päivi Kaukoranta, Said Mahmoudi, Allan Rosas, Gregory Simons, Geir Ulfstein and the late Alyson Bailes (2016), succeeded by Willy Østreng, whose knowledge I have benefited.

The warmest expression of gratitude, as always, goes to my husband Asko, daughter Karoliina and son Henri.

Pirjo Kleemola-Juntunen
Rovaniemi, July 2018

Abbreviations

COLREGS	International Regulations for Preventing Collisions at Sea
DW	Deep water
EEZ	Exclusive Economic Zone
EU	European Union
ICAO	International Civil Aviation Organization
ICJ	International Court of Justice
ILA	International Law Association
ILC	International Law Commission
ILM	International Legal Materials
IMO	International Maritime Organization
ITLOS	International Tribunal for the Law of the Sea
LNTS	League of Nations Treaty Series
LOSC	United Nations Convention on the Law of the Sea
MARPOL	International Convention for the Prevention of Pollution from Ships
NATO	North Atlantic Treaty Organization
PCIJ	Permanent Court of International Justice
PCTS	Parry Consolidated Treaty Series
SOLAS	International Convention for the Safety of Life at Sea
TSC	Convention on the Territorial Sea and the Contiguous Zone
TSS	Traffic Separation Scheme
UN	United Nations
UNGA	United Nations General Assembly
UNTS	United Nations Treaty Series
US	United States

CHAPTER 1

The Åland Islands and the Åland Strait Region

The Åland Islands are located between Finland and Sweden. The Islands are a self-governing, demilitarised and neutralised area under Finnish sovereignty, this status initially granted by the 1921 Åland Convention.[1] They extend from the coast of Finland to more than halfway across the mouth of the Gulf of Bothnia as it opens to the Baltic Sea. The main island is called 'Åland mainland', and the eastern part of this area, consisting of small islands, are collectively called 'the archipelago'. The total extent of the Province of Åland is 13,324 km², including the land and surrounding sea areas; most of the area consists of water (roughly 80%), of which 11,740 km² is sea. Nowadays there are around 28,500 inhabitants on the islands, of which around 11,300 people reside in Mariehamn (in Finnish: *Maarianhamina*). The Åland Islands were demilitarised for the first time in 1856, after the Crimean War. Since 1921 the area is also now a neutral zone.

The waters separating the Islands from the Finnish mainland are shallow and therefore the passage is not easy to navigate. Prior to the 1809 Peace Treaty of Fredrikshamn, the Gulf of Bothnia was regarded as Swedish inland sea, but today west of the Åland Islands, the Finnish and Swedish territorial waters meet. Finland and Sweden also have a land border in the area, within the strait on Märket Reef (MR). There is a deep-water passage as well as open sea between the Åland Islands and Sweden. The open waters area in the Åland Sea is about 40 km in breadth and the passageway between the Baltic Sea and the Gulf of Bothnia is an international strait referred to as the 'Åland Strait' (in Finnish: *Ahvenanrauma*, in Swedish *Södra Kvarken*), located within the Åland

---

1 Convention relating to the Non-Fortification and Neutralisation of the Åland Islands, adopted 20 October 1921 entered into force 6 April 1922, Finnish Treaty Series 1/1922; English translation available in 17 Am. J. Int. Law Supplement: Official Documents 1–6 (1923), Hereinafter the '1921 Åland Convention'; Treaty concerning the Åland Islands between Finland and the Union of Soviet Socialist Republics, adopted 11 October 1940 entered into force 11 October 1940, Finnish Treaty Series 24/1940; Reactivation of the Treaty concerning the Åland Islands between Finland and the Union of Soviet Socialist Republics, adopted 10 February 1947 entered into force 17 April 1948, Finnish Treaty Series 9/1948, Peace Treaty with Finland, adopted on 10 February 1947 entered into force 15 September 1947, Finnish Treaty Series 19–20/1947: English translation available in 42 Am. J. Int. Law Supplement: Official Documents 203–223 (1948).

© KONINKLIJKE BRILL NV, LEIDEN, 2019 | DOI:10.1163/9789004364189_002

Sea and its width measured at its narrowest point is no more than 6 nautical miles.

It is also important to mention that the border at Märket Reef is also the border of the demilitarised and neutralised zone, due the fact that the Swedish half is outside of the Convention. The main route through the strait is located between the Understen islet on the Swedish side and the Märket Reef. Eastward of Märket Reef the strait belongs to Finnish internal waters and is demilitarised and neutralised by the terms of the 1921 Convention. Thus, there does not exist through the Åland Strait a high-seas route or a route through an Exclusive Economic Zone (EEZ).[2]

The Åland Strait serves as a route for the bulk of the Swedish and Finnish shipping trade and the Strait is one of the chokepoints in the Baltic Sea. The strategic importance of the Åland Islands rests in their geographic position. From the Åland Islands it is possible to block the entrance to the Gulf of Bothnia or to threaten shipping in the northern Baltic Sea. Due to its crucial geographical position, the area can be either a threat to Finland and Sweden or a basic element in their defence. The significance of the Åland Islands to Sweden illustrates the active role of Sweden in the demilitarization of the Åland Islands, which was premised on the basis of Swedish security claims.[3] Although the Åland Islands and the Åland Strait represent a minor part of the Baltic Sea and the Northern Europe, the object and purpose of demilitarisation and neutrality should be seen within this larger context.

Passage through the Åland Strait is fundamentally different from transit through the straits connecting oceans as there has never been an international waters area in the Åland Strait where foreign vessels enjoy freedom of passage. Foreign vessels do not need the Gulf of Bothnia for passage to enter another sea or ocean. To reach the ocean, passage through the Åland Strait is most important for Sweden and Finland, as the only coastal states of the Gulf of Bothnia. The issue that makes passage in the territorial waters of the Åland Islands international is the international legal framework that demilitarises

---

2   Charles Noble Gregory, *The Neutralization of the Aaland Islands*, 17 Am. J. Int. Law 63–76, 65 (1923); Holger Rotkirch, *The Demilitarization and Neutralization of the Aland Islands: A Regime 'in European Interests' Withstanding Changing Circumstances*, 23 J. Peace Res. 357–376, 359 (1986); Sia Spiliopoulou Åkermark, Saila Heinikoski & Pirjo Kleemola-Juntunen, *Demilitarisation and International Law in Context: The Åland Islands* 48–49 (2018); Pirjo Kleemola-Juntunen, *Straits in the Baltic Sea: What Passage Rights Apply?*, in *Regulatory Gaps in Baltic Sea Governance* 21–44, 34 (Henrik Ringbom ed., 2018). More information about the Åland Islands see official homepage http://www.aland.ax [last access 24.3.2018].
3   Anders Gardberg & Kate Törnroos, *Åland Islands: A Strategic Survey* 17–18, 19 (1995).

and makes neutral not only the Åland Islands but the surrounding area of the sea. In addition to the demilitarised and neutral special status, the Province of Åland enjoys political and cultural self-governance, granted in 1920, and is currently regulated by the self-government of Åland Act of 1991, which entered into force in 1993.[4]

---

4 Rotkirch, *supra* note 2 at 358; Allan Rosas, *The Åland Islands as a Demilitarised and Neutralised Zone*, in *Autonomy and demilitarisation in international law: the Åland Islands in a Changing Europe* 23–40, 23 (Lauri; Hannikainen & Frank Horn eds., 1997). Act on the Autonomy of Åland, Statutes of Finland 1144/1991.

CHAPTER 2

Historical Background

1 Pre-World War I Era

Until the 1809 Peace Treaty of Fredrikshamn (in Finnish: *Hamina*), Finland was part of Sweden and the Åland Islands a part of the Finnish administration. Thus, both coasts of the Gulf of Bothnia were Swedish territory and the Gulf of Bothnia was an inner sea. As a result of the 1808–1809 war between Sweden and Russia, Finland separated from Sweden, and joined Russia. The development of the Åland Strait regime followed the development of the Åland Islands regime. The Åland Islands, already incorporated within the Finnish provinces of Åbo and Björneborg, joined the split from Sweden.

This was not the first time that Åland had become a part of Russia. The Islands had been occupied by Russia twice during the 18th century due to two wars between Sweden and Russia. In 1714 Russia defeated a Swedish navy detachment at Hangö udd (in Finnish: *Hankoniemi*) and occupied the islands. The occupation of the Åland Islands allowed the Russian army to raid the Swedish coast. The Great Northern War lasted until 1721 and concluded with the Peace Treaty of Nystad (in Finnish: *Uusikaupunki*), putting an end to the Russian occupation. Peace between Sweden and Russia only lasted about twenty years, after which another war broke out between Sweden and Russia from 1742–1743. This shorter war concluded with the Peace Treaty of Åbo (in Finnish: *Turku*), which allowed another Russian occupation of the Åland Islands.[1]

Finland's final separation from Sweden happened after the 1808–1809 war and the 1809 Peace Treaty of Fredrikshamn, during which time Finland was conquered by Russia. After this period a new strategic position was affirmed by Sweden, namely that Finland and the Åland Islands, as a part of Russia, constituted a threat to Swedish sovereignty. At the time of peace negotiations Sweden had attempted to retain the Åland Islands, but her diplomatic efforts

---

1 Gregory in Chapter 1 note 2 at 66; Rotkirch in Chapter 1 note 2 at 359–360; Tapani Mattila, *Meri maamme turvana, Suomen meripuolustuksen vaiheita Ruotsin vallanaikana* 38–51 (1983); Arvo Komulainen, *Taistelu Ahvenanmaasta, Oolannin iäisyyskysymys* 13–15 (2005); Pertti Luntinen, *The Imperial Russian Army and Navy in Finland 1808–1918* 20 (1997); Kenneth Gustavsson, *Ålandsöarna – en säkerhetsrisk? Spelet om den demilitariserade zonen 1919–1939* 15 (2012).

© KONINKLIJKE BRILL NV, LEIDEN, 2019 | DOI:10.1163/9789004364189_003

fell upon deaf ears. Sweden also proposed the non-fortification of the Islands but this, too, was rejected by Russia.[2]

After the Peace of Fredrikshamn, Russia took precautions to reinforce its permanent occupation of the Åland Islands. This initiative included the construction of a fortress in Bomarsund on Åland mainland. Work on the Bomarsund fortress began in the early 1830s; however, only 3 of the 12 defence towers were completed before the war broke out. The Oriental War (later known as the Crimean War) broke out in 1854 and signified a great misfortune for the Bomarsund fortress, which was still under construction. During the war, France and Great Britain were allied with Turkey. Both of their naval and land forces successfully destroyed Bomarsund and took control of the Åland Islands in a joint effort. As a result of the Crimean War and the demolition of Bomarsund, a discussion ensued in Sweden over whether Finland should be returned to Sweden. Further to this discussion, France and Great Britain suggested that Sweden should be granted sovereignty over Åland. However, Sweden had stabilised its relations with Russia in 1812 when it restated its position as a neutral country and declared itself neutral in 1854. If Sweden had then occupied the Åland Islands the country would have been at risk of compromising its neutral status and King Oscar I recognised this.[3]

Although choosing neutrality instead of occupying Åland, Sweden had not given up on the idea of regaining the islands. When King Oscar I first heard about the peace negotiations, he had pressured Britain and France into adovcating that the islands should be restored to Sweden. The second alternative was to declare Åland an independent, neutral State under the collective guarantee of France, Britain and Sweden. Nonetheless, Sweden's claim for sovereignty over Åland only drew support from Great Britain, while Russian opposition and a lack of support from France meant that Sweden was obliged to give up these efforts. The outcome of the peace negotiations, held in Paris

---

2   Lage Staël von Holstein, *Sverige och Åland* 4 (1916); Gregory in Chapter 1 note 2 at 66; R.C.S. Hamburger, *Twee Rechtsvragen aangaande Finland: de demilitarisatie der Alandgroep en de autonomie van Oost-Kareleie* 19 (1925); J.O. Söderhjelm, *Démilitarisation et neutralisation des Iles d'Aland en 1856 et 1921* 86 (1928); Norman J Padelford & K Gosta A Andersson, *The Aaland Islands Question*, 33 Am. J. Int. Law 465–487, 466 (1939); Rotkirch in Chapter 1 note 2 at 359–360; Komulainen, *supra* note 1 at 15–18; Gustavsson, *supra* note 1 at 15. Peace Treaty of Fredrikshamn available at https://histdoc.net/history/fr/frhamn.html [last access 24.3.2018].

3   Padelford and Andersson, *supra* note 2 at 467; Martin Isaksson, *Kring Bomarsund* 67–68, 72, 177–179 (1981); Rotkirch in Chapter 1 note 2 at 359–360; Graham Robins, *Bomarsund: Imperiumin etuvartio* 15 (2004); Komulainen, *supra* note 1 at 19–21; Gustavsson, *supra* note 1 at 15–16.

on 30th March 1856, was that Great Britain, France and Russia had agreed to a Convention which demilitarised the Åland Islands.

Sweden was not party to the Convention since it did not take part in the Peace Conference. However, Sweden did achieve two goals: first, to assist Great Britain and France in weakening Russia's geopolitical position in the region; and second, to secure Swedish timber imports from the Gulf of Bothnia during times of war. This Convention was annexed to the 1856 Paris Peace Treaty despite strong resistance by Russia. The Paris Peace Treaty ended the Crimean War and as part of the Treaty the 1856 Convention became binding for Austria, Prussia (Germany), Sardinia (Italy) and the Ottoman Empire (Turkey), who had also been parties to the Treaty. The 1856 Convention on demilitarisation consists of two articles and is often referred as to the Åland Islands' 'servitude'.[4] This means that the regulation is unchangeable despite possible changes to the islands' ownership. The 1856 Convention is short and only covers demilitarisation. There is no clear definition in the Convention regarding the territory to which it is applied to. However, Article 1 of the 1856 Convention refers to the islands of Åland and has therefore only been applied to this specific land area. Thus, it is still possible for military operations to be carried out within the waters of Åland's archipelago. The 1856 Convention is also silent regarding defence arrangements during times of war. Additionally, Russia had interpreted the 1856 Convention to mean that it permitted them to build radio stations for military purposes as well as establishing impermanent fortifications there. Russia held that the demilitarisation obligation only applied during peace time and for this reason the islands' fortification should be allowed during times of armed conflict.[5]

---

4   Holger Rotkirch, *A Peace Institute on the War-Path: The Appilication of the Treaty on Open Skies to the Neutralized and Demilitarized Åland Islands and the Powers of the Åland Autonomy*, in *Nordic Cosmopolitanism – Essays in International Law for Martti Koskenniemi* 61–88, 65 (Jarna Petman & Jan Klabbers eds., 2003); Gustavsson, *supra* note 1 at 16. In the case of the Åland Islands 'servitude' means that regulation is permanent and is not allowed to be altered if ownership over the Islands were to change.

5   Padelford and Andersson, *supra* note 2 at 467–468; Erik Castrén, *Ahvenanmaan linnoittamattomuus ja neutralisointi*, Lakimies 255–273, 258 (1939); Tore Modeen, *De folksrättliga garantierna för bevarandet av Ålandsöarnas nationella karaktär* (1973); Rotkirch in Chapter 1 note 2 at 260–261; Isaksson, *supra* note 3 at 188–190; Christer Ahlström, *Demilitarised and Neutralized Zones in a European Perspective*, in *Autonomy and demilitarisation in international law: the Åland Islands in a changing Europe* 41–56, 51–52 (Lauri Hannikainen & Frank Horn eds., 1997); Komulainen, *supra* note 1 at 19–21. The intention of Great Britain when it suggested demilitarisation might have also been to prolong and intensify the Crimean War, as Graham Robins has pointed out in his speech 'Fred som provocation on the Demilitarisation' Day of Åland 30th March 2006, referred to by Sia Spiliopoulou Åkermark, *Åland's Demilitarisation and Neutralisation: Continuity and Change*, in *The Åland Example and Its*

Although the 1856 Convention was considered as a limitation to its sovereign rights, as well as prejudicial to its interests, Russia had unwillingly agreed to the demilitarisation of the Åland Islands. Russia therefore felt obliged to comply with the 1856 Convention throughout the nineteenth century. However, events in the middle of the first decade of the twentieth century had made Sweden more reliant on the Baltic region.[6] After this course of events Russia believed that it was time to renegotiate the situation in the Scandinavian Peninsula, as established by the treaties drawn up after the Crimean War. Russia's intention was to detach itself from its demilitarisation obligations and sent its warships along with 750 men to the Åland Islands in 1906. The force's task was to stop smuggling and to prevent the Åland Islands from being used by revolutionaries as an escape route to Sweden. Russia believed that these activities were desirable in order to maintain internal order. As a result of their deployment, the British Parliament questioned Russia's actions but came to the conclusion that they had not acted in violation of the 1856 Convention. Although there was no official protest, Russian was reminded of the Islands' status. The troops were later withdrawn the same year leaving only 30 men to maintain the new wireless telegraph station in Prästö. Russia approached Germany the following year, asking for their support in abrogating the 1856 Convention, and on 29th October 1907 a secret convention was signed between the two states in St. Petersburg in order to preserve the *status quo* within the Baltic region. Additionally, Russia and Germany agreed to an abolition of 'servitude' towards the Åland Islands, provided that Sweden agreed to it.[7]

Russia's efforts to effect an abrogation of the 1856 Convention ensued. The status of the Convention was also vital for Sweden, especially in consideration of views suggesting that the status of the Åland Islands should be modified

---

Components – Relevance for International Conflict Resolution 50–71, 55, fn 197 (Sia Spiliopoulou Åkermark ed., 2011). See also Graham Robins, *Bomarsund och fredsavtalet i Paris. Fred som Provokation, Åland – fredens öar? Seminarium 19 Oktober 2006, Ålands Landskapsregering.* 12 (2007).

6   These events being the breakup of the Swedish–Norwegian union and defeat of Russian fleet against Japanese in 1905. The Anglo–French Treaty of Guarantee was also terminated, which was made between Great Britain, France and Sweden in 1855 during the ongoing Crimean War. According to this Treaty, Great Britain and France guaranteed the Swedish–Norwegian territories against a Russian attack. Rotkirch in Chapter 1 note 2 at 361.

7   Padelford and Andersson, *supra* note 2 at 368; Martin Isaksson, *Ryska positionen Alandskaja. En översikt av Ålands militära historia åren 1906–1918* 19–24 (1983); Maximilian Boeck, *Die Alandsfrage* 17–18 (1927); Erik Sjöstedt, *La Question des Iles d'Aland* 23 (1919); Raymond Boursot, *La Question des Iles d'Aland* 47–49 (1923); James Barros, *The Aland Islands Question: Its Settlement by the League of Nations.* 12–14 (1968); Söderhjelm, *supra* note 2 at 123; Rotkirch in Chapter 1 note 2 at 361; Gustavsson, *supra* note 1 at 17.

in connection with the Baltic question. Thus, from Sweden's point of view there was a danger that interested States such as Great Britain or Germany might agree to the abrogation of the Convention if it were to benefit their strategic interests. Russia's submission was unveiled to public scrutiny and as a consequence, there was expressly strong opposition to the plan in Britain and Sweden. Thereafter it was politically impossible to abrogate the 1856 Convention. After negotiations between Germany, Denmark, Russia and Sweden were concluded in 1908, the resulting Baltic Declaration confirmed the territorial *status quo* within the Baltic region but did not abolish previous restrictions imposed upon Russian sovereignty over the Åland Islands. Britain and France were not signatories to the Declaration.

Russia's change of Foreign Minister put an end to negotiations concerning the Åland Islands question because the opinion of the new Foreign Minister, Sergei Sazonov, was contradictory to previous views held by the former Foreign Minister, Alexander Petrovich Isvolsky. Sazonov's opinion was that it was not necessary to fortify the islands during peace time and that it was not difficult to defend the islands during wartime. He also believed that fortifying the islands would encourage Sweden to ally with Germany.[8]

2   During the First World War

The First World War broke out on 1st August 1914 and soon reached the Åland Islands. The 1856 Convention demilitarised the islands but did not mention anything about its means of defence. Germany was active in the Northern Baltic Sea at the end of 1914 and its submarines navigated within the Gulf of Bothnia. As a party to the Paris Peace Treaty, Germany was bound by the provisions of the 1856 Convention.[9]

Russia was under the impression that Germany's active presence posed a threat to the Åland Islands and its surrounding area. The possibility that the islands could be occupied by Germany was a great threat, thought to have a chance of taking place either during the winter or early spring of 1914–1915. The islands constituted an ideal operations base for submarines and other naval vessels, and thus Germany would be in a position to control navigation within

---

8   Declaration on the Subject of the Maintenance of the Status Quo in the Territories Bordering Upon the Baltic, available at 2 Am. J. Int. Law, no. 3, Supplement: Official Documents, 270–272 (1908); Padelford and Andersson, *supra* note 2 at 468; Isaksson, *supra* note 7 at 25–31; Rotkirch in Chapter 1 note 2 at 361–362; Komulainen, *supra* note 1 at 21–22.
9   Barros, *supra* note 7 at 21; Isaksson, *supra* note 7 at 47.

the Gulf of Bothnia. This kind of situation would have been disadvantageous for Russia and would have also had a negative impact on commercial relations between Russia and Sweden. Russia informed Sweden that it was prepared to undertake military measures due to German activities but explained that the character of such measures would be solely defensive. Sweden informed Russia that it did not oppose military measures in defence of the Åland Islands; in fact Sweden approved of any action taken to secure maritime commerce between the two states.[10] Russia's allies at the time, namely Britain and France, were not contacted at this stage but probably acted in silent agreement over the fortification of the Åland Islands in spite of the 1856 Convention. As a result, the fortification work was extensive and by the end of the war the area was developed into an enormous fortress.[11]

A German assault took place during August 1915 at Utö in the Archipelago but was turned back after a brief skirmish.[12] After this event took place, questions regarding the status of the islands became of topical interest in the Swedish press. Discussion in the media also touched upon possible Swedish retaliation if German troops were to occupy the area. There was a public outcry when the truth regarding the fortification of the Åland Islands became public knowledge, i.e. that it had been ongoing since the beginning of 1915. Various protests took place in Sweden when the idea of joining the war on Germany's side was proposed, since this would have led to the renunciation of neutrality. This possibility was also noted by the Entente Powers. Negotiations on the status of the Åland Islands were conducted between Sweden and Russia. This process finally peaked when an interpellation was made by the Swedish Parliament (the *Riksdag*) in May 1916.[13] The course of events activated Britain and France,[14] who suggested that Russia should make a public statement to inform people that the Åland Islands' fortifications were impermanent, built only to protect Russia against Germany, and would be destroyed as soon as conflict was over. Britain and France would also agree to validate such a statement since, given that both were signatories to the 1856 Convention, they would be in a position to confirm that the Åland Island's status was legitimate.[15]

---

10   Barros, *supra* note 7 at 22–23; Gustavsson, *supra* note 1 at 18.
11   Rotkirch in Chapter 1 note 2 at 362; Gustavsson, *supra* note 1 at 18.
12   Isaksson, *supra* note 7 at 62–64.
13   Barros, *supra* note 7 at 34–36.
14   The Entente Powers (Britain, France and Russia) considered that it was in their interest to do everything possible to avoid armed conflict with Sweden. Barros, *supra* note 7 at 35–37.; Rotkirch in Chapter 1 note 2 at 362–363.
15   Barros, *supra* note 7 at 37; Rotkirch in Chapter 1 note 2 at 363.

After negotiations had taken place between three of the Parties to the 1856 Convention (i.e. Britain, France and Russia), the Czar accepted an invitation to provide an official statement to the Swedish Government. The statement was intended to ensure that when the war was over the Åland Islands would be non-fortified during peacetime, on the condition that the Swedes remained neutral during present hostilities. It is worth mentioning that there was no explicit reference made to the 1856 Convention. Also noteworthy is that Britain and France both had similar intentions of giving similar statements to the Swedish Government at the same time. However, these statements were never made, since Russia had been informed that Sweden was willing to accept less than Russia was prepared to give her. Instead of providing the above-mentioned statement, Russia gave Sweden a statement of a different kind, explaining the reasons for fortifying the Åland Islands and stressing that Russian motives were of a defensive type which were only applicable during present hostilities.[16]

It was obvious that the Åland question was of 'vital importance' to Sweden, in the sense that many recognised that the war had created a new situation for Sweden. Sweden realised that any questions related to the Islands should be negotiated directly and formally with Russia. Sweden took the initiative in most discussions, with Russia often responding positively to suggestions, especially when they concerned the post-war period. In the meanwhile, Russia had not forgotten its ambition to release itself from restrictions imposed by the 1856 Convention.[17]

To attain this goal, Russia needed support from Great Britain and France. It was agreed, for example, that the threat along the frontiers between France and Germany was to be resolved by Russia in its support for France. At the time of this proposal, the war was fully engaged and France was afraid that if it favoured the release of Russia from its 1856 Convention obligations, then Sweden might ally with Germany. For that reason, France did not give any clear answer to Russia. French foreign policy would also influence Britain's position. Sweden had its suspicions and doubts regarding Russia's intentions, so its contact with Germany was of particular importance, especially when the status of the Åland Islands was concerned. Germany wanted to contribute to Sweden's cause, even by proposing that the islands should return to Sweden after the war. However, remaining neutral was such an important issue for Sweden that it felt it could never relinquish its status. Another option was to make the islands properly neutral, by drawing up an agreement between Germany, Russia

---

16   Barros, *supra* note 7 at 37–52; Rotkirch in Chapter 1 note 2 at 363.
17   Barros, *supra* note 7 at 52–55; Rotkirch in Chapter 1 note 2 at 363.

and Sweden. Such a neutralisation would have put additional strain on the Swedish army and navy because neutralisation would have been entrusted to units of the Swedish army and navy. After the Bolshevik seizure of power, Germany suggested that it would be able to occupy the islands until they could be handed over to Sweden, on the grounds that the islands could be occupied by Swedish military personnel and not surrendered to any other State.[18]

2.1   The Treaty of Brest-Litovsk, 1918

A peace treaty was the outcome of diplomatic negotiations held in Brest-Litovsk between Soviet Russia (the Russian Soviet Federative Socialist Republic was formed in January 1918) and the Central Powers (Germany, Austria-Hungary, Turkey and Bulgaria). Sweden did not participate in the negotiations, but it submitted a note to Germany, Austria-Hungary and Turkey, who had been parties to the 1856 Paris Peace Treaty. Sweden insisted that concerns about Åland's status had to be paid attention to during the Brest-Litovsk talks. It is noteworthy that Sweden's request was made in December 1917, some two weeks after Finland's declaration of independence and before Sweden had recognised Finland (which occurred on 4 January 1918 without restrictions or conditions). The main question was whether Russia would destroy its fortifications built on the islands. There were no discussions regarding the sovereignty of the islands. Sweden also made the suggestion that the islands would be neutral but because Sweden had not recognised the Bolshevik government, it did not make this request to Soviet-Russia. Nonetheless Soviet-Russia was informed of Sweden's actions unofficially.[19]

The situation was politically and legally complicated. Finland had declared its independence, and everything seemed to indicate that Finland also wanted the Åland Islands to be considered a part of Finnish sovereign territory. It was important to Sweden to maintain good relations with Finland and so, by demanding the possession of the islands Sweden would have endangered such rapport. The primary objective of Sweden was still to neutralise the islands. Germany raised the Åland question during discussions at Brest-Litovsk. First of all, the states had to figure out whether the matter should be dealt with by the Soviets or the new State Republic of Finland. The leader of the Soviet delegation, Leon Trotsky, responded and claimed that Finnish independence had not changed the question of the Åland Islands. Second, during negotiations Germany showed no interest in maintaining the neutrality of the islands

---

18   Barros, *supra* note 7 at 43, 55–61; Rotkirch in Chapter 1 note 2 at 363–364.
19   Barros, *supra* note 7 at 60–69; Rotkirch in Chapter 1 note 2 at 364.

whilst the war was ongoing.[20] As a result there was no reference in the Treaty of Brest-Litovsk about neutralisation. It only included a demand for Russia to withdraw its troops and members of the Russian Red Guard from the islands and to demolish their military installations built during the war. There was the intention, between Germany, Finland, Russia and Sweden, to conclude a special treaty concerning the future use of the islands for military and navigational purposes as well as any permanent non-fortification of the islands. It was also intended that other countries bordering on the Baltic Sea were to be invited to take part in this treaty. A similar Article in the Finno-German Peace Treaty was signed in Berlin on 7 March 1918 four days after Brest-Litovsk.[21]

Both of the aforementioned treaties refer to sea areas, unlike the 1856 Convention, which only mentioned land. Perhaps the chances of warfare at sea influenced common intentions to expand the permanent demilitarised zone. The technological development of naval weapons, as well as the ships carrying them, had significantly advanced by the beginning of the First World War. As a result of this development, destroyers and torpedo boats were bigger, faster and more seaworthy. One of the most important new weapons was the submarine, which could operate effectively in waters inaccessible to surface ships and therefore bring warfare closer to enemy forces. An assault against of the Åland

---

20   Rotkirch in Chapter 1 note 2 at 365. Proceedings of the Brest-Litovsk Peace Conference 1918, p. 119, available at http://archive.org/details/cu31924027837396 [last access 24.3.2018].

21   The Peace of Brest-Litovsk – The Treaty of Peace between Russia and Germany, Austria-Hungary, Bulgaria and Turkey, 3 March 1918, art. VI (3), (4) says that:

> Finland and the Aland Islands will be also, without delay, cleared of Russian troops and the Russian Red Guard and Finnish ports of the Russian fleet and of Russian naval forces. While ice renders impossible the conveying of warships to Russian ports there must remain on board only a limited crew. Russia ceases all agitation or propaganda against the government or public institutions of Finland.
>
> The fortifications constructed on the Aland Islands must be razed at the first opportunity. As regards the prohibition to erect fortifications of these islands in the future, as well as the question of their future in general in a military respect and in respect to the technical side of navigation, a special agreement must be concluded between Germany, Finland, Russia and Sweden; the parties consent that at Germany's desire other countries bordering the Baltic Sea may be called upon to take part in the above agreement.

Available at http://avalon.law.yale.edu/20th_century/bl34.asp#art6 [last access 24.3.2018]; see also Treaty of Peace between Finland and Germany, Finnish Treaty Series 3 /1918, art. 30, translation in English available at https://histdoc.net/history/153_1C.html [last access 24.3.2018]; Proceedings of the Brest-Litovsk Peace Conference 1918, pp. 119, 227, 861, Texts of the Finland 'Peace', with Map, p. 26, available at http://archive.org/details/cu31924027837396 [last access 24.3.2018]; see also Barros, *supra* note 7 at 69–75; Rotkirch in Chapter 1 note 2 at 364.

Islands could take place quickly and effectively, creating an additional danger that the waters surrounding the islands might become a theatre of war.[22]

As a result of the Treaty of Brest-Litovsk, Sweden attained one of its basic objectives: the demolition of Åland's fortifications. The Treaty touched upon the potential for the permanent demilitarisation of the islands, which Sweden could actively participate in. Finland and Sweden cooperated in the demolition of military installations between April and October 1919, in accordance with a separate Treaty between Finland, Sweden and Germany which was signed on 30 December 1918. Germany did not wish to take part in this operation because it had been defeated during the war and was preparing for its own peace negotiations with the Allied Forces in Versailles, France. It is also worth mentioning here that the Brest-Litovsk Peace Treaty was dissolved by the Treaty of Versailles in 1919. While peace negotiations ensued in Brest-Litovsk, a civil war erupted in Finland during January 1918. This crisis had an effect on relations between Finland and Sweden, which were already soured by a dispute over the presence of Swedish troops on the Åland Islands. Sweden's military presence had been justified on the grounds of humanitarianism, while from a Finnish perspective this was viewed as a ruse to gain control of the islands.[23] The following section looks briefly at this turn of events.

3   Sweden and Germany on the Åland Islands, 1918

A difficult situation arose on the Åland Islands in the beginning of 1918. A separatist movement on Åland, which had gained considerable support from the Swedes, delivered a petition on 2nd February 1918 to the Swedish government. More than 7,000 Ålanders had signed the petition, calling for the reunion of the islands with Sweden. Finland's internal situation was unstable due to civil unrest as a war between the 'Whites' and the 'Reds' had broken out at the end of January 1918. There were Russian troops stationed in Finland who supported the 'Reds' while the 'Whites' tried hard to expel them. There was a Russian garrison stationed on Åland whose behaviour became anarchic. Many of the islanders hoped that Sweden would provide assistance and protection to them if they made their pleas heard. The Swedish government's reaction

---

22   'The First World War 1914–1918', in 'Most Dangerous Service': A Century of Royal Navy Submarines, available at http://www.lutonmodelboat.co.uk/history_submarines.html [last access 24.3.2018].

23   Barros, *supra* note 7 at 75; Rotkirch in Chapter 1 note 2 at 365; Treaty of Peace between the Allied and Associated Powers and Germany, available at http://avalon.law.yale.edu/subject_menus/versailles_menu.asp [last access 24.3.2018].

was to dispatch ships to Åland, which were given instructions to evacuate all persons who wished to be transferred to Sweden. Also aboard the expedition was a Bolshevik agent, V.V. Vorovsky, whose personal task was to persuade the Russian garrison to depart for Sweden, and to proceed from there to Russia.[24]

The situation became more complicated after the Nystad Corps (a Finnish detachment about 600 men strong) had arrived on the islands. This 'White' corps was warmly greeted by the islanders, after which fighting broke out between the corps and the Russian garrison. This battle was brought to an end on 20 February through Swedish mediation, as it was agreed by all the parties that the Nystad Corps would be immediately evacuated to Sweden while the Russian troops would follow as soon as possible; no later than five weeks hence. The Ålanders and the Nystad Corps both stipulated that Swedish troops should be stationed on Åland during the remaining period of time that the Russian garrison was staying there, in order to guarantee the safety of the locals.[25]

At the same time there were other events happening elsewhere. Russia decided to break off negotiations at Brest-Litovsk. Germany moved to seize the rest of the Baltic Sea coast still under Russian control, to force the Russians to agree to a peace settlement and to push the Bolshevik insurgence as far to the east as possible. After Russia broke off peace negotiations, Finland requested a dispatch of German troops to assist Finland against the Bolsheviks. Germany informed Sweden that it had decided to accede to Finland's request for assistance against the Bolsheviks, and that the Åland Islands would be used as a base for these operations. To make sure that no complications or accidents took place, Germany also requested that Sweden recall all its ships and vessels from Åland's waters. Due to the rapport between the two States, Germany acknowledged that the total recall of Swedish troops was unnecessary and that both States could occupy separate areas of the islands. Area limits were to be settled by a mutual agreement between the commanders of each army upon reaching the islands. Sweden informed Germany that once an evacuation of Russian troops had been completed, Sweden would recall its expedition. German troops arrived on Åland, on 5th March 1918. However, prior arrangements between Swedish and Russian troops were not respected by the Germans, as the remaining Russian troops were captured and taken as prisoners of war on 9th March 1918. Prisoners of Russian origin were transferred to Libau

---

24 US Department of State, *Papers Relating to the Foreign Relation of the United States, 1918. Russia. Volume II*, 751–752 (1918), available at http://digital.library.wisc.edu/1711.dl/FRUS .FRUS1918Russiav02 [last access 24.3.2018]; Barros, *supra* note 7 at 75–79; Rotkirch in Chapter 1 note 2 at 365; Gustavsson, *supra* note 1 at 23–26.

25 Barros, *supra* note 7 at 79; Rotkirch in Chapter 1 note 2 at 365.

(Latvia) and other nationalities were transferred by Swedish ships to Oskar-ham (Sweden).[26]

These events were a strain upon Finnish–Swedish relations for a long time. Swedish activities were carried out beneath a veil of 'humanitarianism', while Finns were often in doubt as to whether their neighbour's good intentions were genuine or not. In Finland many considered Sweden's military occupation of the Åland Islands an attempt to occupy the islands permanently, after which the islands would be annexed.[27]

4   Finland's Independence (1917) and the Åland Question

Discussions that took place throughout this time period between Russia, Sweden, Britain and France all indicate that the 1856 Åland Convention was in force despite the First World War. The three Contracting Parties had originally been Allies during the First World War; the demilitarisation of the Islands, namely Article 6 of the 1918 Peace Treaty of Brest-Litovsk, had been approved of by the Soviet Government.

Finland's declaration of independence prompted new questions regarding the 1856 Convention and whether it should be binding for Finland. It was Finland's opinion that the treaties concluded by Russia did not bind Finland as a newly independent State.[28] Finland particularly refused to accept the 1856 Convention. Nevertheless, their opinion on the 1856 Convention did not hinder Finland's approval of demolishing the fortifications on the Åland Islands. Sweden was totally in favour of the 1856 Convention and contended that its obligations constituted 'servitude', which meant that it remained in force even if the islands' sovereignty changed. From the perspective of international law, however, the concept of 'servitude' is questionable.[29]

The League of Nations set up the Commission of Jurists in 1920. The Commission agreed with the Swedish position when it decided that the 1856 Convention was in force and had been instituted out of a common will to protect 'European interests'. Because of such implications for regional security, every State was required to enforce the respective legal provisions. Thus, whichever

---

26   Barros, *supra* note 7 at 84–88; Rotkirch in Chapter 1 note 2 at 365–366; Gustavsson, *supra* note 1 at 26–31.

27   Rotkirch in Chapter 1 note 2 at 366. For more, see Barros, *supra* note 7 at 89–95.

28   Nowadays the principle can be found in the Vienna Convention on Succession of States in respect of Treaties, 1946 UNTS 3.

29   Rotkirch in Chapter 1 note 2 at 366. See P.B. Potter, *The Doctrine of Servitudes in International Law*, 9 Am. J. Int. Law, 627–641 (1915).

State held sovereignty over the islands would still be obliged to adhere to the 1856 Convention. When Russia had controlled the Islands it had been bound to the Convention's requirements, and when Russia recognised Finland the same obligations devolved on Finland. As an interested Power, Sweden also had a right to put forward its claim for compliance with the Convention.[30]

Another question was whether the Åland Islands resided within Finnish sovereignty. This matter was brought to the fore by Sweden. In this sense, there were two important issues. First of all, should the islands stay demilitarised? And second, did the islands belong to Finland or should Ålanders have the option to join Sweden? The Commission of Jurists believed that the scope of the issues at hand was international in nature, and that the League Council would be more competent when dealing with the problem. It was also argued that the issue had derived from a time when Finland had not been a sovereign State. Before the declaration of Finnish independence, a separatist movement took place on the Åland Islands that aimed to unify Åland with Sweden once more. The separatists were actively supported by Sweden because the islands had previously belonged to Sweden and because of their strategic value. Officially Sweden expressed that the language, culture, and wishes of the majority of Ålanders were important factors.[31]

Finland contested that the Commission of Jurists had not taken into account the fact that Finland had been given its status as a State as early as 1809, although with restricted sovereignty in regard to various competences. It is noteworthy that although Finland's sovereignty had indeed been restricted during those times, this restriction had not applied to the full extent of its territory.[32] Regardless, Finland did not oppose a settlement made in regard to the Åland question by the League of Nations. Finland concurred that the 1856 Convention on the non-fortification of the Åland Islands was inconclusive, yet it

---

30   *The Report of the Commission of Jurists*, Leag. Nations Off. J. 3–19, 17–19 (1920); Barros, *supra* note 7 at 288, 291–292; Bo Johnson, *Kolliderande suveränitet*, Tidskr. i Sjöväsendet 172–242, 237 (1973). See also Philip Marshall Brown, *The Aaland Islands Question*, 15 Am. J. Int. Law 268–272 (1921).; Gregory in Chapter 1 note 2 at 64.

31   Rotkirch in Chapter 1 note 2 at 358, 366. Finland's perspective on its sovereign territory was based on both the area it had as a Russian Grand Duchy as well as the Åland Islands. Sweden was especially interested in Åland's legal status as a demilitarised zone. Sweden concurred that Finland was bound by the 1856 Convention, and also that non-parties of the Convention could appeal. Finland's opinion was contrary to Sweden's. Barros, *supra* note 7 at 290; Johnson, *supra* note 30 at 237.

32   Conduct of foreign policy and defence matters remained outside of Finland's authority; otherwise Finland had all elements of a State: a defined territory, citizens and an independent government. Furthermore, legislation dating back to the Swedish period remained in force.

was ready to come to an agreement over the future demilitarisation and neu-trali of the islands. On the other hand, Sweden proposed that the inhabitants of Åland should hold a referendum on a reunion with Sweden. Finland refused to accept this proposal.[33]

Both Finland and Sweden presented drafts for a convention on the demili-tarisation and neutralisation of the Åland Islands to the Commission of In-quiry. Both countries remarked on the other party's draft. The League Council made a formal decision on 24th June 1921, which contained a clause relating to the demilitarisation and neutralisation of the Åland Islands. According to the Council's decision, all Governments concerned were expected to conclude the proposed Treaty. The Conference was convened in Geneva by invitation of the Secretary General of the League of Nations in October 1921. The States who took part were Denmark, Estonia, Finland, France, Germany, Great Brit-ain, Italy, Latvia, Poland and Sweden. Soviet Russia did not take part due to its negative sentiments about the Åland Islands agreement.[34]

The Entente powers had been informed in 1919 by Soviet Russia that it would never recognise any arrangement regarding the Islands to which it was not a party. Soviet Russia once again voiced its objections during the settle-ment procedure of the League of Nations. After the Convention Relating to the Non-fortification and Neutralisation of the Åland Islands had been signed in October 1921, the Russian Government informed all signatories with dip-lomatic ties to Soviet Russia that they disagreed with the Convention. The Russian Government denied the Convention's existence and declared that its provisions were not legally binding for Soviet Russia. In accord with its pre-decessor's policy, the Soviet Union[35] also did not accede to the Convention.[36]

5   The Geneva Conference, 1921

In spite of the Russian Government's negative attitude, the Conference was held in Geneva during 10–20 October 1921. An invitation to the Conference was

---

33   Barros, *supra* note 7 at 291–292; Johnson, *supra* note 30 at 237; Rotkirch in Chapter 1 note 2 at 367.

34   The decision of the League Council on 24th June 1921 also recognised that the sovereign-ty of the Åland Islands belonged to Finland, LNOJ, September 1921, p. 697; Rafael Erich, Suomen valtio-oikeus *I* osa 180 (1924); Castrén, *supra* note 5 at 265.

35   The Union of Soviet Socialist Republic was established on 30 December 1922.

36   In July 1921 the Russian Government made an official protest to Finland. Rotkirch in Chapter 1 note 2 at 367–368; Johnson, *supra* note 30 at 237; Bertil Stjernfelt, *Ålands hav och öar – brygga eller barriär? Svensk-finsk försvarsfråga 1915–1945* 45 (1991).

sent to Denmark, Estonia, Finland, France, Germany, Great Britain, Italy, Latvia, Poland and Sweden. Both Finland and Sweden had prepared new drafts for the Convention's text.

There were two Commissions taking part in the Conference: one that consisted of maritime experts whose task was to delimit the Åland Islands zone; the other's task was to examine the Convention drafts submitted by Sweden and Finland and to propose a decision. One of the main questions was to define the Åland Islands' area. This would be specified, by means of a system of coordinates and zones, to cover all islands and islets within the archipelago as well as the sea area between them extending to three nautical miles from the outermost islands. Finland proposed that the territorial waters of the Åland Islands would be equivalent to the breadth of the Finnish territorial sea.[37] This proposal was rejected by the participants of the Conference because several States agreed to only three nautical miles. Finland agreed to this because the demilitarised zone was located within Finland's territorial sea.[38]

The drafts submitted by Sweden and Finland were basically similar in scope. Both proposals included the principle of demilitarisation, the reassertion of the 1856 Convention, and that the Convention was made in regard to European interests. Particularly under scrutiny were the exceptions to the general rules and measures of protection against sudden offences. At first, cooperation between Finnish and Swedish delegates proved to be a difficult task due to several misunderstandings over the notion of sovereignty. The Swedish draft Convention challenged Finnish sovereignty over the Åland Islands, and its first draft article contained an obligation to hold a plebiscite to decide which State held true sovereignty over them. The Finnish Government refused to accept any doubts pertaining to its sovereignty over the Åland Islands. After the issue was resolved, cooperation became easier. Finland's right to deploy troops, warships and military aeroplanes in the neutralised zone was the most troublesome of problems. Matters concerning its navy seriously impaired the Conference and the Great Powers (France, Italy and Britain) had to work hard to reach a mutual understanding on all issues. The Convention was signed by all participants after its adoption on 20th October 1921 and the Convention entered into force in Finland on 6th April 1922.[39]

---

37 This had been four nautical miles at the time.
38 Rotkirch in Chapter 1 note 2 at 367–368.
39 Rotkirch in Chapter 1 note 2 at 368; *Ahvenanmaankysymys: Kansainliiton neuvoston asettaman selostajakomissionin lausunto liitteineen*, 74 (1921).

6   The Åland Convention, 1921

The 1921 Geneva Convention on the Non-Fortification and Neutralisation of the Åland Islands[40] includes a Preamble and ten Articles. The Preamble refers to the Resolution of the League of Nations made on 24 June 1921, which states a recommendation formulated by the League of Nations expressly calling for the Convention on the demilitarisation and neutralisation of the Åland Islands to be concluded between interested Powers, with the intention of reducing the islands' potential as a military threat. There is also a reference made to the 1856 Convention on the Demilitarisation of the Åland Islands, which had originally been committed by Russia and annexed to the Treaty of Paris. Furthermore, under Article 1, Finland recognises its binding commitment to the 1856 Convention, which it originally rejected in 1917 as Russia's successor.[41]

Article 2 delimits the area of the Åland Islands. The 'Åland Islands' includes all islands, islets and skerries within its respective zone. Besides land areas, the zone also includes territorial waters belonging to the Åland Islands, extending to three nautical miles from the outermost islands, islets and skerries. Together these areas comprise the demilitarised and neutralised zone to which the Convention is applied. The demilitarisation provisions of the Convention are included in Article 3, which prohibits the maintenance or setting up of any military or naval building, operational base, or installation to be used for war purposes within the zone. Neutralisation provisions are included in Articles 4 and 6. According to Article 4, no military, naval or air force of any State may enter or remain in the zone described in Article 2. The Article especially notes that manufacturing, importing, transporting and re-exporting weapons or war materials is forbidden inside the zone. In other words, this article does not allow for any fortification of the islands and therefore reinforces its neutralisation. Article 6 stipulates that in times of war the zone is to be considered a neutral area. The area must not in any way be used for purposes related to military operations.[42]

However, these articles are not given without an exception: they are only applicable to Finland during peacetime and allow Finland to execute an armed response if ever forced to take action in extraordinary circumstances. Armed forces can supplement regular police forces. Finland also has the right to use, from time to time, one or two light surface warships for the inspection of the

---

40   Parties to the Convention include: Denmark, Estonia, Finland, France, Germany, Great Britain, Iceland (Union with Denmark in 1921) Italy, Latvia, Poland and Sweden.

41   Brown, *supra* note 30 at 268–272; Rotkirch in Chapter 1 note 2 at 368–369.

42   Rotkirch in Chapter 1 note 2 at 369.

Islands. During these visits, warships have the right to temporarily anchor in the zone. If special circumstances demand, Finland has a right to bring other surface warships into the waters of the zone but the joint displacement of these ships cannot exceed 6,000 tons. It is worth noting that the article explicitly states that ships in question must navigate on the surface, i.e. the reference excludes Finland's submarines.[43] During the Second World War the issue of Finnish submarines was valid but currently the issue is academic because Finland does not have submarines.

The normal mode used for navigating submarines is submersion. However, this mode of navigation for submarines is restricted through territorial seas belonging to foreign States in accordance with international law. Regulations pertaining to international law grant submarines right of innocent passage through foreign territorial waters on the condition that they navigate on the surface and display their flag. However, it is up to the discretion of coastal States to permit a foreign submarine to navigate submerged through its territorial seas, or even through its internal waters. Under these circumstances a submarine is not covered by right of innocent passage. In the case of the Åland Islands it appears that the 1921 Åland Convention does not make any difference between Finnish and foreign submarines.[44]

The 1921 Convention does not refer to the airspace above the zone. There is only a restriction upon Finnish army or naval aircraft using the zone's airspace, whilst the Finnish air force is allowed to fly there without landing except in cases of *force majeure*. The exception is interpreted as applying to rescue operations, in which military helicopters can be used. The Contracting Parties have been informed of this issue in 1969 and no objection was raised to this interpretation.[45]

There is also a possibility for foreign warships to enter and temporarily anchor in the zone during peacetime. Yet a foreign warship's visit is restricted by the Convention, in the sense that the Finnish Government may only grant a right to enter and anchor in the zone to one foreign warship at a time. This provision was applied when two warships escorted HMS Britannia in 1976 during Queen Elisabeth II's visit. The British warships were not allowed to enter the demilitarised and neutralised zone while the Queen visited Mariehamn.

The problem arose again in 1988 when military-registered foreign sailing-ships taking part in the Tall Ships Race visited Mariehamn, the capital of the

---

43   *Id.* at 369.
44   Spiliopoulou Åkermark, Heinikoski, and Kleemola-Juntunen in Chapter 1 note 2 at 63.
45   Rotkirch in Chapter 1 note 2 at 369. Article 4(2)(c) is consistent with the recognized sovereignty the State enjoys over its airspace.

Åland Islands. The Finnish Government ultimately held that the restrictions set by the 1921 Åland Convention did not apply to these unarmed sailing ships which entered the zone solely with the aim of participating in a peaceful sailing contest. The visit of many of the sailing-ships was not in contravention to Article 4 paragraph 2 of the 1921 Convention, since the 'one warship' rule appears to apply to each foreign State separately. This interpretation makes it possible for more than one warship to visit the demilitarised and neutralised area simultaneously as long as they belong to different States. However, two of these eleven ships were Swedish, *Falken* and *Gladan*. In a memorandum made by the Finnish Ministry for Foreign Affairs, which was sent to the parties of the 1921 Åland Convention on 14th April 1987, the Finnish Government clearly stated that because these ships were unarmed and took part in a peaceful yacht race with the intention of promoting international cooperation and understanding, their presence in the zone was not a breach of the 1921 Åland Convention. But then on the other hand, Finland prohibited access of the Russian school sailing ship *Kruzenstern* to the port of Mariehamn in August 2017.[46]

Article 4 does not influence the right of innocent passage. According to Article 5 the prohibitions shall not prejudice the right of innocent passage, which is governed by international rules and custom. Passage in times of war is covered in Article 6. The zone, as described in Article 2, is a neutral area which shall never be directly or indirectly used for any purpose related to military operations. Nonetheless Finland has the right to lay mines temporarily if the Baltic Sea is ever involved in a war. If Finland were to undertake such measures, however, it should immediately inform the Council of the League of Nations.[47]

If there happened to be a sudden attack against the Åland Islands, or through them during an assault against the Finnish mainland, then Finland has the right to take necessary measures to resist and counter-attack. Finland's right to undertake such countermeasures lasts until other Contracting Parties to the 1921 Convention get involved and enforce respect for the neutrality of the islands according to the Convention. However, as already noted, if ever provoked to undertake such retaliatory measures, Finland would also have a duty to inform the Council of the League of Nations. In such a case, Contracting Parties to the Convention would be allowed to approach the Council and ask it to decide which measures could be taken to ensure that Åland's status

---

46   Rosas in Chapter 1 note 4 at 32; Ove Bring, *Ålands självstyrelse under 80 År: Erfarenheter och utmaningar* 64 (2002); Ove Bring, *Ålands demilitarisering – alive and kicking!, Åland – fredens öar? Seminarium 19 Oktober 2006, Ålands landskapsregering* 17 (2007); Spiliopoulou Åkermark, Heinikoski, and Kleemola-Juntunen in Chapter 1 note 2 at 44.

47   Rotkirch in Chapter 1 note 2 at 369–370; Mikaela Björkholm & Allan Rosas, *Ålandsöarnas demilitarisering och neutralisering* 71 (1990); Rosas in Chapter 1 note 4 at 32.

as a neutral zone was respected. Contracting Parties were committed to providing mutual assistance when enacting countermeasures agreed upon by the Council. Contracting Parties had a right to intervene or come to Finland's aid but solely on the basis of permission granted by the Council of the League.[48]

The weakness of the guarantee system, as a result of Article 7, was that the procedural system was very heavy and posed ineffectiveness. The League of Nations dissolved in 1945, after which the guarantee provision became insignificant to the Contracting Parties. For Finland, however, its duty to inform the Council of the League of measures taken had lost its status, while Article 7 contained further obligations; therefore, the dissolution of the League of Nations did not change their validity.[49]

The content of Article 8 is interesting because it stipulates that provisions belonging to the Convention shall remain in force, regardless of any changes occurring in the status quo of the Baltic Sea region. This means that the principle of changing circumstances (clausula *rebus sic stantibus*) is not applicable to this Convention. Article 9 concedes that the Åland Islands form an integral part of the Republic of Finland. After having ratified the Convention, then, Sweden subsequently ended the long debate over sovereignty. Furthermore, the Council of the League was required to inform all other Member States about the Convention so that they could duly respect its provisions in the interest of peace. The treaty arrangements relating to the Åland Islands are still in force. The character of the demilitarisation and neutrality of the Åland Islands as a permanent settlement is discussed later.

7   **Between the World Wars**

The geopolitical situation in the Baltic Sea changed after the First World War. Russia had lost Finland and the Baltic Countries, as well as strategic bases located within their territories. Russian navy incursions into Åland's waters could be traced using Finnish surveillance stations, but its submarines, built in Leningrad during the beginning of the 1930s, could pass by unobserved. From a naval strategic point of view, Germany, Sweden and Finland were in better positions. Furthermore, the deepening of the Kiel Canal was completed in 1916, which made it possible for the first time to transfer big warships from Germany directly to the Baltic Sea. Considering the size of the German and Russian navies, the Baltic Sea was principally under their control. When the

---

48   Rotkirch in Chapter 1 note 2 at 370; art. 7 of the 1921 Åland Convention.
49   Rotkirch in Chapter 1 note 2 at 370.

Baltic Countries attained their independence, Germany and the Soviet Union became interested in the Åland Islands. The Islands were a possible rest area for their navies when operating in the Baltic Sea or Gulf of Bothnia. The Åland archipelago also formed an ideal area to lay mines, thus offering ample opportunities for establishing a defence against foreign navies trying to invade the Gulf of Bothnia and the Turku and Stockholm archipelagos.[50]

The volume of Finnish foreign trade increased between the World Wars and most goods were transported by sea. Navigation through the Åland Strait to the Baltic Sea was also important to Sweden. For this reason, Finnish and Swedish collaboration was deemed to be beneficial in a state of war. If a third country were to occupy the Åland Islands, Finland would be cut off from the rest of Europe. In order to secure sea transportation, it was important that the Åland Islands remained under uncompromised sovereign control.[51]

Germany had strengthened its position as a great power in the Baltic Sea area and the Soviet Union had also increased its military activity there. The Åland Islands, located in between these two power centres, was known to be a key strategic position for both States. By the end of the 1930s the League of Nations had weakened significantly due to political reasons. It became possible that, were a conflict to ever break out, the League of Nations would be unable to react. As a result, the guarantee system of the 1921 Convention was thrown into doubt. If imminent danger were to occur, the procedure of the 1921 Convention could not effectively strengthen the defence of the Åland Islands. In addition to this major insecurity, the political situation in central Europe had become unstable. Finland's response to these crises was to plan an alteration of the 1921 Convention with the aim of improving its military standing in the event that a foreign country occupied the Åland Islands. Finland took the initiative during preliminary negotiations with Sweden in 1937, after which official talks between Finland and Sweden began in April 1938 on the defence of the Islands.[52]

---

50   Komulainen, *supra* note 1 at 55–56.

51   Martti Turtola, *Torniojoelta rajajoelle: Suomen ja Ruotsin salainen yhteistoiminta Neu-vostoliiton hyökkäyksen varalle vuosina 1923–1940: puolustuspoliittinen vaihtoehto* 6, 64, 70, 76 (1984); Gardberg and Törnroos in Chapter 1 note 3 at 11. Ore was transported from Northern Sweden through the Gulf of Bothnia to Germany, and it was vital to Germany that transports were not endangered.

52   The Soviet Union was not a Contracting Party to the 1921 Convention and Germany had left the League of Nations in 1933. The crisis of Abessinia 1935–36 had decimated the authority of the League of Nations. Krister Wahlbäck, Maija-Liisa. Vuorjoki & Asko Vuorjoki, *Veljeys veitsenterällä* 73–74 (1968); Rotkirch in Chapter 1 note 2 at 370; Komulainen, *supra* note 1 at 62, 73, 81; Gustavsson, *supra* note 1 at 147–149, 152–153.

After a long period of bilateral diplomacy, the so-called Stockholm Plan was drawn up in 1939. A proposal was submitted to both Finnish and Swedish Parliaments in 1939. Finland and Sweden also submitted similar proposals to Contracting Parties to the 1921 Åland Convention, as well as to the Soviet Union regarding the Islands' fortification. According to Finnish and Swedish wishes, the 1921 Convention would be respected in a more realistic sense. But the main purpose of the Stockholm Plan was to protect the islands against a surprise attack by revising the concept of demilitarisation. The proposal suggested that the Convention's demilitarisation provisions concerning the southern part of the zone should be changed, thereby allowing Finland to employ all necessary military measures if necessary. The northern part of the zone would be jointly defended by Finland and Sweden over the course of a ten-year period. Fortifications on the Åland Islands would be connected to Finnish and Swedish coastal artillery positions, creating a network extending from the Swedish archipelago to Hanko, Finland. The Stockholm Plan also included compulsory military service for male Ålanders, which would be carried out on the islands. However, military service was deemed to be undesirable by the local population. The aim of the Stockholm Plan was to show that Finnish and Swedish competencies were necessary, which would then encourage others among the Parties not to revoke the 1921 Convention. All Contracting Parties approved the proposed amendments but the Soviet Union rejected them. The Stockholm Plan was submitted to the Council of the League of Nations but due to a Soviet veto the Plan was never adopted. The Soviet Union's negative attitude was the principal reason why the matter was withdrawn from the Swedish Parliament. After Sweden's formal withdrawal and Finland's reluctance to pursue the matter alone, the Stockholm Plan fell through.[53]

8   During the Second World War

8.1   *The Winter War*
During the autumn of 1939 the Soviet Union invited Finland to participate in negotiations concerning bases and frontiers. When the first negotiation with Russia began, Finland took measures to strengthen its defensive preparations.

---

53   Aaro Pakaslahti, *Talvisodan poliittinen näytelmä: UM:n poliittisen osaston päällikön päiviä ja öitä* 19, 21, 34–37, 70–79 (1970); Rotkirch in Chapter 1 note 2 at 370–371; Komulainen, *supra* note 1 at 93, 109–113; see also J.K. Paasikivi, *Toimintani Moskovassa ja Suomessa 1939–41: 2, Välirauhan aika* 90–93 (1958); Max Jakobson, *Paasikivi Tukholmassa: J.K. Paasikiven toiminta Suomen lähettiläänä Tukholmassa 1936–39* 148–153 (1978); Gardberg and Törnroos in Chapter 1 note 3 at 11–12; Gustavsson, *supra* note 1 at 152–168, 350–359.

The Finnish Government felt determined to improve its competencies on the seacoast and implemented an extra military refresher course, which in practice called for a mobilisation. The main task for Finland's navy was to insure sea routes to the west of its territory. To succeed in its task, the navy had to safeguard sea routes within the Finnish Archipelago, the Åland Island's Sea and the southern part of Gulf of Bothnia against submarines, torpedo boats and air forces. Or to put it more simply, the navy had to hinder any enemy invasion within the Finnish territorial waters.[54]

During September 1939 the Germans had undertaken to control and check up on merchant vessels within the Baltic Sea. Some vessels were taken to German harbours because they were said to be carrying war contraband. Two Finnish vessels in transit to Great Britain were sunk by German forces in Skagerrak It was claimed the vessels' cargo contained contraband. In addition to this, mines had destroyed four merchant vessels before the Winter War began. Germany extended its activities into the Gulf of Bothnia, whilst Finland convoyed Finnish and neutral State vessels from Åland to Sweden.[55]

The Winter War between the Soviet Union and Finland began on 30th November 1939. On the 1st December the Finnish Government dispatched its troops to the Åland Islands. The Finnish Government also asked Sweden to dispatch troops to Åland in accordance with the Stockholm Plan, but Sweden rejected this petition. The task for the Finnish troops was to defend Åland's neutrality. Finland laid mines in the Åland Strait (permitted according to the 1921 Convention), erected other temporary defences and coastal artillery points, and subsequently informed the League of Nations and Contracting Parties to the Convention about its actions; all of whom approved of these measures discretely.[56]

The Soviet air force bombed western ports in Finland. There were also several offensive actions carried out against Finnish armoured ships within the archipelago of Turku and Åland. The Finnish coastal fleet was ordered to cover any merchant vessel navigating the Turku-Åland-Sweden route. During the beginning of December the Soviet Union blockaded Finland (including Åland).

---

54   Stig Jägerskiöld & Kai Kaila, *Mannerheim rauhan vuosina 1920–1939* 364 (1973); Komulainen, *supra* note 1 at 138.

55   Komulainen, *supra* note 1 at 139–140.

56   Britain and France did not protest as the other signatories to the 1856 Convention the Russian fortifications which were built on the Åland Islands during the First World War. Barros, *supra* note 7 at 291; Rotkirch in Chapter 1 note 2 at 371; Komulainen, *supra* note 1 at 141; *Suomen laivasto I* 227–229, 238, 250 (1968). The coastal fleet was responsible for defence of the Åland Islands until 20th December and thereafter the Åland Islands' defence troops were responsible for defence.

Neutral merchant ships were given an opportunity to leave the blockaded area during definite periods. Inside the blockaded area submarines were commanded not to begin combat until 9th December, while outside the area they had to comply with international conventions.[57]

Submarines belonging to the Soviet Union were patrolling sea routes within the Gulf of Finland and facing the Åland Islands. The submarines sank several ships. Submarines navigated within the Gulf of Bothnia via the Åland Strait, nearby Märket Reef, and avoided mines. During the Winter War, the Soviet Union devised a strategy to occupy the Åland Islands by means of its navy forces, thereby cutting off Finnish maritime traffic. From these new naval bases, submarines and military aircraft located on Åland could hinder the Finnish navy when trying to take cover within the archipelago, thus rendering the fleet vulnerable and easy to destroy. This strategy, however, was never realised. In spite of various Soviet naval activities, Finland was able to continue transit within its sea regions. The Åland Islands' area was a particular advantage to Finland as merchant and convoy vessels could rely on the ports of Åland. For instance, merchant ships could anchor in the Åland area while waiting for their convoys. By constructing fortifications, the Åland Islands were prepared for military operations, yet Finland chose not to use the fortifications as military bases during the Winter War.[58]

The Peace Treaty, which ended the Winter War between Finland and the Soviet Union, was signed on 13th March 1940. The Åland Islands were not brought up during the peace negotiations. The Soviet Union, however, had put forward a proposal for the Åland Islands' demilitarisation during July of the same year.[59] Perhaps one reason for such a proposal was the Soviet Union's simultaneous preparations to occupy the Islands.[60]

Finland and the Soviet Union concluded a bilateral treaty concerning the demilitarisation of the Åland Islands in September 1940. The Treaty is short and includes just four Articles. The first Article obliges Finland to demilitarise the Åland Islands, which includes destroying existing cannon foundations. The demilitarisation obligation is equivalent to the 1921 Convention. Furthermore, Finland commits itself not to make the islands accessible to any other State for

---

57   Komulainen, *supra* note 1 at 142–143.
58   Ohto Manninen, *Kilpapurjehdus Ahvenanmaalle?*, Sotilasaikakauslehti 248–250 (1992); Ohto Manninen, *Hanko – 'ampumavalmis pistooli' 1940–1941*, Sotilasaikakauslehti 28–31 (1993); Komulainen, *supra* note 1 at 144–145; *Suomen laivasto 1 supra* note 56 at 255.
59   The Soviet Union was not a Contracting Party to the 1921 Convention.
60   Erik Wihtol & Ohto Manninen, *Pohjois-Itämeren lukot: Ahvenanmaa ja Gotlanti, Neuvosto-laivaston toiminta-alueen laajentuminen Itämerellä 1939–1941*, Sotilasaikakauslehti 61–65 (1994).

military purposes. The second Article then defines the demilitarised zone and also complies with the 1921 Convention.[61]

According to the third article, however, the Soviet Union is granted a right to establish a Consulate on the islands. The Consulate performed regular assignments, including a particular obligation to ensure that the demilitarisation and non-fortification provisions of the Treaty were conformed with. The Soviet Consulate representative has a right to inform authorities of anything of a contradictory nature to the provisions laid out in the Treaty. In the event of this happening, any communication shall be delivered to Finnish authorities via Åland's County Administrative Board with the intention of beginning a formal investigation. Any investigation is expected to be carried out as soon as possible by the Finnish Government and the Soviet Consulate representative. Results of any joint investigation shall then be sent to the Governments of both Contracting Parties for necessary actions.[62]

8.2   *The Continuation War*

In accordance with the Peace Treaty, the Soviet Union had a right to lease a land area in Hanko. As a result of this, Finland people feared that the Soviet Union would use the bases in Hanko and the Baltic countries to launch further offensive attacks against them. The demilitarised Åland Islands were especially threatened. Finnish fears were not groundless. The Baltic Fleet's historical archives contain strategic blueprints of a plan, drawn up in September 1940, outlining a possible Soviet invasion of the Åland Islands. The task of the invasion was to break enemy connections within the Baltic Sea, the Gulf of Bothnia, and the Finnish archipelago. To achieve this aim, it was primarily essential to occupy the Åland Islands.[63] The Soviet Union was not the only State which intended to occupy the Åland Islands: Germany, too, had plans to take over Åland, dating back to 1939. Germany's strategy was kept operational until the autumn of 1944.[64]

---

61   Treaty concerning the Åland Islands between Finland and the Union of Soviet Socialist Republics, Finnish Treaty Series 24/1940, arts. 1, 2.

62   Treaty concerning the Åland Islands between Finland and the Union of Soviet Socialist Republics, Finnish Treaty Series 24/1940, art. 3. Reactivation of the Treaty concerning the Åland Islands between Finland and the Union of Soviet Socialist Republics. Concluded on 10th October 1940, Finnish Treaty Series 9/1948.

63   Treaty of Peace between Finland and Soviet Socialist Republics, Finnish Treaty Series 3/1940, art. 4; Gardberg and Törnroos in Chapter 1 note 3 at 14.

64   Ohto Manninen, *'Operaatio Tanne' Ahvenanmaan uhkana*, Sotilasaikakauslehti 61–65 (1994).

War between Germany and the Soviet Union broke out on 22nd June 1941 when Germany attacked the Soviet Union. This also led to military operations carried out against Finland by the Soviet Union. Finland had made preparations for the outbreak of war, including a plan for the occupation of the Åland Islands. The plan was called 'Sailing Race' (in Finnish: *Kilpapurjehdus*). The same day as the war broke out, ships belonging to Operation Sailing Race transported Finnish troops overnight to the islands. The Finnish coastal fleet mined sea routes within the Åland area; the Åland Strait was mined jointly by Finland and Sweden. Furthermore, the outermost part of the Gulf of Finland was mined.[65] Thus the Soviet navy was contained within the innermost part of the Gulf of Finland, which probably limited their acts against the Åland Islands considerably.[66]

The Åland Islands had an important role to play in the Baltic Sea strategy during the autumn of 1941, when the Gulf of Finland was split between different naval operational spheres belonging to Finland and Germany. The German navy operated to the west of Åland and counted on the Soviet Baltic Fleet attempting to break through to Sweden. The German navy was tasked with destroying the Soviet Baltic Fleet as it attempted to navigate within the Baltic Sea. The 'Baltenflotte', containing its famous battleships, *Tirpitz* and the heavy cruiser *Admiral Scheer*, reached the Åland Islands on 24th September. This was the first time ever that a German naval fleet of this magnitude had entered the Åland area. However, the operations that had been carried out by the German air force had damaged the Soviet Fleet so efficiently that it was not able to sail on the sea. After their short visit, German vessels sailed away from the Åland Islands on 25th September.[67]

During the winter of 1941–42, the Soviet Union had refitted submarines and had begun to navigate within the Baltic Sea as well as the Åland Sea As early as 23rd June 1941, a submarine was seen near Märket on its way northward. When Soviet submarine activities increased during the summer of 1942, the Åland Strait was mined by Sweden and Finland. Because of the mining the Åland Strait was closed off. Finnish submarines operated actively within the Åland Sea sinking three Soviet submarines and convoying other merchant ships. The sea was freezing over and therefore made any submarine activities impossible until sea routes were re-opened in January 1943. During the spring

---

65   Gardberg and Törnroos in Chapter 1 note 3 at 14–15; Komulainen, *supra* note 1 at 191–192, 207. See also Juuso Säämänen, *Operaatio 'Kilpapurjehdus' Ahvenanmaan miehitysoperaatio kesällä 1941*, Sotilasaikakauslehti 60–65 (2005).

66   Gardberg and Törnroos in Chapter 1 note 3 at 15.

67   Per-Olof Ekman, *Sjöfront: Sjökrigshändelser i Norra Östersjöområdet 1941–1944* 101–105 (1981); Gardberg and Törnroos in Chapter 1 note 3 at 15; Komulainen, *supra* note 1 at 195.

of 1943, Germany planned to occupy Sweden, planning 'Operation Schweden'. An attack against Stockholm would have happened via the Åland Strait.[68] This fact bears significance when arguing that the status of the Åland Islands was important to Sweden for security reasons, and that their requirement in the League of Nations was reasonable.

The war between Finland and the Soviet Union ended in September 1944 as a result of the Armistice Agreement.[69] But war continued in Europe and its northern parts were still in focus. The Åland Strait, in front of Märket, was mined for the third time in October 1944 after several German submarines were seen in the Åland Sea Germany had prepared to occupy the Åland Islands after becoming aware in the early spring of 1944 that Finland was going to withdraw from the war. The German plan of action was referred to as 'Tanne West', and its aims were numerous: to secure Germany's ore transports from northern Sweden and nickel transports from Finland; to transport troops and war material to northern Finland; and to later use the same route for evacuation. Furthermore, Germany wanted to limit Soviet naval navigation between the Gulf of Bothnia and the Baltic Sea. However, Germany withdrew its plan and its troops operated elsewhere. For the duration of the Second World War, the Åland Islands became an area of operations chiefly used by the Soviet navy.[70]

Article 5 of the 1947 Peace Treaty, signed after the end of hostilities, says 'the Åland Islands will remain demilitarised according to the present situation'. The Treaty does not mention the status of the Åland's demilitarisation, nor does it mention the neutralisation of the Åland Islands; the Treaty simply refers to existing international regulations. The phrasing of the Article is a notable compromise, since the Soviet Union wanted to include the 1940 Treaty but not the 1921 Åland Convention, while Great Britain could not agree to a reference to the 1940 bilateral Treaty without referring to the 1921 Convention as well. However, by mentioning the Åland Islands, the Contracting Parties to the 1947 Peace Treaty recognised that the Åland Islands have a special status.[71]

---

68   Gardberg and Törnroos in Chapter 1 note 3 at 16; Komulainen, *supra* note 1 at 206–208. The
      Plan is found on microfilm from The Finnish Military Archives SA F 43/1061.
69   By the Armistice Agreement 19.10.1944, the bilateral treaty between Finland and the So-
      viet Union concerning the demilitarisation of the Åland Islands was re-confirmed. This
      meant that fortifications on the Åland Islands had to be destroyed.
70   Stjernfelt, *supra* note 36 at 178–180; Manninen, *supra* note 64 at 61–65; Komulainen, *supra*
      note 1 at 199–219.
71   1947 Peace Treaty, Finnish Treaty Series 19–20/1947:
      'The Union of Soviet Socialist Republics, the United Kingdom of Great Britain and North-
      ern Ireland, Australia, the Belorussian Soviet Socialist republic, Canada, Czechoslovakia,

9   Post-war Developments

The dissolution of the League of Nations also had an impact upon the 1921
Åland Convention as Article 7 specifically sets the procedure to follow to ren-
der the guarantee that the Åland Islands may never become a threat from the
military point of view. Article 7 focuses upon possible armed conflicts which
may come to bear upon the neutralisation of the Åland Islands. Its provisions
would also be applicable to any situation where Finland acted against its obligations to the Convention. In the case of a sudden attack against either the
Åland Islands or against Finland through them, Finland should take necessary
measures inside the neutral zone to check and repulse aggressors until the
Contracting Parties shall, in conformity with the Convention's provisions, be
in a position to intervene out of respect for the island's neutrality. The Convention states an obligation for Finland to carry out actions although Finland
ultimately feels this obligation to do so as a sovereign State.

   Erich (1924) maintains that after Finland reports to the Council it then has
a right to ask other Contracting Parties to contribute towards efforts to fend
off an attack if Finland's own measures are not sufficient. It is noteworthy, too,
that if the Council could not reach unanimity, then the Contracting Parties
are authorised to take measures recommended by two-thirds of a majority.
The Convention is silent about any case in which the Council cannot obtain
two-thirds of a majority. Castrén (1959) is of the opinion that other Contracting Parties are not authorised to take measures without requesting Finland's
permission. Nevertheless, the guarantee system was only a part of the Convention, and therefore key principals on demilitarisation and neutralisation have
not been affected by the dissolution of the League of Nations. Furthermore,
Finland's obligation to defend the Åland Islands continues and, according to
the Convention, Finland has a right to ask for help from other signatory States.
However, events which unfolded as a result of the League of Nations' dissolution affected other Contracting Parties to the 1921 Åland Convention. As a
result of its dissolution, the League of Nations' authorisation as a decision-
making institution according to Article 7(1) disappeared as well. Consequently,

---

India, New Zealand, the Ukrainian Soviet Socialist Republic, and the Union of South
Africa, as the States which are at war with Finland and actively waged war against the European enemy states with substantial military forces, hereinafter referred to as "the Allied
and Associated Powers", of the one part, and Finland, of the other part'.
Tuomo Polvinen, *Suomi kansainvälisessä politiikassa* [*1941–1947*]. *Jaltasta Pariisin rauhaan
/ 3, 1945–1947* 168–169, 171, 176 (1981); Arto Kosonen, *Suomen aseviennin oikeudelliset rajoitukset I*, 80 Lakimies 205–240, 239–240 (1982); Björkholm and Rosas, *supra* note 47 at 44.

other Contracting Parties lost a way of ensuring that the provisions of the Convention were maintained.[72]

The demilitarisation and neutralisation of the Åland Islands have been renewed after both World Wars. After the Second World War the area has been spared from any military operations. Recent discussions regarding the interpretation of the Convention have touched upon the geographic area defined in the 1921 Åland Convention.[73] Parties to the 1921 Åland Convention, as well as the Soviet Union as a party to the 1940 Treaty, have been informed about the border revision between Finland and Sweden, drawn through Märket Reef in 1984. States did not comment on this minor revision of the borderline, except for Great Britain, when it informed Finland that it had taken note of this new information.[74]

The 1921 Åland Convention contains some exceptions regarding both demilitarisation and neutralisation. Some of these exceptions only consider Finland's access and sojourn within the zone, whereas others consider other Parties and States outside of the Convention. For this reason it would be important to note that the borderline of the demilitarised and neutralised area should be clearly indicated on charts.[75] The borderline of the Åland Islands is solely drawn over the sea (excluding Märket Reef). This means that the borderline is defined by coordinates in accordance with certain charts. However, British, Finnish and Russian maps referred to by the Convention do not correspond to the modern cartographic reference system. In the late 1990s, this point was made by Martin Ekman who remarked upon the interpretation of coordinates mentioned by the 1921 Åland Convention. One of the problems raised was to do with the existing differences between the zone defined by the 1921 Convention and area covered by the Act on the Autonomy of Åland.[76]

---

72   Erich, *supra* note 34 at 187–188; Söderhjelm, *supra* note 2 at 308; Erik Castrén, *Suomen kansainvälinen oikeus* 126 (1959); Björkholm and Rosas, *supra* note 51 at 31.

73   Spiliopoulou Åkermark, *supra* note 5 at 58.

74   Suomen ja Ruotsin välisen valtakunnanrajan vuoden 1981 rajankäynnin osittaisesta vahvistamisesta tehty sopimus.
      Finnish Treaty Series 36/1985; UaVM n:o 9/1985; Government Proposal HE 70/1984; Rotkirch in Chapter 1 note 2 at 373; Björkholm and Rosas, *supra* note 47 at 38.

75   Finnish Ministry of Justice, *En utredning om gränserna för Ålands demilitarisering* (2006).

76   The Autonomy Act from 1920 has been dated in 1951 by another Act, which also became outdated and the present Act on the Autonomy of Åland entered into force on 1st January 1993 and has been passed by the Finnish Parliament in constitutional order and with assent given by the Åland Parliament. In spite of the Act on the Autonomy of Åland, Finland has legislative authority relating to foreign relations, merchant shipping and shipping lanes, aviation, nuclear energy, civil defence, armed forces and border guards, the actions

In addition, the discussion has touched upon the consequences of a gradual uplift of land.[77] The so-called Boundary Working Group, named by the Finnish Ministry of Justice in 2005, stated that it is necessary to mark demilitarisation boundaries on new maps.[78] The Ministry for Foreign Affairs of Finland asked in 2012 the National Land Survey to perform the technical delimitation of the areas defined by the Åland Convention. The geographical points that refer to certain British, Finnish and Russian nautical charts were transferred into the modern ETRS89 system and new coordinates published on 25th March 2013.[79]

Discussions regarding military activities have touched upon the air force's flights over the islands, navy visits to the islands, and the coast guard's use of warning fire against unknown underwater objects.[80] In past times, violations in conjunction with the demilitarised area had involved Finnish and Swedish aircraft. However, in more recent years NATO aircraft have violated the zone as well.[81] Also Finland's accession to the Treaty on Open Skies[82] led to a lively debate about Treaty's compatibility with the 1921 Åland Convention. Discussion was started by Åland Islands Peace Institute and it included Ålandic politicians and local newspapers.[83] Eventually the Åland authorities found that there was no need for a territorial exception to be made for the Åland Islands because the Treaty of Open Skies is in conformity with the 1921 Åland Convention.[84]

Finland's and the Åland Islands' membership to the European Union has brought new instruments to the interpretation of the 1921 Åland Convention.

---

of the authorities to ensure the security of the State, state of defence and readiness for a state emergency.

Act on the Autonomy of Åland available in English http://www.finlex.fi/en/laki/kaannokset/1991/en19911144.pdf. The original text in Swedish and Finnish: 16th August 1991/1144 amended 31st December 1994/1556, 12th July 1996/520, 28th January 2000/75 and 30th January 2004/68 (in Swedish also in Ålands författningssamling 1991/71,1995/6, 1996/59, 2000/38 and 2004/11). Markku Suksi, *Ålands konstitution : en sammanställning av material och tolkningar I anslutning till självstyrelselag för Åland* 15–16 (2005).

77   See Martin Ekman, *Det självstyrda och demilitariserade Ålands gränser – historiska, geovetenskapliga och rättsliga synpunkter* (2000).

78   Finnish Ministry of Justice, *supra* note 75 Section 4.4.1.

79   Technical Delimitation of the Åland Convention 25th March 2013, Finnish Treaty Series 31/2013.

80   Björkholm and Rosas, *supra* note 47 at 39; Gardberg and Törnroos in Chapter 1 note 3 at 56; Spiliopoulou Åkermark, *supra* note 5 at 64–68.

81   Spiliopoulou Åkermark, *supra* note 5 at 67.

82   Treaty on Open Skies, Finnish Treaty Series 40/2003. Finland and Sweden submitted their applications on the same day in 2002. Rotkirch, *supra* note 4 at 61.

83   See more on the position of Åland's authorities, Rotkirch, *supra* note 4 at 78–85; the Åland Islands Peace Institute's letter and press releases.

84   Rotkirch, *supra* note 4 at 88.; Bring, *supra* note 46 at 18–19.

The Åland Island's special status was referred to in Protocol No. 2 attached to the 1994 Accession Treaty, where it referred to the special status the Åland Islands enjoyed under international law. The EU Commission also referred to the demilitarisation and neutralisation of the Islands in its statement.[85] References to the Åland Islands regime, and a continuously changing pattern of incidents involving it, suggest that the regime is a current topic of debate.

10   The 1921 Åland Islands Convention under International Law

The 1921 Åland Convention established coordinates to clearly define the geographical space encompassing the demilitarised and neutralised zone within the Åland Islands sea area. Without taking into account the possible inaccuracy of available charts used to define this zone, the demilitarised and neutralised space is clearly evident. The Åland Islands have followed their own unique strategic trajectory in the Baltic Sea. This geographical space is divided into islands, islets, and reefs that lie within Åland's surrounding territorial waters. According the preamble, the object and purpose of the 1921 Åland Convention is to guarantee peace and stability in the sense that the Åland Islands and the surrounding three nautical mile sea area that covers in part the Åland Strait shall never become a threat from a military point of view.

From a geographical and political viewpoint, however, the Åland Islands and its surrounding territorial waters are distinguishable from other parts of Finland's archipelago. In this sense, there has been justification for its treatment as a separate region. The phrasing of the preamble to the Convention clearly shows that there was a common interest among States to secure the region, with a particular focus on the Åland Islands. Yet it is understandable that the legal scope of the Convention would have been expanded to cover the Islands' surrounding sea areas because it was desirable to prevent military activities from occurring in the future.

It may also be said the geographical range of the 1921 Åland Convention is connected to various security issues and the ability of States to handle these issues within the limits of the region. The demilitarised and neutralised zone exists as a consequence of localised security threats that were identified by Parties to the Convention. Alexander refers to this kind of sea area as a 'management region'. Alexander believes that if problems were to arise it would be necessary for an area to be geographically distinguishable from other maritime

---

85   Commission opinion on Finland's application for membership on 4th November 1992, 18; Rosas in Chapter 1 note 4 at 35.

areas in order to fully justify treating it as a separate sea region. Alexander also uses the concept of an 'operational region' when he suggests that separate marine areas are sites of one or more formal regional arrangements. Such arrangements may be defined within the scope of a governing treaty by the limits of institutional competences or by the real extent of ocean space. Therefore, an operational region gets its meaning from the aim and purpose of the arrangement. A maritime area becomes an operational region when its respective sea-area arrangement comes into force.[86] From this perspective, the arrangement of the Åland Islands could be understood as an operational region.

It is obvious that when the arrangements regarding the Åland Islands were initially agreed upon, the general intention of States was to create a special international legal status for the Islands. The aim of the parties to the 1856 Convention when designing the 1921 Åland Convention was to extend the influence of the conventions beyond *erga omnes partes*. A Commission of Jurists established by the League of Nations provided its opinion on international legal issues relating to the status of the Åland Islands in 1920. The Commission reported that the provisions of the 1856 Convention and the Peace Treaty were in force. Furthermore, according to the Commission, the 1856 Convention provisions had been created with European interests in mind, which is why the demilitarised status of the Åland Islands 'constituted a special international status relating to military considerations for the Åland Islands'.[87] The Commission also stated that the provisions of the Convention were a part of 'European law' and that any States interested in the procedure at hand would have a right to demand other States to comply with these provisions. The Commission went on to remark how this situation highlights the fact that any State in possession of the Åland Islands must conform to obligations in effect, mainly as a result of the demilitarisation provisions.[88] However, the 1856 Convention

86   L.M. Alexander, *Regional Arrangements in the Oceans*, 71 Am. J. Int. Law 84–109, 92–93 (1977); Marja Lehto, *Itämeren turvallisuusjärjestelmä erityisesti oikeudellisen säännöstön kehityksen kannalta: Aseidenriisunnan neuvottelukunnalle valmistettu raportti* 1–4 (1986).

87   *The Report of the Commission of Jurists, supra* note 30 at 19.

88   *The Report of the Commission of Jurists, supra* note 30 at 17–19. Tauno Suontausta, *La situation juridique des îles d'Aland*, 13 Zeitschrift für ausländisches öffentliches R. und Völkerr. 741–742, 744 (1951); Barros, *supra* note 7 at 291–292; Arnold Duncan McNair, *The Law of Treaties* 263–265 (1986); E.J. Manner, *Some Observations on the Effects and Applications of the New Law of the Sea, with Special Reference to the Baltic*, in *Finnish Branch of the International Law Association* 114–144, 127–128 (1987); Lauri Hannikainen, *The Continued Validity of the Demilitarised and Neutralised Status of the Åland Islands*, 54 Zeitschrift für ausländisches öffentliches R. und Völkerr. 614–651, 619–620 (1994); Katariina Simonen, *Suomi, Ahvenanmaa ja liittoutuminen*, 102 Lakimies 664–678, 666 (2004).

did not demilitarise the surrounding sea areas belonging to the Åland Islands; the Island's territorial waters were established by the 1921 Åland Convention.

One should also bear in mind that during the time when the Commission gave its report, the Permanent Court of International Justice had not yet been established. The Council of the League had set up a Commission of Jurists, whose report had made a strong impression on States and may have played an instrumental role in the outcome of negotiations on the forthcoming convention. Hence, when concluded in 1921, the Åland Convention was complementary to the 1856 Convention.

Also noteworthy is that the 1921 Convention is also supplemented by the 1940 Treaty between Finland and the Soviet Union. The Second World War had an impact on the legal status of the Åland Islands, too. In 1947, Parties to the Peace Treaty had stated that 'the Åland Islands will remain demilitarised according to the present situation'. It is noteworthy that Article 5 of the Peace Treaty mentions neither the 1856 Convention nor the 1921 Convention. Nevertheless, the Article could be seen as a way of effectively preserving the regional status quo because it prevented any military presence whatsoever. Although the 1947 Peace Treaty and the 1940 Treaty between Finland and the Soviet Union cover the same geographical area as the 1921 Åland Convention, they do not address its neutralisation and only agree to the terms of demilitarisation within the context of the 1856 Convention.[89]

There is no doubt that the 1921 Åland Convention is a multilateral international treaty. International treaties are significant because the rules they establish, and the rights and obligations set out by them, are legally binding on their parties. It may be said that all treaties are law-making inasmuch as they each establish rules of conduct that their parties are obliged to obey. If a treaty has a considerable number of parties to it and has an international character in general, then its influence may reach far beyond the limits of formal participation. The abovementioned factors bestow a legislative character upon treaties like the Åland Convention, which all tend to function as instruments whose original provisions are accepted as customary international law. Oppenheim mentions the Hague Conventions regarding the rules of warfare on land and sea as examples of treaties that are considered to have become generally binding rules of international law.[90]

---

89   Paris Peace Treaty Finnish Treaty Series 20/1947; Suontausta, *supra* note 88 at 749; Bo
      Johnson Theutenberg, *Folkrätt och säkerhetspolitik* 203 (1986); Rotkirch in Chapter 1 note
      2 at 372; Bengt Broms, *Kansainvälinen oikeus* 534 (1978).
90   L. Oppenheim, *Oppenheim's International Law, Volume I* 32–33, 1203–1206 (Robert
      Jennings & Arthur Watts eds., 9 ed. 1993). The First Peace Conference at The Hague ad-
      opted 29 July 1899, entered into force 4 September 1900; and the Second Peace Conference

Another type of treaty exists that is contractual in origin but functions independently from parties to the treaty.[91] This kind of situation is illustrated in the *Mandate for South West Africa* case,[92] in which the ICJ declared that '[t]he international rules regulating the Mandate constituted an international status for the Territory recognised by all the Members of the League of Nations, including the Union of South Africa'.[93] Hence, the provisions of the *Mandate for South West Africa* were not affected by the fact that the League of Nations had ceased to exist. In his separate opinion, Judge McNair stated that the survival of the Mandate was based upon the juridical character of the obligations created by it.[94] Correspondingly, treaties that impose a special status upon a territory or create a special regime for an international waterway become a part of the public law of the world and are valid *erga omnes*. This raises an interesting question in regard to the categorisation of such treaties, namely whether they are similar to other law-making treaties that have extra-contractual effects on the grounds of customary international law, or whether they have an inherent and distinct juridical element of their own.[95]

Furthermore, rules may develop customary international law characteristics when they progress to become an accepted normative practice. In some cases, rules may be codified in the treaty or else the treaty may reflect existing rules of customary international law.[96] This sort of instance occurred in Geneva in 1958, when for the first time in history the customary international law of the sea was codified in four conventions. As a result of this historical event, a situation has occurred where the same rules continue to exist in treaty and customary form.[97]

The demilitarisation of the Åland Islands is mentioned in several treaties but their neutral status is only mentioned in the 1921 Åland Convention. This indicates that demilitarisation and neutralisation have a different kind of legal

---

        at The Hague adopted 18 October 1907, entered into force 26 January 1910, Finnish Treaty Series 11/1924.

91   Oppenheim, *supra* note 90 at at 1205.

92   The Treaty was made between League of Nations and South West Africa.

93   I.C.J. Reports, *International Status of South-West Africa, Advisory Opinion*, 132 (1950).

94   Separate opinion by Sir Arnold McNair, I.C.J. Reports, *supra* note 93 at 156–157.

95   Oppenheim, *supra* note 90 at 33, 1295–1206. Also for the neutrality of Switzerland and demilitarisation of the Åland Islands, see the Kiel Canal, *S.S. Wimbledon*, PCIJ 1923, available at http://www.icj-cij.org/pcij/series-a.php?p1=9&p2=1 [last access 24.3.2018], the Danube, Jurisdiction of the European Commission of the Danube, PCIJ 1927, available at http://www.icj-cij.org/pcij/series-b.php?p1=9&p2=2 [last access 24.3.2018]; McNair, *supra* note 88 at 257–268.

96   Oppenheim, *supra* note 90 at 33.

97   *Id.* at 34.

status. However, a treaty may have *erga omnes* effects if parties intend to create general obligations and rights relating to a particular region. From this it follows that the international status of the region has been established by a treaty without the additional influence of customary practice.[98] The Report of the Commission of Jurists reflects this latter kind of interpretation of the Åland Islands' demilitarised status according to the 1856 Convention, despite the fact that the Convention does not directly or indirectly mention any third party having any rights under its provisions.[99] Nowadays, demilitarisation is confirmed in several treaties, whereas the Islands' neutral status is only mentioned in the 1921 Åland Convention. For this reason treaties cannot be the sole means of assessing neutrality. A direct quote from the Decision of the Council of the League of Nations suggests that:

> An international agreement in respect of the non-fortification and the neutralisation of the Archipelago should guarantee to the Swedish people and to all the countries concerned, that the Aaland Islands will never become a source of danger from the military point of view. With this object, the convention of 1856 should be replaced by a broader agreement, placed under the guarantee of all the Powers concerned, including Sweden. The Council is of the opinion that this agreement should conform, in its main lines, to the Swedish draft Convention for the neutralisation of the Islands.[100]

This Decision illustrates how crucial it is that the Åland Islands never exist as a military threat and makes it clear that this objective will be achievable by means of demilitarising and neutralisation of the region. The phrasing of the text clearly shows that the main objective of the States was to attain a neutral status that was similar to that already attained for demilitarisation. The Decision also proved that European interests were still prominent. Keeping in mind the fact that European interests were the basis for opinions advanced by the Commission of Jurists, Finland could not escape obligations imposed by the 1856 Convention and had to give Sweden a right to insist on compliance with the provisions of the Convention. Furthermore, both Finland's and Sweden's

---

98   *Yearbook of the International Law Commission 1964 Volume II, Documents of the Sixteenth Session Including the Report of the Commission to the General Assembly*, 26–27, draft article 63.

99   *The Report of the Commission of Jurists, supra* note 30 at 17–19.

100   *Decision of the Council of the League of Nations on the Åland Islands Including Sweden's Protest, Minutes of the Fourteenth Meeting of the Council, June 24th*, Leag. Nations Off. J. 697 (1921).

drafts of the Convention mentioned that the regulations concerning the de-
militarisation and neutralisation of the Åland Islands were already part of
European public law.[101] European interests were still prevalent when the 1856
Convention was supplemented by a broader agreement, namely the 1921 Åland
Convention. Nevertheless, the only direct reference to customary international
law is Article 5 of the 1921 Åland Convention, which deals with the freedom of
innocent passage for warships navigating the Islands' territorial waters. The
Article says that such acts shall remain subject to the existing international
rules and usages. At this point in history the formulation of Article 5 referred
to customary international law, regardless of the fact that States held different
opinions on the right of innocent passage and its applicability to warships.

10.1   Permanent Settlement

The 1921 Åland Convention includes two elements: demilitarisation and neutralisation. The characteristics of these two elements as a permanent settlement, as an objective regime, or as part of customary international law are quite
significant, particularly with respect to passage through the Åland Strait.[102]

The Vienna Convention on the Law of Treaties does not include a special
Article regarding the permanent settlement even though it was included in
draft Article 63 of the Convention. Submitted for the ILC by the Special Rap-
porteur, Humphrey Waldock, draft Article 63 states that treaties concluded
for the demilitarisation and neutralisation of specific territories or localities
constitute an analogous form as an 'international regime' or 'international
settlement'. Had intentions of the Parties to the 1921 Åland Convention been to
prohibit military activities, this would have created an international status for
the territorial area. The maintenance of such an area might have been of vital
interest to third-party States as well to the treaty parties themselves.[103]

The demilitarisation of the Åland Islands was initiated by the 1856 Convention and the concept was also used in later arrangements made in 1921, 1940,

---

101   *The Report of the Commission of Jurists, supra* note 30 at 3–19.
102   The LOSC includes a concept of transit passage that is applied to straits used for international navigation. The aim of this new concept was to secure freedom of navigation
through straits which would become a part of the territorial sea of a coastal state. However, transit passage is focused chiefly upon straits where there had previously existed a
high sea route.
103   *Yearbook of the International Law Commission 1964 Volume II, Documents of the Sixteenth
Session Including the Report of the Commission to the General Assembly, supra* note 98 at
22–23, 26–27. On the other hand, Article 35 of the Vienna Convention on the Law of Treaties says that 'An obligation arises for a third State from a provision of a treaty if the parties to the treaty intend the provision to be the means of establishing the obligation and
the third State expressly accepts that obligation in writing'.

and 1947. The Report of the Commission of Jurists refers to the objective regime in saying that

> [t]he Powers have, on many occasions since 1815, and especially at the conclusion of peace treaties, tried to create a true objective law, a real political status the effects of which are felt outside the immediate circle of contracting parties.[104]

On grounds of treaty law, it appears that 'demilitarisation' has achieved a different status in general international law when compared with 'neutralisation'. This treaty law–centred analysis is supported by Lehto who believes that the demilitarisation of the Åland Islands achieves the status of an objective regime, thus becoming legally binding for third-party States as well.[105] The status of a permanent settlement is supported by Fagerlund and McNair.[106] Fagerlund forms the opinion that the Åland Islands' status, as it was established in 1921 by the Åland Convention, subsequently creates a permanent settlement.[107] McNair refers to the Report of the Commission of Jurists established by the Council of the League of Nations in claiming that the demilitarisation of the Åland Islands was established with European interests in mind. McNair comments on two expressions found in the report, 'European Law' and 'the objective nature of the settlement', which he thinks both reflect the Commission of Jurists' high degree of authority; he feels that States cannot act against the Åland Convention, regardless of whether or not they are party to it.[108]

Bring does not use the term 'permanent settlement'; instead he refers to the international conventions affecting the Åland Islands and also State practices that assert a commonality of interests in such a way that demilitarisation and neutralisation are considered to be sanctioned by general international law.[109] The demilitarisation and neutralisation of the Åland Islands as a rule of customary law, for instance, has been recognised by Rosas, Johnson Theutenberg, Rotkirch, Bring and Hannikainen.[110] Rosas considers that the Åland arrangement is part of a European international legal order that derives its

---

104   *The Report of the Commission of Jurists, supra* note 30 at 17.
105   Lehto, *supra* note 86 at 57–60.
106   McNair, *supra* note 88 at 263–265; Niklas Fagerlund, *Ålands folkrättsliga status och EG* 98–99, 106 (1993).
107   Fagerlund, *supra* note 106 at 106.
108   McNair, *supra* note 88 at 263–265.
109   Ove Bring, *Nedrustningens folkrätt* 327–328 (1987).
110   Johnson Theutenberg, *supra* note 89 at 205–206; Rotkirch in Chapter 1 note 2 at 373; Bring, *supra* note 109 at 327–328; Björkholm and Rosas, *supra* note 47 at 112–117; Lauri

competencies from customary international law. Johnson Theutenberg writes
that the demilitarisation and neutralisation of the Åland Islands has become
a part of European public law. Rotkirch similarly regards the special status of
the Åland Islands to be a part of customary international law, which is legally
binding for the international community as a whole.[111] Hannikainen concludes
that the demilitarisation and neutralisation of the Åland Islands constitute a
permanent settlement that is grounded in the international treaties and customary international law applicable to the Baltic Sea region.[112]

One should keep in mind that the special legal status of the Åland Islands
is recognised by the 1947 Peace Treaty and the Second Additional Protocol of
the EU Treaty of Accession, which came into force when Finland joined the
European Union in 1995. The latter is included in primary legislation, so all
EU member States have committed themselves to an acknowledgement of
the Åland Islands' legal status. In addition to increasing the number of States
bound indirectly to the Åland regime, by joining the EU Finland has acknowledged another institution capable of interpreting the legal status of the Åland
Islands – the Court of Justice of the European Union – whose job is to ensure
that EU legislation is interpreted and applied correspondingly in all member
States. The added interest from EU member States is linked to the preservation
of the special legal status of the Åland Islands and the Court can ultimately
define the content of this legal status.[113]

The 1921 Åland Convention only mentions the Council of League of Nations
as a body to approach when deciding on measures to be taken when ensuring that the provisions of the Convention are adhered to by its Parties. After
the dissolution of the League of Nations, however, Article 7 of the 1921 Åland
Convention became a dead letter because certain tasks were not transferred to
the United Nations. Nonetheless, Finland and Sweden signed bilateral treaties
in 1924 and 1926 regarding different kinds of dispute settlements. Despite the
fact that the League of Nations came to an end both States had agreed that
organs of the United Nations would replace those formerly belonging to the
League of Nations.[114] In the 1950s, Finland and Sweden declared their common

---

Hannikainen, *Ahvenanmaan itsehallinnon ja ruotsinkielisyyden kansainoikeudelliset perusteet* 104–110 (1993); Rosas in Chapter 1 note 4 at 29.

111 See also Ulf Linderfalk, *International Legal Hierarchy Revisited – The Status of Obligations Erga Omnes*, 80 Nord. J. Int. Law 1–23, 4–5 (2011). Linderfalk believes the demilitarisation and neutral status of the Åland Islands to constitute an objective regime.

112 Hannikainen, *supra* note 110 at 104–110; Hannikainen, *supra* note 88 at 626.

113 Simonen, *supra* note 88 at 668.

114 Suomen ja Ruotsin välinen sovintomenettelyä koskeva sopimus, Finnish Treaty Series 29/1924, Suomen ja Ruotsin välinen sopimus riitaisuuksien sovinnollisesta ratkaisemisesta,

recognition for the jurisdiction of the International Court of Justice in accordance with Article 38(2) of the ICJ-Statute.[115] Nowadays, all Parties to the 1921 Åland Convention are also EU member States and emphasise European interests. Therefore, the EU fills some existing legal gaps that arise from an absence of a comprehensive international institution, particularly in regard to its treaty-based system which successfully recognises the 1921 Åland Convention in its 2nd Additional Protocol.[116]

It seems that most scholars tend to regard the demilitarisation and neutralisation of the Åland Islands as a permanent settlement enshrined within the international treaties and customary international law. These conventions restrict the territorial supremacy of a State over the Åland Islands. However, unlike the 1856 Convention and the bilateral Convention between Finland and the Soviet Union, the 1921 Åland Convention includes exceptions to the rules governing demilitarisation and neutralisation. The 1921 Åland Convention allows Finland to send armed forces and warships into the special zone in certain circumstances, therefore allowing Finland a right to use its warships when inspecting the demilitarised and neutralised zone. Finland also has the authority to grant special passage rights and the right to temporarily anchor to one foreign warship at a time within this zone. In addition, Article 5 refers to the right of innocent passage of warships through the territorial waters of the Åland Islands. Article 5 also refers to the international rules and usages in force with respect to the right of innocent passage, which indicates that there is no difference between passage undertaken by vessels belonging to Parties and non-parties. Article 6 effectively confers a neutral status on the Åland Islands, extends the 1921 Åland Convention to cover wartime, and permits Finland to 'temporarily to lay mines in its territorial waters, and for this purpose to take such measures of a maritime nature as are strictly necessary'.

When the Åland Convention was signed in 1921, Article 5 referred to the rules of customary international law regarding the right of innocent passage and rules applied to passage through straits and territorial seas as well. Furthermore, regarding the dispute settlement, the 1921 Åland Convention refers to the Council of the League of Nations, which holds no relevance today.

Finnish Treaty Series 12/1926, Suomen ja Ruotsin välinen sopimus lisäyksestä 29 päivänä tammikuuta 1926 tehtyyn sopimukseen riitaisuuksien sovinnollisesta ratkaisemisesta, Finnish Treaty Series 17/1953; see Hannikainen, *supra* note 110 at 135–136.

115 Finland on 21st June 1958 and Sweden on 6th April 1957, available at http://treaties.un.org/doc/Publication/MTDSG/Volume%20I/Chapter%20I/I-4.en.pdf [last access 24.3.2018].

116 Ulkoasiainministeriö, *Ahvenanmaa Euroopan Unionissa, 176/2005* 38 (2005).

Nevertheless, the development of the law of sea has brought with it new instruments to regulate the right of innocent passage: the 1958 Convention on the Territorial Sea and the Contiguous Zone (TSC)[117] and the United Nations Convention on the Law of the Sea (LOSC).[118] Both the TSC and LOSC include articles to regulate passage rights. Moreover, the LOSC has created new institutions like the International Tribunal for the Law of the Sea (ITLOS), whose task is the adjudication of various aspects of the Convention. In essence then, the LOSC allows States to exclude any disputes concerning military activities of warships or government vessels, aircraft engaged in non-commercial service, and law enforcement activities from compulsory adjudication or arbitration in accordance with Article 298(1)(b).[119] Under LOSC, however, international tribunals may not have any authority to adjudicate disputes concerning transit rights. This disparity between legal regimes is of significant concern.

---

117   Convention on the Territorial Sea and the Contiguous Zone, adopted 29 April 1958 entered into force 10 September 1964, 516 UNTS 205.
118   United Nations Convention on the Law of the Sea, adopted 10 December 1982 entered into force 16 November 1994, 1833 UNTS 397.
119   Art. 298(1)(b); Natalie Klein, *Dispute Settlement in the UN Convention on the Law of the Sea* 280 (2009).

CHAPTER 3

Development of the Norms Concerning Passage through International Straits

Lying on a major sea route between the Gulf of Bothnia and the Åland Sea, the Åland Strait is potentially subject to the provisions of the LOSC on international straits. The provisions would affect navigation within the waters of the Strait, especially with respect to passage of submarines and the right of overflight. Accordingly, it is appropriate to examine the development of the content of the international law of straits and the LOSC in particular, on this topic.

There is no precise definition of an 'international strait'. This lack of precision leads to a number of functional problems. It is necessary to specifically determine whether a strait is international because international conventions and customary rules are only applicable to international straits. In legal literature, international straits have been distributed into three categories according to their functions. One such category is the 'geographical' function of straits: in the geographical sense a strait must be a part of the ocean, which means that it cannot be artificially created. Straits must also be an area of water that separates two land territories. The size of area connected with water (the breadth or length) is not determined. Another feature of a strait is that it must be international. The 'internationality' of a strait focuses on the important role a strait plays in international navigation for vessels and overflight for planes. There are rules in international law concerning straits but some do not apply to all straits. Finally, during the 1958 Geneva Conference the 'usage' of a strait became a topical discussion. Only straits that were considered important to international navigation fell within the scope of rules of the Convention. This indicates that the use of straits is an important matter for coastal States and the international community as a whole.[1]

Straits constitute highways between parts of the seas and oceans. As a result of adoption of the law of the sea conventions, straits are governed by specific regulations. However, these regulations are only applied to straits that are international. Straits that situated completely within internal waters are not 'international'. However, some exceptions to this rule do exist and are

---

1 Eddy Somers, *The Legal Regime of the Danish Straits*, in *The Proceedings of the Symposium on the Straits Used for International Navigation, 16–17 November 2002, Ataköy Marina, Istanbul, Turkey* 12–20, 12 (Bayram Öztürk & Reşat Özkan eds., 2002).

mentioned in Article 35(a) of the LOSC.[2] Straits that are connected to the world's oceans have an important role in implementing the doctrine *mare liberum*.[3] Straits have also been important to historical naval powers, such as the United States, Russia (or the former Soviet Union) and Great Britain. Straits were particularly important during the Cold War.

Also noteworthy is that the 1958 TSC separated the regime of straits from the regime of territorial seas in three respects. First, coastal States may not suspend the right of innocent passage through straits, whereas States may temporarily suspend innocent passage in their respective territorial seas for security reasons. Second, discussions on the right of innocent passage for warships have tended not to touch upon straits because a well-established rule already exists, which presently includes innocent passage for merchant ships and warships through straits. Third, the evaluation of 'innocence' with respect to passage through straits may only be made by using objective criteria, whereas in cases of regular passage through territorial seas subjective considerations might be lawfully relevant.[4] The idea of implementing a separate regime for straits used for international navigation was a chief concern for States attending the Third United Nations Conference on the Law of the Sea, which led to the establishment of a new concept, 'transit passage'. A former 'normal' right of innocent passage is different from transit passage, as it allows more freedom: it permits both submerged passage for submarines and overflight for aircraft through international straits.

1   A Short Historical Overview of Straits in International Law

1.1   *Scholarly View*
As States made claims for full sovereignty over certain parts of the ocean during the second half of the Middle Ages, freedom of navigation evolved into a *mare clausum* regime. At this point in time the existing legal regimes for territorial seas and international straits had not yet diverged. Straits were considered to

---

2 LOSC art. 35: 'Nothing in this Part affects: (a) any areas of internal waters within a strait, except where the establishment of a straight baseline in accordance with the method set forth in article 7 has the effect of enclosing as internal waters areas which had not previously been considered as such'.

3 Christos L. Rozakis & Petros N. Stagos, *The Turkish Straits* 62–63 (1987).

4 Ruth Lapidoth, *Straits, International*, in *Max Planck Encyclopedia of Public International Law* [MPEPIL] (2006), http://opil.ouplaw.com.ezproxy.ulapland.fi/view/10.1093/law:epil /9780199231690/law-9780199231690-e1226?rskey=hv3GBT&result=4&prd=EPIL [last access 24.3.2018].

be part of the ocean and the same rules of international law were applicable to them. Hugo Grotius had written on the question of transit rights through territorial waters and straits in his work, *De Jure Belli ac Pacis*, during the seventeenth century. According to Grotius, States are not allowed to prohibit innocent passage through parts of the ocean that fall under State jurisdiction. Furthermore, coastal States have a right to levy tolls if they do so with the intention of preserving international navigation by keeping sea routes through straits lit and marked off.[5] Bynkershoek did not share Grotius' view, however, as he thought that the Power in command of any given sea area would have the right to say whether it is part of the outer sea or maritime belt, especially when navigation is concerned. Consequently, sea area owners could forbid transit or innocent passage irrespective of whether the vessel in question carried weapons or intends to do harm. To give an example, Bynkershoek refers to the Danish kings who made use of sovereign rights in straits leading to the Baltic Sea.[6]

Nevertheless, the Grotian doctrine on freedom of the seas was a threat to Western European motives to expand trade routes and control the New World. Unlike Grotius, Selden favoured the *mare clausum* doctrine which presupposes State control over the seas and suggests that customary use and control of the sea justifies acquisition. Grotius and Selden tended to ignore the possibility of straits becoming viewed as a separate concept with respect to the freedom of the seas doctrine. The first scholar to directly address the concept of straits was Pufendorf,[7] who emphasised the necessity to secure coastal State harbours and control parts of straits adjacent to coasts.[8] Pufendorf also discussed the right of collecting tolls and offers the opinion that tolls are acceptable if they are used to cover costs needed to maintain lighthouses or mark off potential dangers within straits. However, Pufendorf further points out how tolls related to land passage are more feasible than tolls collected at sea.[9]

---

5   H. Grotius et al., *De Jure Belli Ac Pacis 1625, English Translation* lib. II, Chap. 3, Secs 12, 14 (2005), available from http://www.lonang.com/exlibris/grotius/index.html [last access 24.3.2018].
6   Cornelius van Bynkershoek, Ralph van Deman Magoffin & James Brown Scott, *De dominio maris dissertatio* 374–375 (1995). See also pp. 57–58 for an English translation.
7   Samuel Pufendorf, *De Jure Naturae et Gentium, Libri Octo, 1688, English Translation by C.H. and W.A. Oldfather, Classics of International Law, No. 17* 386 (James Brown Scott ed., 1934). See also p. 565 for an English translation.
8   Pufendorf, *supra* note 7 at 240–241. See also pp. 354–358 for an English translation; Erik Brüel, *International Straits, Volume I* 50 (1947); Hugo Caminos, *The Legal Régime of Straits in the 1982 United Nations Convention on the Law of the Sea*, 205 Recl. Des Cours/ Hague Acad. Collect. Courses 1987 V 13–245, 25–26 (1989).
9   Pufendorf, *supra* note 7 at 384–386.; see also pp. 563–565 for an English translation; Brüel, *supra* note 8 at 49–51.

Vattel also made note of straits in his work as he made a distinction between straits serving as a means of communication between two points within the ocean, which should be free and open for all nations to navigate, and all other kinds of straits. In straits connecting two separate seas, however, passage cannot be denied if it is considered innocent and harmless by the coastal State.[10] Vattel also believed in the importance of coastal State rights to serve the interests of international navigation as a whole, which calls for the use of moderate toll charges for passage.[11] During the eighteenth century, many scholars failed to draw any conclusive distinction between territorial seas and straits when discussions on territorial sea breadths came up. In other words, straits were only considered to be part of territorial seas.[12]

Discussions on the issue of passage through straits were fervent. By the nineteenth century various scholars shared different opinions on the right of passage through straits. Vattel's doctrines influenced a great deal of scholarly work in international law at the beginning of the nineteenth century. Technological and economic development also started to influence liberal notions on the right of passage through straits. Several scholars have linked the concept of straits to limited breadths of territorial seas or geographical functions in order to further emphasise freedom of navigation. Hautefeuille most strongly advised the international community on the freedom of navigation in straits.[13] The same issue was discussed in the context of peacetime and wartime by Holland, who expressed the opinion that in peacetime the passage of all vessels through straits must be considered 'innocent' and could not be hampered. Nevertheless, Holland thought that in times of war the belligerent coastal State may 'deal with the ships of the enemy as it pleases'.[14]

Towards the end of the nineteenth century Godey published *La Mer cotiére* (1896), which dealt specifically with the legal status of straits. It seems that Godey was the first to comprehensively argue that straits ought to be subject to a specific regime.[15] Godey's argument is based on thoughts on limiting the

---

10   '[S]ervent á la communication des deux mers, dont la navigation est commune á toutes les Nations, ou á plusieurs', 'pourvu que ce passage soit innocent et sans danger', see Emmerich de Vattel, *Le droit des gens* lib. I, cap. 23, §292 (1758).

11   Vattel, *supra* note 10 at lib. I, cap. 23, §292.

12   Brüel, *supra* note 8 at 54; Caminos, *supra* note 8 at 26.

13   L.B. Hautefeuille, *Des droits et des devoirs des nations neutres en temps de guerre maritime* 97, 99 (1868). For more opinions from relevant nineteenth century scholarly authors, see P. Godey, *La mer cotiére* (1896); Brüel, *supra* note 8 at 54–60; David P. O'Connell & I.A. Shearer, *The International Law of the Sea, Volume I* 300 (1982).

14   T.E. Holland, *Studies in International Law* 278 (1898), http://archive.org/stream/ studiesininternoohollgoog#page/n290/mode/2up [last access 24.3.2018].

15   Godey, *supra* note 13 at 32.

breadths of territorial waters to three nautical miles if they are a part of international straits.[16] Godey insists in spite of the fact that straits might sometimes include territorial waters or be subject to a domestic legal regime of some sort, they should also be subject to the customary rights of the high seas. Nevertheless, coastal States enjoy similar sovereign rights in straits than they do in their respective coastal waters.[17]

A growing tendency towards a more liberal interpretation of the right of passage continued into the twentieth century. Most scholars considered the right of innocent passage to be applicable for merchant ships and warships in peacetime.[18] Schüking expressed an opinion on straits that were in between high seas, which he considered to be of considerable value to international shipping and therefore ought to be subject to a special set of rules. When deliberating on this issue further, however, Schüking came to the conclusion that the crucial question in relation to passage through straits was whether the territorial waters of coastal States would be encroached upon while vessels navigated through straits. Schüking would have extended special rules to cover straits that included high sea corridors by modifying the general rules of international law, particularly by limiting any warlike manoeuvres in straits.[19]

1.2 The Institute of International Law, International Law Association, and the Hague Peace Conference of 1907

In addition to contemporary scholarship, scientific associations and other kinds of institutions were interested in the legal status of international straits. The Institute of International Law, for instance, played an instrumental role in wording the principle of innocent passage through straits in 1894. The Institute's intention was to shape and clarify the existing rules of law, which was the motive for establishing a special class of straits. Straits were then classified according to territorial rights of coastal States and transit rights of foreign vessels. The decisive matter in this classification was the recognition that the waters of a strait not exceeding double the territorial sea in width would be classified as territorial waters. Concerns about whether coastal States could close straits was brought to the attention of the Institute. Thus, it was generally understood that if straits were widely regarded to be indispensable to traffic between two or more States other than the coastal State in question, then a

---

16   '[D]ans tout l'espace inférieur á douze milles au minimum', see Godey, *supra* note 13 at 34.
17   Godey, *supra* note 13 at 26–34.; Brüel, *supra* note 8 at 59; O'Connell and Shearer, *supra* note 13 at 300.
18   See more about opinions of scholarly authors in Brüel, *supra* note 8 at 61–69.
19   W. Schüking, *Die Verwendung von Minen im Seekrieg*, Zeitschrift für Int. Priv. und Öffentliches R. 121–152, 140–146 (1906).

movement to separate the regime of straits from territorial sovereignty would be desirable. The Institute adopted a resolution to formerly recognise the interests of coastal States by allowing them the right to extend their territorial seas to cover the entire strait if the waters fell within their coastal areas. The catch of this resolution, however, was that the Institute forbade coastal States from closing the straits.[20]

In terms of the proportion and dimension of straits, very often straits would simultaneously exist both as part of the ocean and as a part of a coastal State's territorial sea, which is why a separate legal regime was proposed to cover straits that would effectively restrict coastal States from suspending passage through straits. Since this time, however, coastal States have each been obliged to grant a continuous right of passage to foreign vessels through straits, which has remained a common characteristic with respect to transit rights through straits. The other crucial point to mention is that the expression 'habitual passage', which was used in a draft text for the Institute of the International Law, was later replaced by the term 'indispensable'.[21] Another substitution for 'indispensable' occurred as a result of the 1958 TSC, which favoured the phrase 'used for international navigation', in order to denote a liberal interpretation of passage through straits. The significance of this formulation became apparent in the *Corfu Channel* case, when the ICJ emphasised the importance of a strait's geographical quality, namely when connecting two parts of the high seas, as well as its functional quality with regard to its use for international navigation.[22]

The Institute continued its discussion on straits during a meeting held in Paris in 1910. Among other things on the agenda, the passage of warships and the matter's relation to the law on neutrality was under discussion.[23] There were different kinds of opinions held during the meeting in Paris as some

---

20   *Resolution II "Règles sur la définition et le régime de la mer territoriale", art.10, Session de Paris – 1894*, Institute of International Law (Institut de Droit International), available at http://www.idi-iil.org [last access 24.3.2018]; *The 1894 Report of the Institute of International Law: Annuaire Abridgment, Volume III*, 393; Brüel, *supra* note 8 at 70–71; O'Connell and Shearer, *supra* note 13 at 301; Caminos, *supra* note 131 at 28.

21   An expression 'habitual passage' stresses the importance what is accustomed while the term 'indispensable' lay stress on the absolute indispensability of the passage. Brüel, *supra* note 8 at 43; O'Connell and Shearer, *supra* note 13 at 301.

22   I.C.J. Reports, *Corfu Channel case (United Kingdom v. Albania)*, 4, 28–29 (1949); Brüel, *supra* note 8 at 71; O'Connell and Shearer, *supra* note 13 at 301; Francis Ngantcha, *The Right of Innocent Passage and the Evolution of the International Law of the Sea: The Current Regime of 'Free' Navigation in Coastal Waters of Third States* 87 (1990).

23   Brüel, *supra* note 8 at 70–71; O'Connell and Shearer, *supra* note 13 at 301; Caminos, *supra* note 8 at 28.

members chose to limit the right of passage if there were more straits than one; in which case the coastal State concerned could decide the main route of passage. Some of those members present at the meeting sympathised with the right of passage for belligerent warships; others also felt that a distinction should be made between 'indispensable' straits and straits used for only minor navigational purposes.[24] There was an attempt to reach a compromise between different viewpoints, especially in order to prevent the loss of a coastal States' neutral status in the event that belligerent warships were to navigate through straits that were a part of territorial seas. However, the Institute could not reach a resolution on the issue at hand. Two years later, in a meeting held in Oslo, the same divergence in opinion was evident when the matter of laying automatic shock mines was discussed. In regard to this issue a proposition was made at the meeting, whereby the prohibition of laying mines should be limited to straits that were considered to be indispensable or those that were a part of the high seas. Regardless of this progress, however, the meeting in Oslo did not bear fruit and no resolution was attained.[25]

The Institute of International Law was not the only institution concerned with straits. Straits were also relevant to the International Law Association and its work. In its 1895 meeting held in Brussels, the ILA had seconded a resolution adopted by the Institute of International Law, which emphasised the role of straits in regard to communications. The ILA meeting adopted a crucial norm for communications and stated that straits may never be closed. The norm focused particularly on straits with a width that is less than double the breadth of territorial seas.[26] On the matter of the right of belligerents to close straits, however, the standards proposed by the ILA varied. Therefore, it was agreed in 1906 that belligerents should not be allowed to close straits.[27] Four years later the Interparliamentary Union appointed a commission to examine the regime of straits.[28] The purpose of this commission was to examine the possibilities for the extension of the existing regime covering the Strait of Magellan, the Suez Canal, and the Panama Canal, as well as to cover all straits and canals

---

24   Brüel, *supra* note 8 at 73–74; O'Connell and Shearer, *supra* 13 note at 301.

25   For different opinions, see Brüel, *supra* note 8 at 75–78; O'Connell and Shearer, *supra* note 13 at 301–302.

26   *Report of the Seventeenth Conference*, 102–116 (1895); Brüel, *supra* note 8 at 78–79; O'Connell and Shearer, *supra* note 13 at 302; Ana G. Lopez Martin, *International Straits: Concept, Classification, and Rules of Passage* 4–5 (2010).

27   Report of the Twenty-Third Conference, 87–89 (1906); *Report of the Twenty-Fourth Conference*, 251–259 (1907); O'Connell and Shearer, *supra* note 13 at 302.

28   Brüel, *supra* note 8 at 81; O'Connell and Shearer, *supra* note 13 at 302; Lopez Martin, *supra* note 26 at 6.

connected to the ocean. In other words, the intention was to grant a neutral status to other straits and canals of equal importance. Yet despite this progress, no decision was reached regarding the draft convention before the First World War.[29]

During the beginning of the twentieth century, the legal status of straits was also discussed, for example at the Hague Peace Conference, held in 1907. During this particular Conference, the status of straits was understood to be connected to both Convention No. VIII covering the laying of mines and Convention No. XIII, which covered the obligations and rights of neutral States. The Netherlands proposed that the right of laying mines does not apply to straits. When this matter was decided upon by a special examining committee, the notion of avoiding any application of the rule to straits that united two open seas ('de laisser une passage dans les détroits qui unissent deux mers libres') was not opposed.[30] In the end, however, the provision concerning a special status for straits was never included in the Convention text.[31]

Sweden posed questions on the topic of straits in a discussion on the interpretation of Convention No. XIII. During this debate on the obligations and rights of neutral States, Denmark insisted that if the right of passage was not limited to neutral waters linking two parts of the high seas it would be difficult to prevent belligerents from benefiting from a lack of regulation in neutral waters. It was generally accepted that coastal States should be permitted a right to prevent passage through their respective territorial seas in order to preserve their neutral status. Nevertheless, issues related to straits connecting two parts of the high seas, the preservation of coastal State neutrality, and the right of passage, could not be tied together.[32] Thus, many questions on the status of straits remained unresolved during the Conference. And yet, as O'Connell has

29 Debates of the 16th Interparliamentary Union Conference see Brüel, *supra* note 8 at 81–87. Convention between Great Britain, Germany, Austria-Hungary, Spain, France, Italy, the Netherlands, Russia and Turkey, Respecting the Free Navigation of the Suez Maritime Canal, available at http://www.suezcanal.gov.eg/Files/Constantiople%20Convention .pdf [last access 24.3.2018]; Convention for the Construction of a Ship Canal (Hay-Bunau-Varilla Treaty), available at http://avalon.law.yale.edu/20th_century/pan001.asp [last access 24.3.2018].

30 *Deuxiéme Conférence Internationale de la Paix, La Haye 15 Jun–18 Octobre 1907, Actes et Documents, Volume III*, Annex 12, 661–662 (1907); O'Connell and Shearer, *supra* note 13 at 302.

31 Ibid.

32 *Deuxiéme Conférence Internationale de la Paix, La Haye 15 Jun–18 Octobre 1907, Actes et Documents, Volume I*, 304–305 (1907); O'Connell and Shearer, *supra* note 13 at 303.

indicated, international straits had an exceptional position that required alternative codification.[33]

The First World War interrupted progress made on the legal status of straits. The matter was breached again in 1927 by the Institute of International Law in pursuance of the legal status of territorial seas but this only concerned the measurement of straits.[34] Straits were also included in the agenda of the International Law Association in 1924, whereby the ILA's committee on neutrality handled the issue. It was then proposed that coastal States had the authority to legislate on passage through straits and that subsequent provisions should be uniform in nature, which meant that they could not hamper the freedom of navigation.[35]

1.3   The 1930 Hague Codification Conference

In September 1924 the Assembly of the League of Nations invited its Council to appoint a Committee whose task would be to examine among other things the question of the breadth and legal status of territorial waters. The reporter for one of the Sub-Committees was Walther Schücking. As straits were often part of territorial waters, matters related to straits fell within the scope of the Committee's working agenda.[36] Schücking's report made a distinction between two types of legal status for straits. The first type to be distinguished in the report was characterised by straits whose widths were less than double the breadth of the territorial sea and whose coasts belonged to one State. The second type of strait referred to those sharing similar characteristics as the other type of strait, except that they shared coasts with two or more States. The former type of strait also included rules related to principles of law concerning bays where the right of passage is not applicable. In regard to the latter type, however, principles of law concerning territorial waters were applicable.[37] For instance, if the coastal area of a strait were to belong to more than one State, then provisions concerning territorial seas would apply. However, where a strait's coastal area only overlapped with a single State's territorial sea, provisions concerning bays would apply. According to an interpretation based on the plurality or

---

33   Ibid.

34   Thomas Barclay et al., *Project de reglement á la mer territoriale en temps de paix Institute of International Law Session de Stockholm – 1928*, 1928. http://www.idi-iil.org/idiF/resolutionsF/1928_stock_03_fr.pdf [last access 24.3.2018]; O'Connell and Shearer, *supra* note 13 at 303.

35   International Law Association, *Report of the Thirty-Third Conference* 259–261 (1924); O'Connell and Shearer, *supra* note 13 at 303.

36   At the time straits did not have a separate legal status. Brüel, *supra* note 8 at 175.

37   O'Connell and Shearer, *supra* note 13 at 303.

singularity of States, innocent passage is only applicable if coastlines of straits belong to more than one State. The consequence of this interpretation is that there would be no requirement for an exceptional right of passage through straits. However, Schücking's report stated that straits that are part of a territorial sea must not be closed.[38]

The issue of straits became more complicated when the Preparatory Committee asked Governments to determine the parts of their respective territorial waters that were part of an international strait used to connect two areas of the high seas. As regards navigation through territorial seas, the Preparatory Committee made no distinction between straits forming a part of a territorial sea and other parts of territorial seas.[39] Most solutions provided by the Committee centred on issues related to the breadths of territorial seas in straits rather than the nature of passage.[40] Germany, however, had made some insightful comments, the first of which highlighted the fact that coastal States may never claim any part of seas belonging to straits connecting two parts of 'inland waters'. The other point raised related to international custom, which made the point of suggesting that there should be a special zone of a territorial sea which would lie beyond the frontier of every coastal State. The latter point meant that the width of a strait must be less than double that of a territorial sea and that sovereign rights of coastal States would therefore be extended to the median line of the strait. Germany added to their comment made on the matter of sea vessels, declaring that the right of passage should also be applied to overflight as well. The opinions of Germany were supported by Greece and France, but the majority of States were not partial to the same views and maintained that the Conference should not deal with questions on overflight, which should be examined at some other opportunity.[41]

During the conference there were two key issues to resolve. The first issues concerned the demarcation of territorial seas with respect to cases involving several coastal States. The other issue on the agenda dealt with the right of innocent passage as it was applied to straits of the above kind. Matters concerning the demarcation of territorial seas were linked to provisions related

---

38   Shabtai Rosenne, *Conference for the Codification of International Law* (*1930*) 411 (1975); O'Connell and Shearer, *supra* note 13 at 304.

39   Rosenne, *supra* note 38 at 1382.

40   Rosenne, *supra* note 38 at 273–277; O'Connell and Shearer, *supra* note 13 at 304.

41   Germany referred to the Lausanne Convention during the conference, which stated that aircraft have a right of overflight and are even allowed to fly over narrow strips of land. Rosenne, *supra* note 38 at 273–274, 1317–1320; O'Connell and Shearer, *supra* note 13 at 304.

to geography, whereas the right of innocent passage involved a legal definition and was separate from geographical interpretations of any kind.[42]

The 1930 Hague Codification Conference came to regard the right of innocent passage through straits as being linked to warships' rights of passage through territorial seas. Three committees were formed to discuss each of the three topics presented to the Conference.[43] The Second Committee was appointed to examine the Bases of Discussions drawn up by the Preparatory Committee regarding territorial waters. The Second Committee formed two Sub-Committees. Innocent passage was examined by the First Sub-Committee and subjects related to straits were examined by the Second Sub-Committee.[44] The First Sub-Committee succeeded in drafting and adopting thirteen Articles as a result of discussions. Nevertheless, the Articles produced by the First Sub-committee did not contain provisions on the breadth of territorial seas.[45] The Second Sub-committee left aside questions relating to straits belonging to several States and instead focused either on straits connecting two parts of the high seas or straits providing access to internal waters. The draft Convention mentions that coastal States are prohibited from preventing passage of warships through straits connecting two parts of the high seas.[46] A common limit for the breadth of territorial seas was closely linked to draft articles covering straits and other matters dealt with by the Second Sub-Committee. Given the work of the two Sub-Committees, the Second Committee therefore came to the conclusion that the absence of an agreement on the breadth of territorial seas prevented the Committee from taking a provisional decision of any kind on passage through straits.[47] Owing to disagreements on the breadth of territorial seas, the 1930 Hague Codification Conference was unable to adopt a convention that regulated passage through territorial waters.[48]

Between 1894 and 1930 various legal definitions of straits were suggested. Out of these suggestions two common features are evident, which relate to the geographical context and phrasing of the definitions. In other words, the definitions touched upon straits connecting parts of the same ocean and those

---

42   O'Connell and Shearer, *supra* note 13 at 304.

43   The three topics were: nationality laws of various States, territorial waters, and State responsibility within their territorial seas concerning damages caused to foreigners or their properties.

44   Rosenne, *supra* note 38 at 825.

45   *Id.* at 828–833.

46   Rosenne, *supra* note 38 at 835–836.; O'Connell and Shearer, *supra* note 13 at 305.

47   Rosenne, *supra* note 38 at 827.

48   The Conference also failed to reach an agreement on State responsibility.

that were 'used for navigation'. The term 'used' ranged from mere 'use' of the strait to the way in which it was seen as 'indispensable' to communications.[49] Several questions were left unanswered, such as whether straits have a separate legal status or whether the right of passage is separate from the rules applicable to territorial seas. Furthermore, it was unsure whether straits were part of territorial seas and therefore regulated according to the same legal regime.[50] It was generally acknowledged that warships have a right to navigate through straits during war and peacetime. Yet it was also agreed that coastal States enjoy a right to exclude warships from their territorial seas, which proved to be the only exceptional circumstance applied to the legal regime of straits. The question of whether coastal States had a right to deny passage of warships was complex and the ambiguity tied to this particular issue lasted until the *Corfu Channel* case.[51] During the 1930 Hague Codification Conference, the dominant attitude towards navigation through straits was that the rules relating to passage through territorial seas also applied to straits.[52]

However, after the draft articles were written they provided important material for further investigations on the legal status of straits. These studies were based on geographical and functional criteria. Nevertheless, limited attention was paid to the role that straits play in shipping. The questions concerning innocent passage through straits, i.e. whether an exceptional right could be established, or whether rules governing territorial seas could be applied, were vaguely addressed. However, with warships in mind, Brüel claims that the 1930 Hague Codification Conference has to some extent clarified the status of warships. In principle, Brüel writes, a warship is generally understood to enjoy a right of passage through territorial seas within straits during peacetime, regardless of whether they may have the same right in other parts of the territorial sea.[53]

---

49   Charles E. Hill, *Le regime international des détroits maritimes*, 45 *in* Recueil Des Cours/
      Hague Academy Collected Courses 1933 III 475–556, 479 (1933); Brüel, *supra* note 8 at 137;
      O'Connell and Shearer, *supra* note 13 at 305; Caminos, *supra* note 8 at 34.
50   O'Connell and Shearer, *supra* note 13 at 305.
51   C. de Visscher, *Le droit international des communications: cours professe a l'institut des
      hautes etudesi internationales de Paris (1921 et 1923)* 99 (1924); G Gidel, *Le droit interna-
      tional public de la mer: le temps de paix. 3, La mer territoriale et la zone gontigue* 728–764
      (1934); O'Connell and Shearer, *supra* note 13 at 305.
52   O'Connell and Shearer, *supra* note 13 at 305.
53   Brüel, *supra* note 8 at 202; O'Connell and Shearer, *supra* note 13 at 305.

2   Legal Status of Straits Used for International Navigation

2.1   *Corfu Channel Case*

The ambiguous legal status of international straits was evident until the *Corfu Channel* case (United Kingdom of Great Britain and Northern Ireland v. Albania). The ICJ presented a definition of the legal status of straits during the *Corfu Channel* case and determined various characteristics that were important to straits, such as its geographical location and purpose for international navigation. A strait need not exist as an indispensable route connecting two parts of the high seas; nor does the volume of vessels passing through it need to be substantial when deliberating whether a strait is international or not. The ICJ came to the conclusion that the Corfu Channel is an optional route, which is useful for international navigation because the Channel has a recognised status as an international strait. The Court also stated that it is

> generally recognised and in accordance with international custom that States in times of peace have a right to send their warships through straits used for international navigation between two parts of the high seas without any previous authorisation of a coastal State, provided that such passage is innocent. Unless otherwise prescribed in an international convention there is no right for a coastal State to prohibit such passage through straits during peacetime.[54]

The Court indicated that innocent passage was an exceptional right and stated that '[t]he Court is of opinion that Albania, in view of these exceptional circumstances, would have been justified in issuing regulations in respect of the passage of warships through the Strait, but not in prohibiting such passage or in subjecting it to the requirement of special authorisation.'[55] The 'exceptional circumstances' referred to territorial claims being expressed by Greece at the time regarding a part of the Albanian territory bordering on the Channel.[56] Furthermore, States were prohibited from suspending the right of passage through the Channel, which was later codified in the law of the sea conventions.

---

54   *Corfu Channel* case, I.C.J. Reports, *supra* note 22 at 28. A status given to straits governed by a special convention was also proposed during the 1930 Hague Codification Conference.
55   *Corfu Channel* case, I.C.J. Reports, *supra* note 22 at 29.
56   Ibid.

In 1947 the United Kingdom had stated that warships had the right of innocent passage through territorial seas, which was an *a fortiori* right when straits
were concerned. In comparison, Albania's opinion was that there was no general or specific right relating to straits. The United Kingdom made reference
to previously published regulations by a large majority of States, as well as an
inventory of State practices leading up to the 1930 Hague Conference. By doing so the United Kingdom managed to portray the extent of how the right
of innocent passage through territorial waters had been acknowledged by a
majority of States.[57] However, Albania had never published any regulations restricting navigation in its territorial waters. Furthermore, the United Kingdom
stated that the majority of States that had replied to the Questionnaire had
expressed their views and had agreed that warships have a right of innocent
passage through the territorial waters of another State. It is noteworthy that
the right of innocent passage through territorial waters for warships had been
given formal recognition in Article 5 of the 1921 Åland Convention, which explicitly reserved the right.[58]

The United Kingdom asserted that during wartime and peacetime warships
habitually pass through the territorial waters of other States without being no-
ticed or having authorisation when using them as a mere channel of passage.
Furthermore, the United Kingdom also claimed that passage through the Corfu Channel was special because it implied passage through straits. The Corfu
Channel constituted a route for international maritime traffic between two
parts of the high seas. During the 1930 Hague Conference, the Committee on
Territorial Waters stated that under no pretext may there be any interference
with passage of warships through such a strait. In compliance with this principle, the United Kingdom noted that warships had for a long time exercised
an undisputed right of passage through straits, which have included the Strait
of Bonifacio, entrances to the Baltic Sea, and the territorial waters of Hong
Kong.[59]

In its Counter-Memorial, Albania made a reference to the British delegate
at the 1930 Hague Conference. During the Conference the British delegate had

---

57   See draft arts. 4, 12.
58   *Corfu Channel* case, Section B. Written Statements, The North Corfu Channel, 1. Memo-
      rial Submitted by the Government of the United Kingdom of Great Britain and Northern
      Ireland, I.C.J. Reports, *supra* note 22 at 43.
59   *Corfu Channel* case, Section B. Written Statements, The North Corfu Channel. 1. Memorial
      Submitted by the Government of the United Kingdom of Great Britain and Northern Ire-
      land, I.C.J. Reports, *supra* note 22 at 43.; for more on State practice see David P. O'Connell,
      Innocent Passage of Warships, The Law of the Sea (4th session: September 1976), 7 Thes.
      Acroasium 408–451, 422–424 (1977).

not treated the passage of warships as a matter of right but one of comity and international courtesy. Thus, according to Albania the British followed suit with the United States' opinion which suggested that warships did not have a right of innocent passage.[60] In its Reply the United Kingdom rejected this kind of interpretation, however, and reiterated its position in a statement made to the Preparatory Committee. The United Kingdom claimed that passage of warships should be unequivocally seen as a right but that its article proposal was a compromise. Moreover, the United Kingdom used its previous investigation on State practices to support its own verdict, namely that warships have a general right of innocent passage through territorial sea.[61]

The United Kingdom referred to government regulations that had been issued with respect to the entry of warships to territorial waters. Overall, out of the laws or regulations of thirty-seven States, thirty-four had mentioned that there were no restrictions affecting entry into ports; twenty-one had mentioned promulgated rules concerning entry into ports or internal waters; and just thirteen had mentioned anchoring in territorial waters. Additionally, some States were noted to have special rules applicable in times of war. However, not one single State out of the thirty-four that had unrestricted access to their ports had mentioned the right of passage of warships in territorial waters. The United Kingdom concluded that this omission was of great significance because it seemed to indicate how the regulations issued by the thirty-four governments had been made based on an assumption that foreign warships do not require notification of right of entry during peacetime. Coastal States only held a limited right to regulate the right of innocent passage of warships through their territorial waters. The United Kingdom endorsed the fact that State practice strongly supported its view on the matter and that warships possessed a general right of innocent passage.[62]

The International Court of Justice minimised the scope of its judgement affirming a right of innocent passage of warships through territorial waters by

---

60 *Corfu Channel* case, Section B. Written Statements, The North Corfu Channel, 4. Counter-Memorial submitted by the Government of the People's Republic of Albania, I.C.J. Reports, *supra* note 22 at 129, 133.

61 *Corfu Channel* case, Section B. Written statements, 5. Reply Submitted, under the Order of the Court of 26th March, 1948, by the Government of the United Kingdom of Great Britain and Northern Ireland, I.C.J. Reports, *supra* note 22 at 289–292.

62 *Corfu Channel* case, Section B. Written statements, 5. Reply Submitted, under the Order of the Court of 26th March, 1948, by the Government of the United Kingdom of Great Britain and Northern Ireland, I.C.J. Reports, *supra* note 22 at 292.; *Regulations Governing the Visits of Men-of-War to foreign Ports*, 10 Am. J. Int. Law 121–178 (1916); O'Connell, *supra* note 59 at 428.

limiting the right to cases concerning straits. Thus, the Court deliberations refrained from referring to a general right of passage through territorial seas.[63]

The Court judgement was not unanimous, however, and there were several dissenting opinions expressed. Judge Alvarez took notice of the different purposes merchant ships have when compared to warships. He claimed that warships' missions are only to secure the legitimate defence of the countries to which they belong. Therefore, coastal States are entitled to regulate the passage of warships but are not entitled to prohibit it.[64] Judge Krylov pointed out that there was no convention that regulated the innocent passage of warships through territorial waters belonging to foreign States. The Hague Conference had failed in 1930 to regulate the regime of territorial waters. At the time of The Hague Conference, State practice was inconsistent and impossible to evaluate in order to see whether an international norm existed concerning innocent passage. Judge Krylov considered how there was no such thing as a common regulation for a legal regime of straits because every strait is regulated independently.[65]

Judge Azevedo similarly mentioned how no significant or consistent facts existed to indicate that States had agreed to recognise a customary right of freedom of passage for warships through their territorial seas. He supported the adoption of a general regime of straits of a certain kind, supplemented by special rules for individual cases. In this sense, then, ordinary straits would be dealt with in conformity with the general principles on the use of territorial seas. In Judge Azevedo's words, this can be summarised as: '[n]o doubt, this transit is founded on freedom of navigation; but here the same means serves different ends. And in consequence we arrive at different conclusions'.[66] Hence, the status of warships with regard to passage rights was different from that of merchant ships because freedom of passage for merchant ships is closely connected to freedom of trade.[67]

It is obvious that questions on the right of innocent passage for warship were left wide open during the early part of the twentieth century. O'Connell

---

63   *Corfu Channel* case, I.C.J. Reports, *supra* note 22 at 28.

64   *Corfu Channel* case, Individual opinion by Judge Alvarez, I.C.J. Reports, *supra* note 22 at 46–47.

65   Judge Krylov referred to conventions regulating the Turkish Straits, the Danish Straits and the Strait of Magellan. *Corfu Channel* case, Dissenting Opinion by Judge Krylov, I.C.J. Reports, *supra* note 22 at 74.

66   *Corfu Channel* case, Dissenting Opinion by Judge Azevedo, I.C.J. Reports, *supra* note 22 at 98.

67   *Corfu Channel* case, Dissenting Opinion by Judge Azevedo, I.C.J. Reports, *supra* note 22 at 98–99, 104–105.

claimed that State practice alone cannot provide an answer to this question because there are not enough cases to follow up on. Other writers had different opinions, however, so there was an availability of many answers. Those who favoured passage of warships linked such a question to the law on neutrality. Therefore, one argument that can be made is that if there is a right of passage for belligerent warships in neutral waters during wartime then there must be a general right of passage in times of peace.[68]

This question was on the agenda of The Hague Peace Conference in 1907 when States expressed differing views on a neutral State's right to limit navigation within its territorial sea area if it was deemed necessary when striving to preserve its neutral status. The British draft, for example, proposed an unlimited right of passage, but this was never adopted. However, States agreed that where straits connecting two parts of the high seas are concerned, neutral coastal States cannot prohibit navigation; whereas in other parts of a neutral coastal States' territorial sea the right to limit navigation was arguable.[69]

2.2   The First United Nations Conference on the Law of the Sea

The legal regime of international straits has its roots in the historical arguments made by Grotius and Selden. From the seventeenth century until the middle of the twentieth, the notion of straits having their own separate legal regime was slow in developing due to international trade requirements, such as freedom of passage for merchant ships, which were fundamental to international commerce. Freedom of passage through international straits later became applicable to warships as well. There were several criteria proposed to classify straits according to whether they were 'indispensable' or just 'useful'.

The definition of an international strait remained ambiguous throughout the codification processes between 1894 and 1930. As discussed above, during the *Corfu Channel* case the ICJ addressed matters related to straits and discussed criteria that might define or categorize types of straits.[70] During the same year as the *Corfu Channel* case the International Law Commission (ILC) started its work on the codification of the law of the sea. Regimes for the high seas and territorial seas were considered worthy of codification.[71] In 1953, the General Assembly of the United Nations considered problems

---

68   O'Connell, *supra* note 59 at 414.

69   *Deuxiéme Conférence Internationale de la Paix, La Haye 15 Jun–18 Octobre 1907, Actes et Documents, Volume III, supra* note 30; Brüel, *supra* note 8 at 73; O'Connell, *supra* note 59 at 414; O'Connell and Shearer, *supra* 13 note at 302.

70   *Corfu Channel* case, I.C.J. Reports 1949; Caminos, *supra* note 8 at 45.

71   *Yearbook of the International Law Commission 1949 Summary Records and Documents of the First Session Including the Report of the Commission to the General Assembly* 43.

relating to the high seas, territorial waters of coastal States, contiguous zones, continental shelves, and superjacent waters, which were all juridically connected and shared similar geographic features that needed further examination and added these to the mission of the ILC.[72] The ILC gave its final report in 1956 and recommended that an international conference should be assembled in order to examine legal, technical, biological, economic, and political aspects of the law of the sea.[73] On 21st February 1957 the General Assembly of the United Nations requested the Secretary-General to convene a Conference on the Law of the Sea in March 1958. Furthermore, the General Assembly decided that the ILC report, which contained draft articles with detailed commentaries for each article as well as verbatim records of relevant debates in the Assembly, should be received as the basis for the Conference's agenda to rectify the various problems existing in relation to the development and codification of the law of the sea.[74]

Four conventions were adopted in the Conference: 1) the Convention on the Territorial Sea and Contiguous Zone (also known as the 1958 Territorial Sea Convention); 2) the Convention on the High Seas; 3) the Convention on Fishing and Conservation of the Living Resources of the High Seas; and 4) the Convention on the Continental Shelf.[75] When considered as a whole, all of the Conventions seem to adopt a traditional stance towards the freedom of the seas. However, the Conventions are not comprehensive and only include provisions on the matters agreed upon by States. There was no consensus on the breadth of territorial seas, the size of fishing zones, or the definition of a continental shelf. The question of the breadth of territorial seas was later brought to the attention of the Second United Nations Conference on the Law of the Sea in 1960, but States did not reach an agreement at this point either.[76]

---

72   UNGA Resolution 798 (VIII) (1953); see also Resolution 899 (IX) (1954).
73   Report of the International Law Commission, Eighth Session in 1956, Articles concerning the Law of the Sea, United Nations, *Yearbook of the International Law Commission 1956 Volume II, Documents of the Eighth Session Including the Report of the Commission to the General Assembly* 256–264 (1957). Articles concerning the Law of the Sea with commentaries, see at 265–301.
74   UNGA Resolution 1105 (XI) (1957), *Yearbook of the International Law Commission 1956 Volume II, Documents of the Eighth Session Including the Report of the Commission to the General Assembly, supra* note 73 at 256–301.
75   See Caminos, *supra* note 8 at 45.
76   David Larson, *Innocent, Transit, and Archipelagic Sea Lanes Passage*, 18 Ocean Dev. Int. Law 411–444, 412 (1987).

2.3   Straits According to the 1958 Convention on the Territorial Sea and the Contiguous Zone

The role that the *Corfu Channel* case played in determining the legal status of straits in the 1958 TCS was quite significant. One topic that the ILC's preparatory work focused on was the codification of passage rights in straits used for international navigation, which was particularly important for warships with respect to their rights of innocent passage through straits. Another topic that the ILC focused on was determination of the definition of 'straits used for international navigation'.[77] In fact, the *Corfu Channel* case was the basis for codification. The ILC assessed the functional aspects of straits in light of the *Corfu Channel* decision. Eventually it was agreed that the 'use' of straits must be referred to instead of a strait's 'indispensable' character. This was due to the fact that the word 'use', which was rather general, could be interpreted more widely. Whereas the word 'indispensable' entailed some order of importance and was too restrictive.[78]

The ILC Report incorporated international straits within draft articles concerning the law of the sea, which referred to the 'Rights of Protection of the Coastal States'.[79] It was obvious that the ILC wanted to link questions related to transit rights in straits to the general concept of innocent passage through territorial seas. However, a tradition of treating straits as a distinct legal regime of its own, and not merely a geographical concept, remained. If there would have been only one rule concerning innocent passage within the draft text then international straits and territorial seas would have been subject to the same legal regime, regardless of whether they were situated in two distinct geographical areas. The same legal regime of straits and territorial seas would have compromised the concept of freedom of passage, because absolute freedom of passage could only remain applicable to straits where high-sea corridors existed.

---

77   *United Nations Conference on the Law of the Sea, Volume III: First Committee (Territorial Sea and Contiguous Zone)* 209; Caminos, *supra* note 8 at 51; R.Y. Jennings, *General Course on Principles of International Law*, 121 Recl. Des Cours/ Hague Acad. Collect. Courses 1967 323–606, 327, 376.

78   *Yearbook of the International Law Commission 1955 Volume I, Summary Records of the Seventh Session 2 May–8 July 1955* 150–151, 255–261; Caminos, *supra* note 8 at 51.

79   *Yearbook of the International Law Commission 1956 Volume II, Documents of the Eighth Session Including the Report of the Commission to the General Assembly, supra* note 73 at 273. Draft art. 17(4): 'There must be no suspension of the innocent passage of foreign ships through straits normally used for international navigation between two parts of the high seas'.

Fitzmaurice alludes to a difference that existed between territorial seas and straits when the right of innocent passage was concerned. This difference focused upon the right of innocent passage for warships, which was not absolute in the context of passage through territorial seas but could not be denied or suspended in international straits. Therefore, warships enjoyed similar rights of passage as merchant ships when navigating international straits.[80] Straits were considered vital to world trade, maritime communications, and strategic interests of States; so much so, however, that unsuspended innocent passage through straits became a norm that was included in the 1958 TSC. The Convention reflects the *Corfu Channel* case, as the Court declared that coastal States must not prohibit innocent passage through such straits.[81]

The ILC discussions also covered geographical questions related to straits that overlapped with territorial waters of coastal States but did not connect two parts of the high seas. Questions relating to this type of strait coincided with discussions on the Strait of Tiran, which connects the Gulf of Aqaba and the Red Sea. Israel argued that in cases where no other entrance to a coastal State's harbours could be found, straits should not be granted the legal status of a territorial sea where coastal States have a right to suspend innocent passage.[82] During the 1958 Law of the Sea Conference the Strait of Tiran was discussed and security interests of coastal States were prioritised in an effort to control passage through straits used for international navigation.[83]

Even though the autonomous legal regime of straits was never acknowledged within the framework of the First Law of the Sea Conference, naval

---

80   See relevant discussion in *Yearbook of the International Law Commission 1955 Volume I, Summary Records of the Seventh Session 2 May–8 July 1955, supra* note 78 at 150–151; Caminos, *supra* note 8 at 51–52.

81   *Corfu Channel* case, I.C.J. Reports, *supra* note 22 at 28; *United Nations Conference on the Law of the Sea, Volume III: First Committee (Territorial Sea and Contiguous Zone), supra* note 77 at 79, 94; *Yearbook of the International Law Commission 1955 Volume I, Summary Records of the Seventh Session 2 May–8 July 1955, supra* note 78 at 149–151; Caminos, *supra* note 8 at 51–52.

82   See *Yearbook of the International Law Commission 1956 Volume II, Documents of the Eighth Session Including the Report of the Commission to the General Assembly, supra* note 73 at 52, 56. (UN Doc. A/CN.4/99/Add.1); S. Slonim, *The Right of Innocent Passage and the 1958 Geneva Conference on the Law of the Sea*, 5 Columbia J. Transnatl. Law 96–127, 111–115 (1966); Caminos, *supra* note 8 at 52.

83   *United Nations Conference on the Law of the Sea, Volume III: First Committee (Territorial Sea and Contiguous Zone), supra* note 77 at 95–100; Caminos, *supra* note 8 at 52. For a detailed debate see Leo Gross, *The Geneva Conference on the Law of the Sea and the Right of Innocent Passage through the Gulf of Aqaba*, 53 Am. J. Int. Law 564–594, 564, 580–592 (1959); Slonim, *supra* note 82 at 111–115; Ruth Lapidoth-Eschelbacher, *International Straits of the World: The Red Sea and the Gulf of Aden* 172–183 (1982).

powers were satisfied with the provision on straits. It appeared that most concerns voiced by naval powers during the conference were included in the Convention text, such as non-suspendable innocent passage through all straits and unlimited access to corridors in the high seas passing through the most important straits.[84]

Questions related to the right of innocent passage for warships through coastal States' territorial seas have been problematic since the late nineteenth century. Innocent passage through international straits, however, has been seen more positively. The *Corfu Channel* case, for example, confirmed this problem, as the right of innocent passage of warships through straits used for international navigation was agreed upon whereas questions concerning warships' rights of innocent passage through territorial seas were not handled by the Court.[85]

It is apparent that the *Corfu Channel* case had created a different legal status for international straits. This new legal status for straits was then carried forward and codified into international law as a result of the 1958 Conference. Article 16(4) of the 1958 Territorial Sea Convention contains a special rule concerning international straits that provides a stronger legal status for foreign vessels that navigate within certain kinds of strait. However, although coastal States were prohibited from suspending innocent passage through straits used for international navigation, the Convention left it up to States bordering straits to decide whether the nature of passage was innocent or not. Therefore, the type of vessel could be sufficient enough grounds for determining whether passage was innocent or not. For instance, a coastal State would have a regulatory competence to prohibit for example passage of nuclear-powered warships as well as other nuclear-powered vessels, such as icebreakers. However, Article 16(4) of the 1958 TSC re-confirms the same rule as the ICJ had previously established as a result of the *Corfu Channel* case, which is why it seems unlikely that the type of vessels would be the sole reason for denying the vessel's innocent character.

The freedom to navigate within straits used for international navigation has been crucial to the functioning and maintenance of an operational naval strategy of naval States. Hence, the law of the sea has an added value of a military dimension because international straits are vital when connecting allies, which is why it is so important for naval powers to secure unrestricted passage rights for warships in the ocean. The greater and more influential naval powers had each considered the regime of transit rights through international straits

---

84   Caminos, *supra* note 8 at 53.

85   O'Connell and Shearer, *supra* note 13 at 274–293; Caminos, *supra* note 8 at 54.

to be particularly restrictive to their navies. When it comes to air space above straits used for international navigation, however, the 1958 TSC does not make a reference to any specific corridor through the straits. According to conventional air law, aircraft are not permitted to fly over a foreign State's territory without the State's agreement, which is why freedom of overflight has only existed in relation to flying above high seas. Thus, a coastal State is allowed to deny passage of aircraft above straits used for international navigation if the strait in question is located within a territorial sea.

Freedom of overflight is considered vital for States wishing to exert military force from a greater distance. However, the 1958 TSC did not include an article on overflight above territorial seas or straits used for international navigation. Instead the legal regime governing air space above territorial seas came into force through the 1944 Convention on International Civil Aviation. Articles 1 and 2 of the Convention codified one of the fundamental principles of aviation law, namely that States enjoy sovereign rights over their respective air spaces. Aircraft do not have the same rights of innocent passage as vessels.[86] Article 5 of the 1944 Chicago Convention says that

> [e]ach contracting State agrees that all aircraft of the other contracting State, being not engaged in scheduled international air services shall have the right, subject to the observance of the terms of this Convention, to make flights into or in transit non-stop across its territory and to make stops for non-traffic purposes without the necessity of obtaining prior permission.

According to both Article 1 and 2 of the 1944 Chicago Convention, the objective of the Convention is to contribute more to the protection of territorial

---

86   Convention on International Civil Aviation, adopted 7 December 1944 entered into force 14 April 1947, 15 UNTS 295; E. Pépin, *The Law of the Air and Draft Articles concerning the Law of the Sea Adopted by the International Law Commission at its Eight Session, UN Doc. A/CONF.13/4 (1958)*, in *United Nations Conference on the Law of the Sea, Volume I: Preparatory Documents* 64–74, 66–67 (1958). The 1930 Hague Codification Conference recognised that there was no customary law of innocent passage through the air above a State's territory, including its territorial sea. While it is true that the Paris Convention of 1919, the Madrid Convention of 1926, and the Havana Convention of 1928 all granted the right of innocent passage to aircraft over a State's territory, these provisions constituted contractual undertakings between States and were not intended as acts recognising a rule of international law. L. C. Peltier & G. E. Pearcy, *Military Geography* 55 (1966); D.W. Bowett, *The Law of the Sea* 7 (1967); Charles E. Pirtle, *Transit rights and U.S. Security Interests in International Straits: The Straits Debate Revisited*, 5 Ocean Dev. Int. Law 477–497, 482 (1978); Caminos, *supra* note 8 at 57–59; Ken Booth, *Law, Force and Diplomacy at Sea* 102–106 (2014).

sovereignty than to the freedom of overflight for aircraft. Moreover, overflight can only take place with respect to stipulated guidelines made by Parties to the Convention. The Convention confirms that the right of innocent passage of aircraft above territorial seas does not exist. The right of innocent passage for aircraft above territorial seas requires a specific convention in order to ensure that the right is granted and respected. Another topic of discussion that lasted till 1958 was whether aircraft have a right of innocent passage above straits used for international navigation. At this time many writers considered international straits to be part of territorial seas, which is why it was possible to believe that norms of international law prohibiting innocent passage for aircraft above territorial seas are applicable to straits. The 1930 Hague Codification Conference confirmed that the right of innocent passage did not cover air space above State territories, which includes territorial seas. The international conventions did not create any rules of customary international law either. Hence, no right of passage through air spaces above international straits existed without a treaty in force.[87]

However, some scholars were of the opinion that the right of passage through air spaces above international straits was already in force according to customary international law. Thus, the rules applicable to passage above territorial seas did not regulate overflight above straits used for international navigation. For example, Brüel and O'Connell thought that common practice in straits tended to affirm the right of overflight rather than compromise it.[88]

2.4   Towards the Third Law of the Sea Conference

In spite of the success of the Geneva Conventions, many problems lay ahead for the evolving law of the sea. Problems concerning the maximum breadth of territorial seas and exclusive fishing zones, as well as the overall definition of innocent passage, were not easily resolved because provisions had to be agreed with coastal State discretion as a priority.[89] The breadth of territorial seas was proposed to be 6 nautical miles during the 1960 Second United Nations Conference on the Law of the Sea. However, the Conference did not succeed in agreeing on a breadth for territorial seas.[90]

The legal status of innocent passage through straits used for international navigation became a significant issue after coastal States established and implemented jurisdictional claims for 12 nautical mile territorial sea breadths or

---

87   Pépin, *supra* note 86 at 64, 65–67; Caminos, *supra* note 8 at 60.
88   Brüel, *supra* note 8 at 233–234; Erik Brüel, *International Straits, Volume II* 369 (1947); O'Connell and Shearer, *supra* note 13 at 334, 344.
89   Caminos, *supra* note 8 at 62.
90   Broms in Chapter 2 note 89 at 323.

beyond. The legal regime for important international straits was changed after 12 nautical mile breadths had been established. Thereafter, corridors within the most important straits used for international navigation were brought under coastal State sovereignty. The freedom of passage also developed into a more restrictive regime of non-suspendable innocent passage. Naval powers were particularly concerned about this legal development. Therefore, during the 1958 Conference the main naval powers expressed their preferences for non-suspendable innocent passage through straits, which is why since 1958 the legal status of straits seems to be developing towards a global trend for a right of innocent passage as provided by international law. The widening of territorial seas has also led to an impact on passage rights for submarines and aircraft. Previously submarines could navigate submerged along the high sea corridor within straits but later, after straits became a part of coastal State jurisdiction vis-à-vis territorial sea jurisdiction, submarines were required to navigate on the water's surface. The law had a stronger effect on the activities of aircraft because the right of overflight above straits was denied. Primarily due to strategic interests, however, most naval powers opposed the expansion of the breadth of territorial seas.[91]

Breadths of territorial seas were particularly altered after the 1958 Convention as more States started claiming wider territorial seas, continental shelves, and fishing zones. In 1958, 54% of coastal States claimed territorial seas of 3 miles or less; whereas by the end of the 1960s this number decreased to 35%. This 'creeping jurisdiction' affected passage through straits, especially passage of warships and submarines. The narrowest points of the world's largest straits today are over 6 nautical miles in width but are each less than 24 nautical miles in width. The reason why coastal State territorial sea claims tended to be 12 nautical miles wide or more is because 'high sea corridors' through most of the world's largest straits would cease to exist.[92]

---

91   William T. Burke, *Submerged Passage through Straits: Interpretation of the Proposed Law of the Sea Treaty Text*, 52 Washingt. Law Rev. 193–225, 193, 195–196 (1976); R.G. Darman, *The Law of the Sea: Rethinking U. S. Interests*, 56 Foreign Aff. 373–395, 375 (1978); Caminos, *supra* note 8 at 62–63.

92   Caminos, *supra* note 8 at 63. R.H. Kennedy, *A Brief Geographical and Hydro Graphical Study of Straits Which Constitute Routes for International Traffic*, UN Doc. A/CONF.13/6 *and Add.1* (1957), in *United Nations Conference on the Law of the Sea, Volume I: Preparatory Documents* 113–164 (1958); Morris F. Maduro, *Passage through International Straits: The Prospects Emerging from the Third United Nations Conference on the Law of the Sea*, 12 J. Marit. Law Commer. 65–95, 65–69 (1980). It was estimated that widening the territorial sea to 12 nautical miles would enclose some 116 international straits within territorial waters; e.g. Gibraltar, Bab al-Mandeb and Malacca.

Additional security issues like pollution and safety at sea were instrumental to coastal State claims for 200 nautical mile territorial sea breadths. At the time when the 1958 TSC came into force it was generally understood that without the introduction of a new binding convention on the law of the sea every State would be able to view ocean spaces and resources differently. The international community recognised the consequences of an inadequate 1958 TSC. For instance, some believed that the combination of rapidly developing technology and an increasing number of territorial sea claims might eventually lead to the militarisation of ocean spaces. Furthermore, it was also generally understood that without a fair and just legal regime natural resources could be monopolised by a few States.[93]

Following the First Law of the Sea Conference discussions concerning the legal regime of straits, maritime States viewed the issue of passage rights uniformly and wanted to secure a regime of unlimited passage through straits for ships and submarines, as well as overflight for aircraft. The approval of maritime States' views on this issue was crucial when trying to reach an agreement on the extension of territorial sea breadths and other related issues, such as the adoption of a conceptual Economic Exclussive Zone (EEZ). The 12 nautical mile limit for territorial seas was the basis for discussions during the Third Law of the Sea Conference. In addition, a new legal regime for straits used for international navigation emerged as a separate part of the Convention.[94]

When breadths of territorial seas were established at 3 nautical miles only a few straits used for international navigation were included within coastal State territorial seas. After territorial sea breadths were extended to 12 nautical miles, however, international straits that extended to 24 nautical miles in breadth would fall entirely within coastal State jurisdiction vis-à-vis State sovereignty over territorial seas. Passage of foreign vessels would be diverted from an emphasis on freedom in the high seas to an emphasis on non-suspendable innocent passage. Uniform claims for 12 nautical mile territorial sea breadths would contrive more than 100 sea routes passing through straits used for international navigation that would overlap with territorial seas.[95]

---

93   The United States' Sixth Fleet was present in the Mediterranean off the coast of Lebanon in 1958; the Seventh Fleet was off the coast of China; the Fifth Fleet was in the Indian Ocean; and the British Fleet was in the Persian Gulf in 1950. These were examples of what was regarded by the new sovereign as a psychological factor, see Caminos, *supra* note 8 at 63–64. See Bowett, *supra* note 86 at 7–9.

94   Myron H. Nordquist, *United Nations Convention on the Law of the Sea 1982: A Commentary, Volume 2, Articles 1 to 85, Annexes I and II, Final Act, Annex II* 282 (1993).

95   *Id.* at 282.

Besides maritime States many other States whose international sea-borne trade needed to pass through straits were interested in freedom of navigation and overflight through and above straits.[96] Many States were both coastal States and user States, in the sense that they used straits for mercantile and military purposes. Coastal States were mainly concerned about their legitimacy on matters relating to the security of their territorial waters and were also interested in international navigation in general.[97]

Due to the fact that matters concerning the breadths of territorial seas were never fully agreed upon by the First and the Second Law of the Sea Conferences, many States adopted territorial seas that were 12 nautical miles in breadth or more. As a consequence of wider territorial seas the number of straits consisting wholly of territorial seas increased. However, many maritime States believed that a regime of non-suspendable innocent passage through straits would be too ambiguous to secure freedom of transit through and above straits. The 1958 TSC provided coastal States some scope for a subjective interpretation of what might compromised their peace, good order or security. Furthermore, submarines were required to navigate on the surface and aircraft had no general right of overflight.[98]

2.5   The Sea-Bed Committee

During 1971 and 1973 the Sea-Bed Committee worked as the official preparatory committee for the Third United Nations Conference on the Law of the Sea. However, the scope of the Sea-Bed Committee's work was divided into three sub-committees. The task of Sub-Committee II was to prepare a list of subjects and points to be covered in the conference agenda, which would include draft articles. The territorial sea regime, international straits, contiguous zones, continental shelves, fishing, and high seas were all issues to be included in the agenda.[99]

From the outset of preparatory work made by the Sea-Bed Committee, passage through international straits was regarded as a priority. The draft articles

---

96   These included flag States with large merchant marines, States bordering enclosed or semi-enclosed seas, and large island States in both Atlantic and Pacific oceans.

97   Nordquist, *supra* note 94 at 282.

98   *Id.* at 283–284.

99   UN. Committee on the Peaceful Uses of the Seabed and the Ocean Floor beyond the Limits of National Jurisdiction, *Report of the Committee on the Peaceful Uses of the Sea-Bed Committee and the Ocean Floor Beyond the Limits of National Jurisdiction, Official Records, 28th Session, Supplement No. 21 (A/9021), Volume I* 1–6 (1973). List of 'Subjects and Issues to Be Discussed at the Law of the Sea Conference' reprinted in 11 ILM 1174 (1972); Caminos, *supra* note 8 at 68.

on the issue were clearly divided into two groups: one covering developed naval powers; the other covering developing coastal States bordering straits. The United States prepared one of the first drafts,[100] which consisted of three articles: the first, handling 12 nautical mile territorial sea claims; the second, handling matters related to straits; and the third, handling fisheries. The United States regarded Articles I and II to be inherently linked, which is why Article I could only be accepted together with provisions from Article II. Freedom of the high seas was emphasised in Article II, which included rights for all vessels and aircraft traversing straits used for international navigation. For the United States and the Soviet Union, matters concerning unimpeded transit through and above straits were 'non-negotiable'.[101]

In its proposal, the United States tried to strike a balance between the regimes of innocent passage and freedom of the high seas. Although the proposal referred to free transit through straits, this kind of freedom only included a right of passage but not a right to conduct any other activity. The proposal made by the United States granted wider freedom of transit rights than the 1958 Convention did.[102] The position of the United States and the Soviet Union had its roots in the bilateral negotiations between the United States and the Soviet Union on the new law of the sea convention which started in July 1968 and where they reached a preliminary mutual understanding on articles of the draft convention relating to the breadth of the territorial sea, passage through

---

100   With full support from the one of the major naval powers, the Soviet Union.
101   UN. Committee on the Peaceful Uses of the Seabed and the Ocean Floor beyond the Limits of National Jurisdiction, *Report of the Committee on the Peaceful Uses of the Sea-Bed and the Ocean Floor beyond the Limits of National Jurisdiction, Official Records, 26th Session Supplement No.21 (A/8421)* 241 (1971), UN doc.A/AC138/SC.II/L.4 and Corr. 1; UN. Committee on the Peaceful Uses of the Seabed and the Ocean Floor beyond the Limits of National Jurisdiction, *Report of the Committee on the Peaceful Uses of the Sea-Bed Committee and the Ocean Floor Beyond the Limits of National Jurisdiction, Official Records, 28th Session, Supplement No. 21 (A/9021), Volume V* 14 (1973), UN Doc. SC.II/WG/Paper No. 4; see also *Foreign Relations of the United States, 1969–1976, Volume E–1, Documents on Global Issues, 1969–1972, Document 333*, (Susan K. Holly, William B. McAllister, & Edward C. Keefer eds., 2005), http://history.state.gov/historicaldocuments/frus1969-76veo1/d333 [last access 24.3.2018]; Horace B. Robertson Jr, *Passage Through International Straits: A Right Preserved in the Third United Nations Conference on the Law of the Sea*, 20 VA. J. Int. Law 801–857, 807–808 (1980); Caminos, *supra* note 8 at 68–69.
102   Report of the Committee on the Peaceful Uses of the Sea-Bed Committee and the Ocean Floor Beyond the Limits of National Jurisdiction, Official Records, 26th Session Supplement No.21 (A/8421), *supra* note 101 at 241; Report of the Committee on the Peaceful Uses of the Sea-Bed Committee and the Ocean Floor Beyond the Limits of National Jurisdiction, Official Records, 28th Session, Supplement No. 21 (A/9021), Volume V, *supra* note 101 at 14; Robertson Jr, *supra* note 101 at 809, 812; Caminos, *supra* note 8 at 69–70.

international straits and later in December on fishing.[103] It is noteworthy that as early as draft Article II(2) many of the conventions or other international agreements that were currently in force and had related to particular straits were excluded from the application of draft Article II(1). Navigation through these particular straits remained under the jurisdiction of treaty arrangements, which is the main reason why freedom of navigation through straits did not function in the same way as it did in the high seas. It seems that States' intentions to change the legal regime for these sorts of straits were limited, which is why a new convention was called for in order to regulate passage through these parts of the ocean.

The Soviet Union and the United Kingdom supported the United States in its proposal for a legal regime for straits. Australia, the Netherlands and Norway were also inclined to support the United States' proposal.[104] On the other hand, many States considered the regime of innocent passage to be adequate with regard to regulating passage through international straits. Other States like Spain expressed a need for pollution control, especially in regard to oil spills, and also felt concerned about the level of coastal State security as rights of warships, submarines, and military aircraft became more effective.[105]

The Soviet Union agreed with the concept of freedom of passage as it had been described by the United States, which granted in transit between one part of the high seas and another part of the high seas or the territorial sea of a foreign State the same freedom of navigation and overflight as they had in the high seas. Regardless of an agreement on freedom of passage, however, the Soviet Union made a proposal for a legal regime for straits that conflicted with the United States' proposal. The Soviet Union restricted its definition of international straits by only covering straits that were connected to two parts of the high seas. The Soviet proposal also made references to the duties of vessels in

---

103 Finnish Ministry for Foreign Affairs Archives, Documents 4.6.1969 and 11.9.1969 relating to the Third Law of the Sea Conference and discussions between the United States and the Soviet Union.

104 Caminos, *supra* note 8 at 69–70.; Lopez Martin, *supra* note 26 at 25. The United States proposed that '[i]n straits used for international navigation between one part of the high seas and another part of the high seas or the territorial sea of a foreign State, all ships and aircraft in transit shall enjoy the same freedom of navigation and overflight, for the purpose of transit through and over such straits as they have on the high seas'. (Article II(1)), *Report of the Committee on the Peaceful Uses of the Sea-Bed Committee and the Ocean Floor Beyond the Limits of National Jurisdiction, Official Records, 28th Session, Supplement No. 21 (A/9021), Volume V, supra* note 101 at 14.

105 Robertson Jr, *supra* note 101 at 816–817; Caminos, *supra* note 8 at 70–71; Lopez Martin, *supra* note 26 at 25.

transit.[106] One remarkable change in the opinion of the Soviet Union after the adoption of the 1958 TSC was that the Soviet Union did not make any distinction between warships and commercial vessels as it had done in its previous proposal to the 1958 Conference. In 1958 the Soviet Union had made a specific reference to passage rights for foreign warships through territorial seas, which proposed that warships should attain prior authorisation from coastal States before entering their territorial seas.[107]

Many coastal States did not agree with the proposals made by the two superpowers. Coastal States were not reluctant to agree with the United States or the Soviet Union on most issues, but when it came to the topic of innocent passage through territorial sea and straits there were problems. Coastal States were suspicious about the possible motives for the two superpowers' proposals and were afraid that 'free transit' could compromise their sovereignty or national security. Proposals made by the coastal States principally set out to protect themselves against threats to their sovereignty or national security, as well as to ensure that other legitimate security interests were safeguarded.[108] Most coastal States believed that the right of innocent passage was an adequate means to regulate passage through territorial seas and straits overlapping with territorial seas. Moreover, the proposals made by coastal States included much more detailed regulations on the right of innocent passage than

---

106   These specified duties concerned the international rules concerning the prevention of collision between ships, precautionary measures to avoid pollution, and liability. *Report of the Committee on the Peaceful Uses of the Sea-Bed Committee and the Ocean Floor Beyond the Limits of National Jurisdiction, Official Records, 28th Session, Supplement No. 21 (A/9021), Volume V, supra* note 101 at 14–15. UN Doc. SC.II/WG/Paper No. 4. Said Mahmoudi, *Transit Passage*, in *Max Planck Encyclopedia of Public International Law* [MPEPIL] (2008), http://opil.ouplaw.com.ezproxy.ulapland.fi/view/10.1093/law:epil/9780199231690/law-9780199231690-e1231?rskey=YeKq38&result=4&prd=EPIL [last access 24.3.2018].

107   *United Nations Conference on the Law of the Sea, Volume III: First Committee (Territorial Sea and Contiguous Zone), supra* note 77 at 223. UN Doc. A/CONF.13/C.1/L.46. The Soviet Union reservation to Article 23 of the TSC: 'The Government of the Union of Soviet Socialist Republics considers that the coastal State has the right to establish procedures for the authorization of the passage of foreign warships through its territorial waters', https://treaties.un.org/Pages/ViewDetails.aspx?src=IND&mtdsg_no=XXI-1&chapter=21&clang=_en [last access 24.3.2018]; Robertson Jr, *supra* note 101 at 816; Caminos, *supra* note 8 at 71–73.

108   For regulations on nuclear-powered vessels, or vessels carrying nuclear weapons, nuclear substances, or any other materials that could harm the coastal State or pollute its marine environment, see *Report of the Committee on the Peaceful Uses of the Sea-Bed Committee and the Ocean Floor Beyond the Limits of National Jurisdiction, Official Records, 28th Session, Supplement No. 21 (A/9021), Volume V, supra* note 101 at 3. Proposal by Cyprus, Greece, Indonesia, Malaysia, Morocco, Philippines, Spain and Yemen, UN Doc. A/AC.138/SCII/L.18.

the 1958 Convention had done.[109] The debates that took place in the Sea-Bed Committee illustrate the differing approaches of States to the same problems, which was the reason for the failure to reconcile the conflicting interests of naval powers and coastal States bordering straits. As a result, no single preparatory text was provided to the Third United Nations Conference on the Law of the Sea.[110]

2.6   *The Third United Nations Conference on the Law of the Sea*
At the end of 1973, the Sea-Bed Committee could not present a draft treaty to act as a foundation for a multilateral convention. Due to the lack of draft treaty articles the Conference agenda was not determined beforehand. Therefore, the agenda was flexible and could be organised as the conference proceeded over the course of its ten-year period. The Rules of Procedure for the Third Law of the Sea Conference were announced in December 1973.[111] These Rules, which included the 'consensus' and 'package deal' ideas, were embodied in the 'Gentleman's Agreement' – an agreement set up that same year by the President of the Conference.[112] The 'Gentleman's Agreement' to help achieve progress in the negotiations was added to the Rules of Procedure by the Declaration,[113] which the Conference approved during its 19th meeting on 27th June 1974 in Caracas, Venezuela.[114]

---

109   The proposals of coastal States tended to deny submerged navigation and embodied no other provisions on overflight.
110   Robertson Jr, *supra* note 101 at 817–818; Caminos, *supra* note 8 at 73–81; Nordquist, *supra* note 94 at 284–286; Lopez Martin, *supra* note 26 at 26–29.
111   *Third United Nations Conference on the Law of the Sea, Volume I: Summary Records (Plenary and General Committee),* 5–32, http://legal.un.org/diplomaticconferences/1973_los/vol1.shtml [last access 24.3.2018].
112   United Nations General Assembly adopted the 'Gentleman's Agreement' at its 2169th meeting on 16th November 1973, which was endorsed by the Conference at the 19th meeting on 27th June 1974, see *Third United Nations Conference on the Law of the Sea, Volume I: Summary Records (Plenary and General Committee),* *supra* note 111 at 52. See also the discussions in at 10, 12–17, 20–27, 40–59.
113   'Bearing in mind that problems concerning ocean space are closely interrelated and need to be considered as a whole, and the desirability of adopting a convention on the law of the sea, which will secure the widest possible acceptance, '[t]he Conference should make every effort to reach agreement on substantive matters by way of consensus and there should be no voting on such matters until all efforts at consensus have been exhausted'. *Third United Nations Conference on the Law of the Sea, Volume I: Summary Records (Plenary and General Committee),* *supra* note 111 at 52.
114   See UN Doc. A/CONF.62/30/Rev. 1, *Third United Nations Conference on the Law of the Sea, Volume I: Summary Records (Plenary and General Committee),* *supra* note 111 at 52.

The 'package deal' concept was one of the most relevant features of the Third Law of the Sea Conference negotiations, which was also to be included in the first paragraph of the Declaration. The second paragraph of the Declaration incorporated 'consensus', which was to become the primary means to adopting decisions during negotiations. The idea was that votes would only be counted as a last resort, after all efforts to reach consensus had been tried beforehand.[115]

The Third Law of the Sea Conference was organised into three main Committees. The task of the First Committee was to discuss and elaborate on the mechanisms of international governance in the deep seabed beyond the limits of national jurisdiction. The Second Committee handled issues related to the high seas, continental shelves, territorial seas (including matters concerning international straits and archipelagos), contiguous zones, fisheries, and the conservation of living resources in those areas. The Third Committee handled issues related to the marine environment, scientific research, and technology transfer.[116]

States presented various approaches to the regime of straits used for international navigation to the Second Committee during the Second Session of the Conference. Proposals made by many States in the Second Session were similar to other proposals that had already been presented to the Sea-Bed Committee.[117] Some differences of opinion still existed among States with regard to passage through straits. For instance, several States preferred a regime of free passage for all vessels through straits; whereas other States favoured a regime of non-suspendable innocent passage. However, though differences of opinion existed, many States were in favour of balancing legitimate interests of States bordering straits with the general right of navigation for all vessels.[118] One achievement made by the Second Committee, however, was the production of a document containing a collection of alternative agenda items allocated to the working paper of the Second Committee.[119] In addition, a connection made between territorial sea breadths and passage through straits was

---

115 *Third United Nations Conference on the Law of the Sea, Volume I: Summary Records (Plenary and General Committee), supra* note 111 at 52 Rule 37.

116 Caminos, *supra* note 8 at 83–84; *Third United Nations Conference on the Law of the Sea, Volume III: Documents* 93, http://legal.un.org/diplomaticconferences/1973_los/vol3.shtml. [last access 24.3.2018] UN Doc. A/CONF.62/L.8/Rev. 1.

117 Nine proposals relating to international straits.

118 Nordquist, *supra* note 94 at 287.

119 The document was entitled 'Working paper of the Second Committee: Main Trends', *Third United Nations Conference on the Law of the Sea, Volume III: Documents, supra* note 116 at 107. UN Doc. A/CONF.62/L.8/Rev.1; Lopez Martin, *supra* note 26 at 30.

emphasised in the Conference as a result of the growing tendency of States to expand territorial seas. A dispute between coastal State sovereignty and freedom of the seas became apparent as the legal regime of straits used for international navigation was examined. Although the 1930 Hague Codification Conference had indicated a common position among States with respect to the significance of straits used for international navigation, the 1958 TSC had a different focal point: coastal States have exclusive sovereignty in relation to their territorial seas in straits; their sovereignty is only limited by non-suspendable innocent passage. What is also noteworthy is that when compared to earlier conferences that included fewer States, new territorial sea claims were made in the early 1970s as a result of the inclusion of newer States that needed to demarcate their territories after gaining sovereign rights. In the 1970s these kinds of emerging international developments further encouraged States to bring about a separate legal regime for straits used for international navigation.

During the Third Law the Sea Conference many of the problems related to passage rights tended to focus on the regime of straits. Major naval Powers were concerned about the potential effects of introducing 12 nautical mile wide territorial seas, such as the abolishment of high sea corridors through straits with widths that were less than 24 nautical miles. As a result of tensions over these issues, a confrontation between coastal States and naval Powers was not avoidable.[120]

The United Kingdom presented its proposal based on various proposals submitted to the Sub-Committee of the Sea-Bed Committee, particularly those made by the so-called 'straits States group', Fiji, and other texts submitted by the Soviet Union in 1972 and by the United States in 1971. The United Kingdom pointed out that it aimed to find the right balance between the interests of the international community with regard to freedom of navigation and security interests of coastal States.[121] The significance of this proposal was heightened by the fact that it was made by both a major naval Power and a coastal State, and thus complemented both sides of the overall argument. The United Kingdom connected aspects of the regime of innocent passage in the territorial sea with a separate regime entitled 'Passage of Straits Used for International Navigation'.[122]

---

120   Lopez Martin, *supra* note 26 at 29–30.; Kleemola-Juntunen in Chapter 1 note 2 at 25.
121   *Third United Nations Conference on the Law of the Sea, Volume II: Summary Records (1st, 2nd and 3rd Committee)* 101, http://legal.un.org/diplomaticconferences/1973_los/vol2. shtml [last access 24.3.2018].
122   Nordquist, *supra* note 94 at 287.

The proposal was founded on 12 nautical mile territorial seas, and involved three elements: 1) a new concept, the 'right of transit passage', which included freedom of navigation and overflight between parts of the high seas; 2) a regime of non-suspendable innocent passage through straits where transit passage was not applicable; and 3) provisions aiming to safeguard the interests of States bordering straits. Furthermore, the proposal excluded the concept of transit passage through straits that were governed by treaties already in force. In other words, straits like these would remain subject to their respective treaty regimes. This kind of exception was included in the Socialist States' proposal as well. Straits governed by existing treaties were already mentioned in previous proposals submitted to Sub-Committee II of the Sea-Bed Committee, which the United Kingdom closely followed.[123] Thus, it might be said that States that acted in support of free transit through straits for all vessels must have nonetheless recognised the special status of straits governed by existing treaties. Furthermore, the right of passage through these kinds of straits would not be altered by any new convention.

Besides the proposals of the United Kingdom and the Socialist States, a joint proposal presented by Malaysia, Morocco, Oman and Yemen became the subject of much discussion. In this proposal the right of innocent passage was applied to 'any strait which is used for international navigation and forms part of the territorial sea of one or more States'. This proposal presumed that a strait formed a part of the territorial sea, which meant that navigation through territorial seas and straits used for international navigation was not based upon the legal regime for maritime zones connected to straits.[124] Nevertheless, the

---

123   Nordquist, *supra* note 94 at 287–288. Second Committee, 3rd meeting, para. 25, *Third United Nations Conference on the Law of the Sea, Volume II: Summary Records (1st, 2nd and 3rd Committee)*, *supra* note 121 at 101; the Second Committee, at the 11th to 15th meetings in 1974, at 123–142. United Kingdom: draft articles on the territorial sea and straits, UN Doc. A/CONF.62/C.2/L.3, *Third United Nations Conference on the Law of the Sea, Volume III: Documents*, *supra* note 116 at 183–186. Bulgaria, Czechoslovakia, German Democratic Republic, Poland, Ukrainian Soviet Socialist Republic, Union of Soviet Socialist Republics: draft articles on straits used for international navigation, UN Doc. A/CONF.62/C.2/L.11, at 189. The United States' proposal included straits used for international navigation between two parts of the high seas and straits that connected the high seas with territorial seas of one or more foreign States, UN Doc. SC.II/WG/Paper No. 4, *Report of the Committee on the Peaceful Uses of the Sea-Bed Committee and the Ocean Floor Beyond the Limits of National Jurisdiction, Official Records, 28th Session, Supplement No. 21 (A/9021), Volume V*, *supra* note 101 at 14.

124   Malaysia, Morocco, Oman and Yemen: draft articles on navigation through the territorial sea, including straits used for international navigation, UN Doc. A/CONF.62/C.2/L.16, *Third United Nations Conference on the Law of the Sea, Volume III: Documents*, *supra* note 116 at 192–195.

proposal included non-suspendable innocent passage through straits, which meant that straits had a different legal status. Therefore, the proposal reflected the 1958 TSC, and thus referring to passage within the context of the regime of innocent passage through territorial seas. Moreover, the proposal did not involve any reference to the international treaties already in force that related to particular straits.[125]

The three proposals submitted by the United Kingdom, the Socialist States and Malaysia, Morocco, Oman and Yemen, which were the focal point for much of the discussion taking place during the second session of the Second Committee, had included a new concept for transit passage and innocent passage concerning straits used for international navigation. There were supporters for both viewpoints. Many coastal States presented an inflexible position involving only the recognition of innocent passage through straits. Denmark and Finland presented an amendment to the draft articles submitted by the United Kingdom. They suggested that transit passage would be applicable only to straits between 6 and 24 nautical miles wide. Straits that would be no wider than 6 nautical miles between base-lines would remain governable by the rule of non-suspendable innocent passage. However, the proposal made by the United Kingdom had been supported in the Second Committee's initial debates. The aim of the Conference was to reach a compromise between the different points of view, but this was not achieved in the Second Session.[126]

The Third Session of the Conference, held in Geneva in 1975, worked to achieve tangible and lasting results that would lead to a convention on the law of the sea.[127] The Second Committee decided to found a number of consultative groups to meet in place of the Committee in plenum. One of the very first questions discussed by the consultative group on innocent passage was whether the regime of innocent passage should also be extended to cover straits situated within territorial seas. The key problem at stake was whether straits should be used for international navigation in order to cope with an

---

125   In comparison, the proposals of the United Kingdom and the Socialist States did refer to international treaties.

126   *Third United Nations Conference on the Law of the Sea, Volume III: Documents, supra* note 116 at 191–192, UN Doc. A/CONF.62/C.2/L.15 (22 July 1974), Denmark and Finland: Amendment to a document UN Doc. A/CONF.62/C.2/L.3, discussions in the Second Committee at the 11th to 15th meetings, *Third United Nations Conference on the Law of the Sea, Volume II: Summary Records (1st, 2nd and 3rd Committee), supra* note 121 at 123–142.; Lopez Martin, *supra* note 26 at 26, 32.

127   *Third United Nations Conference on the Law of the Sea, Volume IV: Third Session* 72, http://legal.un.org/diplomaticconferences/1973_los/vol4.shtml [last access 24.3.2018], A/CONF.62/C.2/SR.47 (18 March 1975).

autonomous legal regime, which could be distinguished from the regime of innocent passage through territorial seas, or whether the new Convention should follow the 1958 TSC. During the session various State groups presented their positions, but it was difficult to find consensus between differing views. States, however, acknowledged that it was important to find a phrase that might be able to reconcile passage through straits without the use of arbitrary interference in order to respect straits States' legitimate concerns about safety and pollution in the seas.[128]

The United Kingdom's proposal was used as the basis for work done by the informal Private Group on Straits, which was arranged by the shared chairmanship of Fiji and the United Kingdom.[129] This informal group produced a slightly modified version of the United Kingdom's proposal, in which the group combined two approaches: the first preferring some mode of free passage through straits (i.e. transit passage); the second favouring a modified form of non-suspendable innocent passage.[130] The basic structure of the regime adopted by the Informal Single Negotiating Text/Part II was not changed and became Part III of the LOSC. The text managed to distinguish a legal regime for straits used for international navigation that were part of territorial seas, which was the first time this had been achieved by recognising an autonomous legal regime for straits.[131]

During the Fourth Session the Informal Single Negotiating Text/Part II was analysed thoroughly. The discussions held at this time focused on the absence of a definition for 'straits', as well as the meaning of the term 'States bordering the straits', which substituted the term 'coastal States'. During the negotiations Canada had proposed a partial definition of an international strait, which was that

---

128   Lopez Martin, *supra* note 26 at 33; Caminos, *supra* note 8 at 94–105.

129   Myron H. Nordquist, *United Nations Convention on the Law of the Sea 1982: A Commentary, Volume I* 107 (1985).

130   See inclusion of art. 40, which prohibits vessels from carrying out research activities during their passage through straits; see also modification of art. 234. Memorandum by the President of the Conference on document A/CONF.62/WP.10/Add.l, UN Doc. CONF.62/WP.10/Add.1, *Third United Nations Conference on the Law of the Sea, Volume VIII: Informal Composite Negotiating Text* 65–70, http://legal.un.org/diplomaticconferences/1973_los/vol8.shtml [last access 24.3.2018]. Informal Composite Negotiating Text, A/CONF.62/WP.10/Rev.3, at 12–16.

131   Informal Single Negotiating Text/Part II, UN Doc. A/CONF.62/WP.8/Part II; *Third United Nations Conference on the Law of the Sea, Volume IV: Third Session, supra* note 127 at 158–159. Nordquist, *supra* note 94 at 288.; see also Lopez Martin, *supra* note 26 at 33–35; Caminos, *supra* note 8 at 94–105.

[a]n international strait is a natural passage between land formations which:

(a) (i) Lies within the territorial sea of one or more States at any point in its length and

(ii) Joins...

(b) Has traditionally been used for international navigation.[132]

Nevertheless, other delegations had not regarded any specific definition of a strait to be very important. Instead they believed that the meaning of the term was self-explanatory or that any further definition would be unnecessary. This was mainly because the proposed articles expressed legal details so effectively that it was clear which waters were being referred to, regardless of what they were named.[133] The proposal made by the United Kingdom had replaced the specific definition of a strait:

3. This article applies to any strait or other stretch of water, whatever its geographical name, which:

(a) is used for international navigation;

(b) connects two parts of the high seas.[134]

The term 'States bordering the straits' was accepted in the Revised Single Nego-tiating Text/Part II, which clearly distinguished the regime of passage between parts of territorial seas bordering straits and passage through other parts of ter-ritorial seas. Initially the United Kingdom proposed the expression 'strait State', which referred to 'any State bordering a strait to which the Chapter applies'.[135] The term was changed to 'States bordering the straits' because of translation difficulties, particularly with French.[136]

An overview of the regime's historical evolution from territorial sea jurisdic-tion to an autonomous regime of straits used for international navigation has been provided above. After 1976 some effort was made to amend the provisions but only a few minor changes were accepted. The Conference continued until 1982.[137]

---

132 UN Doc. A/CONF.62/C.2/L.83 (26 August 1974); *Third United Nations Conference on the Law of the Sea, Volume III: Documents, supra* note 116 at 241.

133 Nordquist, *supra* note 94 at 289.

134 UN Doc. A/CONF.62/C.2/L.3 (3 July 1974), *Third United Nations Conference on the Law of the Sea, Volume III: Documents, supra* note 116 at 186.

135 UN Doc. A/CONF.62/C.2/L.3 (3 July 1974), Chapter III, art. 11, *Third United Nations Confer-ence on the Law of the Sea, Volume III: Documents, supra* note 116 at 186.

136 Nordquist, *supra* note 94 at 290.

137 See a short summary in Lopez Martin, *supra* note 26 at 35–37.

2.7   Different Conceptions of Straits

2.7.1   The Geographical Conception of Straits

Straits are generally recognised as a place of crossing because they cover the shortest distance between two land areas and are therefore commonly used by vessels navigating the oceans. For instance, the Åland Strait is located between the Swedish mainland and the Åland Islands, hence fulfilling the geographic criterion for judging the status of a strait. Although straits have been an important topic of discussion in debates about the law of the sea for many years now, no precise definition of an international strait exists at this point in time. The 1958 TSC mentions that '[t]here shall be no suspension of the innocent passage of foreign ships through straits which are used for international navigation'[138] but evidently lacks a provision specifically for matters concerning straits. Part III of the LOSC goes by the title 'Straits Used for International Navigation', and yet neither of the Conventions define what the phrase means. It is construed that two phrases, 'international straits' and 'straits used for international navigation', both include three elements relating to: geography (the nature of water connecting two seas and separating two territories), functionality (the purpose of international navigation), and law (whether the waters of a strait form part of a territorial sea belonging to one or more coastal States).[139]

The lack of a precise definition of the concept of international straits leads to various problems regarding the legal regime of international straits as a whole. It is important to find out if a strait is international because international conventions and customary rules are only applied to straits used for international navigation. In a geographical sense, then, a strait is defined as a natural waterway and a part of the ocean separating two land territories. Moreover, a strait is not an artificial creation;[140] the size of the connection (i.e. its breadth or length) is not determined. Another defining feature, namely that a strait must perform an international function, focuses on the importance of straits used for international navigation by ships or overflight by planes. However, the rules of international law concerning straits are not valid for all straits. The 1958 TSC stressed the usage of a strait. Only straits that are important to international navigation fall within the scope of the rules of this Convention. The LOSC, however, also refers to straits that have a width exceeding 24 nautical miles, which implies that an EEZ or high seas area would be included in

---

138   TSC art. 16 (4).

139   J. Westlake, *International Law, Part I, Peace* 197 (2 ed. 1910); Brüel, *supra* note 8 at 18–19; D.P. O'Connell, *International Law, Volume 1* 497 (1970); O'Connell and Shearer, *supra* note 13 at 314; Lapidoth, *supra* note 4.

140   Brüel, *supra* note 8 at 18–19; Jose A. de Yturriaga, *Straits Used for International Navigation: A Spanish Perspective* 5 (1991).

the strait. In this kind of situation, the Convention concurs with the 1958 TSC that there is no need to introduce a special regime for straits.[141] Other relevant provisions of the Convention are applicable to straits and their routes through the high seas and EEZs, such as the provisions on freedom of navigation and overflight.[142]

In his study on 'International Straits', Brüel claims that in order for a strait to be defined geographically it must be part of the sea. Furthermore, a strait has to be 'a contraction of the sea area, i.e. at any rate [a strait must be] compared with the adjoining waters [and] must be of certain limited width'. Therefore, the strait has to separate two areas of land and connect two areas of sea.[143]

Brüel's definition of straits comprises four parts. First, a strait must be a natural part of the sea. In other words, it cannot be artificially created. International man-made canals are excluded, such as the Suez, Panama, and Kiel canals. Also waterways that exist between islands that are not naturally navigable cannot be regarded as straits.[144] Second, the sea area of a strait must be of a 'certain limited width'. Third, a strait must 'separate two areas of land', regardless of the sizes of such land areas. Fourth, the sea area of a strait must 'connect two areas of sea that otherwise if the strait be eliminated, were separated either totally or in that particular place by the territories between which the strait runs'.[145]

As regards transit passage, Froman classifies straits on the basis of geography, which contains three criteria used in the LOSC. First, all ships and aircraft 'enjoy the right of transit passage which shall not be impeded' through straits connecting 'one part of the high seas or an exclusive economic zone and another part of the high seas or an exclusive economic zone'.[146] However, due to a strait's particular geographical nature, some straits fall outside of the provisions established for straits. For instance, straits comprising a 'route through the high seas or through an exclusive economic zone of similar convenience'[147] are excluded from the provisions relating to straits. Transit passage

---

141   Yturriaga, *supra* note 140 at 5; LOSC art. 36 says 'if there exists through the straits a route through the high seas or through an exclusive economic zone of similar convenience with respect to navigational and hydrographical characteristics'.

142   LOSC art. 36.

143   Brüel, *supra* note 8 at 18.

144   For example navigation needs aid from the coastal State, like in the *Anglo-Norwegian Fisheries* case. I.C.J. *Reports, Fisheries case (United Kingdom v. Norway)*, 116, 132 (1951); Brüel, *supra* note 8 at 18.

145   Brüel, *supra* note 8 at 18.; Yturriaga, *supra* note 140 at 5–6.

146   LOSC arts. 37, 38; F.D. Froman, *Uncharted Waters: Non-innocent Passage of Warships in the Territorial Sea*, 21 San Diego Law Rev. 625–689, 647–648 (1984).

147   LOSC art. 36; Froman, *supra* note 146 at 647.

is not always applied in straits comprising an island belonging to a State and its mainland. In these kinds of straits non-suspendable innocent passage is granted to all vessels if an alternative route exists, either through the high seas or through an EEZ of similar convenience that is close by the island's coastline. Non-suspendable innocent passage is also granted in straits connecting a part of the high seas or an EEZ and the territorial sea of a foreign State.[148] All other straits within territorial seas that are not used for international navigation, regardless of their geographical situation, fall within the scope of provisions concerning innocent passage through territorial seas. Due to the fact that these straits fall under jurisdiction of the regime of territorial seas, coastal States have a right to temporarily suspend passage through their territorial waters.[149]

The LOSC contains provisions establishing different regimes in relation to the navigation of vessels through straits. Straits used for international navigation fall under the regime of transit passage if they are being used for international navigation between a part of the high seas or an EEZ, and another part of the high seas or an EEZ. Straits used for international navigation also fall under the regime of innocent passage if they exist between a part of the high seas or an EEZ and the territorial sea of a foreign State.[150]

Geographical reasoning alone is not sufficient from a legal point of view when defining straits. Pharand points to the fact that geography alone fails to identify the width of a strait and does not ascertain whether any overlaps exist between straits and territorial waters.[151] In spite of their insufficiencies, however, geographical arguments cannot be ruled out. In the case of the Åland Islands, for example, the demilitarised and neutralised zone is geographically defined in the Treaties. Therefore, geographical arguments are essential when determining the legal status of the Åland Strait, which is located between the Swedish mainland and the Åland Islands. Hence, it is clear that the Åland strait may be classified as a strait according to its geographical nature. Furthermore, the territorial waters defined by the 1921 Convention partly overlap with the strait.[152] Article 35(c) of the LOSC ensures that all long-standing conventions in question relate wholly or in part to straits. The phrasing of Article 35(c), however, does not make any reference to a strait's geographical or functional character. The fact that the text is silent about these geographical

---

148   LOSC arts 38(1), 45; Froman, *supra* note 146 at 647 at 648.
149   LOSC art. 25(3); Froman, *supra* note 146 at 647 at 648.
150   LOSC arts. 37, 45; Yturriaga, *supra* note 140 at 6.
151   Donat Pharand, *International Straits, The Law of the Sea* (*4th session September 1976*), 7 Thes. Acroasium 64–100, 66 (1977).
152   Marja Lehto, *Restrictions on Military Activities in the Baltic Sea – a Basis for a Regional Regime?*, 2 Finnish Yearb. Int. Law 38–65, 57 (1991).

and functional elements provides scope for an interpretation of conventions concerning straits. The contents of different conventions vary and are therefore not completely compatible with each other.

2.7.2   Legal Conception of Straits

The definitions of international straits also include legal elements. Discussions on the legal nature of straits give rise to questions concerning whether straits also fall within parts of coastal States' territorial seas. The strait as a whole does not need to belong to a particular territorial sea as such; rather it is sufficient that the strait in question is partly included within territorial waters.[153] The legal nature of straits is a new issue. In the early 1900s, Westlake had stated that with regard to international law straits with a width that is twice that of a coastal State's territorial sea width are most important. Westlake's opinion was noted by the Preparatory Committee of the 1930 Hague Codification Conference,[154] which drafted articles for the Conference and claimed that passage rights for vessels navigating through straits was no different from rights of passage through territorial seas.[155]

There is no problem if a high sea route passes through a strait because in such cases the principle of freedom of seas is applicable. Complexities arise when straits are narrow and partly or entirely cover territorial waters belonging to one or more coastal States. Due to situations like these separate legal regimes for territorial seas are necessary. The LOSC requires that a territorial sea's breadth only extends to 12 nautical miles. Thus, 'legal strait[s]' have a width of 24 nautical miles or less.[156] Nevertheless, a strait may be still significant if it is wider than 24 nautical miles and passage through the high seas or an EEZ is not possible due to hydrographical conditions. With regard to cases such as those where straits are wider than 24 nautical miles, the extent to which a strait covers a part of a coastal State's territorial seas is of no consequence. Part III of the LOSC includes regulations for straits connecting two mainland areas or one or more islands.

The establishment of EEZs by the LOSC has introduced new types of straits because the special regime of straits also covers straits that exist between EEZs and territorial seas. Many scholars have presented different views on the types of straits that exist, often combining different features that pertain to various types in order to classify them appropriately. De Yturriaga says that the

---

153   Pharand, *supra* note 151 at 66; Yturriaga, *supra* note 140 at 6–7.
154   Basis of Discussion No. 15, Rosenne, *supra* note 38 at 277.
155   Westlake, *supra* note 139 at 197; Rosenne, *supra* note 38 at 867–871.
156   Pharand, *supra* note 151 at 66.

number of strait types varies depending on the combination of types. If geographical and legal criteria are combined, for instance, three types of straits exist; whereas in cases where geographical and functional criteria are combined, four types of straits exist. However, straits that are wider than 24 nautical miles do not have a legal aspect to them, which is an essential feature of international straits from the perspective of law.[157]

George has defined even more types. She suggests that the combination of geographical criteria, such as high seas or EEZs, and legal criteria, such as straight baseline methods established by the LOSC, collectively establish six different categories of straits:[158]

George categorises[159] straits in the following way:

Category One: whereby high sea routes or EEZ routes run through the middle of the strait. This type is regulated by Article 36 of the LOSC. The Bass Strait in Australia is one such example of a strait used for international navigation where a route exists through a strait that overlaps with high seas or exclusive economic zones of similar convenience, when looking at the navigational or hydrographical characteristics.

Category Two: whereby straits are formed by high seas or EEZs. Article 37 of the LOSC deals with straits that cover territorial seas located between high seas or EEZs and other parts of high seas or EEZs. Article 37 of the LOSC recognises straits of this type. As an example of such straits, George mentions the Straits of Malacca and Singapore.

Category Three: whereby straits are situated between a part of the high seas or EEZs and a territorial sea of a foreign State. This category is regulated by Article 45(1)(b) of the LOSC that refers to straits used for international navigation, which are located between a part of the high seas or an EEZ and the territorial sea of a foreign State. An example of this type would be the Strait of Juan de Fuca, which is located between the United States and Canada, the Strait of Leti between Indonesia and Timor-Leste and the Straits of Tiran between the Red Sea and the Gulf of Aqaba.[160]

Category Four: whereby a strait is formed by an island (belonging to a State situated adjacently to the strait in question) and its mainland. Article 38(1) of

---

157   Yturriaga, *supra* note 140 at 12.
158   Mary George, *Transit Passage and Pollution Control in Straits under the 1982 Law of the Sea Convention*, 33 Ocean Dev. Int. Law 189–205, 190 (2002).
159   *Id.* at 190.
160   Mahmoudi, *supra* note 106; Kresno Buntoro, *An Analysis of Legal Issues Relating to Navigational Rights and Freedoms through and over Indonesian Waters* 200 (2010), http://ro.uow.edu.au/theses/3091 [last access 24.3.2018].

the LOSC refers to this type. An example of this type of strait is the Messina Strait, which is located between Italy and Sicily.[161]

Category Five: whereby straits are regulated by long-standing conventions. This type is an application of Article 35(c), which recognises straits that are regulated in whole or in part by long-standing international conventions concerning the regulation of such straits. This Article does not include a list of straits, however. As an example of this type of strait, George only mentions treaty arrangement regarding the Turkish Straits. However, treaty arrangements regarding the Danish Straits (located between Denmark and Sweden), the Strait of Magellan (located between Argentina and Chile), or the Åland Strait (located between Finland and Sweden) are mentioned by many writers in reference to the application of Article 35(c).[162]

Category Six: concerning straits that previously used to be a part of a territorial sea. Article 35(a) needs to be read in light of Article 8(2) of the LOSC, as its provision refers to straits used for international navigation whose waters were previously a part of a territorial sea area but had since been altered by the introduction of straight baselines. According to these circumstances, the provision declares, these straits are considered a part of a coastal State's internal waters.

With respect to the Åland Strait, declarations made by Finland and Sweden on the eve of signing the LOSC[163] both seem to indicate they believe that the Åland Strait falls within the scope of Category Five above. However, the application of Article 35(c) is ambiguous in the sense that it does not include a list of straits that it covers, which therefore leaves scope for various interpretations. It has been stated by some writers that the Åland Strait does not belong to any category that exists outside of the regime of transit passage.[164] It is noteworthy that no divergence of opinion has occurred when discussing the

---

161   Mahmoudi, *supra* note 106.

162   Pharand does not mention the Åland Strait. Pharand, *supra* note 151 at 66; Caminos, *supra* note 8 at 130–131; Kari Hakapää, *Uusi kansainvälinen merioikeus* 133–134 (1988); Rainer Lagoni, *Straits Used for International Navigation: Environmental Protection and Maritime Safety in the Danish Straits*, in *The Proceedings of the Symposium on the Straits Used for International Navigation, 16–17 November 2002, Ataköy Marina, Istanbul – Turkey* 159–173, 170 (Bayram Öztürk & Reşat Özkan eds., 2002); Lopez Martin, *supra* note 26 at 78.

163   http://www.un.org/depts/los/convention_agreements/convention_declarations.htm #Sweden%20Upon%20signature [last access 24.3.2018].

164   Elmar Rauch, *The Protocol Additional to the Geneva Conventions for the Protection of Victims of International Armed Conflicts and the United Nations Convention on the Law of the Sea: Repercussions of Naval Warfare* 52 (1984); Wolff Heintschel von Heinegg, *The Law of Naval Warfare and International Straits*, in *International Law Studies Volume 71, The Law of Armed Conflict: Into Next Millennium*, 263–292, 279 (M.N. Schmitt &

inclusion of the Turkish Straits within the Convention text. At the State level, the US Department of State has expressed in publication Limits in the Seas[165] that Article 35(c) is not applicable to the Åland Strait because the territorial sea of the Åland Islands only extends by 3 nautical miles from the low-water line. However, the negotiations in the Third Law of the Conference do not support the interpretation that the Turkish Straits are the only straits covered by Article 35(c).

2.7.3   Functional Elements of Straits

It is quite possible that certain straits may be classified as international straits on grounds of geographical and legal characteristics. However, the provisions of the 1958 TSC and the LOSC regulating navigation in straits are only applicable to straits that are used sufficiently enough to be considered 'international'. Therefore, one must also take into consideration the functional elements of straits. The Conventions require that a strait is used for international navigation but do not refer to a limit to the volume of traffic through straits, which would bring the strait within the scope of the 1958 TSC and the LOSC. Hence, the matter has been generally left open to interpretation. To determine the nature of a strait we must first define the factors that are relevant to straits used for international navigation.[166]

According to a functional definition of an international strait, not just the traffic alone but also the volume of traffic passing through straits is important. Traffic volume may even be regarded as one of the key factors in determining the significance of a strait. In its own definition of a strait, the ICJ has emphasised 'the fact of its being used for international navigation'.[167] During the drafting of both the 1958 TSC and the LOSC, the fact that a strait is being used for international navigation was referred to when establishing the conditions for determining whether a strait is international or not. However, the volume of navigation is not explicitly addressed in either of the Conventions' texts. Therefore, issues regarding the volume of navigation must be determined separately according to the character of the strait in question.[168]

Brüel concludes that a strait's significance to international navigation is of importance when considering whether a strait is used for international

---

L.C. Green eds., 1998); J. Ashley Roach & Robert W. Smith, *Excessive Maritime Claims* 284 (2012).

165   US Department of State, *Limits in the Seas No. 112, United States Responses to Excessive Maritime Claims* 66–67 (1992).

166   Pharand, *supra* note 151 at 67.

167   *Corfu Channel* case, I.C.J. Reports, *supra* note 22 at 28.

168   Ytturriaga, *supra* note 140 at 8.

navigation. He also notes that due to the fact that the importance of a particular strait is difficult to determine, a special norm for international law would be likewise problematic. It is difficult to determine how extensive the interests of the international community should be or how long a particular strait should have been important for international sea-commerce when striving to create a special norm of international law for them. As Brüel notes, however, a definition like this is based on facts, which could include 'the number of ships passing through the strait, their total tonnage, the aggregate value of their cargoes, the average size of the ships' or the number of nations represented by vessels in the strait.[169] Nonetheless, all of the abovementioned features merely relate to whether or not a strait is considered to be 'international'.[170] Brüel's conclusion is that only straits playing a significant role in international maritime commerce can attain a legal status as an international strait. In other words, where there are global interests at stake.[171] Going by the definition provided by Brüel, it is not difficult to point to such straits because shipping routes hardly change.[172] Moreover, it is likely that new international straits may emerge over time as a former strait becomes less important for navigation and a newer route becomes more favourable. It is also noteworthy that Brüel only refers to maritime commerce in his definition of a strait. States aiming to secure transit rights through straits for their warships have particularly encouraged debate.

Questions related to the volume of traffic passing through straits were raised during the *Corfu Channel* case. After considering the Corfu Channel to be an international strait, the United Kingdom claimed that the strait fulfilled the requirements as an international strait because the Corfu Channel connected two parts of the high seas and was useful to navigation.[173] The Albanian delegate viewed the situation differently, seeing as though the Corfu Channel could not be characterised as an international strait and was not the main route between the north-eastern corner of Corfu and the Albanian mainland; it was only a secondary route.[174]

---

169   Brüel, *supra* note 131 at 42–43.
170   *Id.* at 43.
171   *Id.* at 43.
172   *Id.* at 43–44.
173   *Corfu Channel* case, I.C.J. Reports, *supra* note 22 at 242; O'Connell and Shearer, *supra* note 13 at 308.
174   Albania considered the Corfu Channel to be a secondary route, I.C.J. Reports, *supra* note 22 at 354; O'Connell and Shearer, *supra* note 13 at 309; Yturriaga, *supra* note 140 at 9–10.

The Court decision stated that the Corfu Channel connects parts of the high seas and is used for international navigation. The volume of traffic and the significance of a strait for international navigation are not decisive criteria. It is adequate enough that a strait is useful to international navigation, which is why the Court rejected any contrary opinion on grounds of more important alternative routes which existed.[175] The Court took the volume of vessels passing through a strait into consideration as well as the total number of flag States that were represented by vessels to be contributory factors when making a judgement on passage through the channel.[176] Brüel also suggests that the total tonnage and value of cargo onboard needs to be considered.[177] One argument made by the United Kingdom was that the British Navy had 'regularly used [the] Channel for 80 years or more'.[178] Thus, it appears that another requirement for an international strait would be the historical or traditional value of a strait.[179]

As a result of the Court's judgement on the legality of passage by the Royal Navy, a draft convention to the 1958 Law of the Sea Conference was prepared, which included a proposal made by the International Law Commission that suggested that non-suspension of innocent passage of ships through straits should only cover straits that were 'normally used for international navigation between two parts of the high seas'.[180] During the *Corfu Channel* case the Court stated that the strait had also traditionally been used by the navies of other States. One could speculate that the word 'normally' in the context of passage was used as a reference to the regular use of the strait by vessels like those of the British Navy. The use of the word 'normally' was removed from the Convention's text during the course of the Conference, which is probably due to the fact that it is too restrictive as it implies that a strait is regularly used for international navigation over a long period of time.[181] The customary rule concerning passage through straits was codified in the 1958 Conference, but the Convention was silent on the volume of traffic through the strait; which would mean

---

175   Pharand, *supra* note 151 at 69.; *Corfu Channel* case, I.C.J. Reports, *supra* note 22 at 28; O'Connell, *supra* note 139 at 497.
176   2884 ships throughout a 21-month period from seven flag States.
177   Brüel, *supra* note 8 at 42–43.
178   *Corfu Channel* case, I.C.J. Reports, *supra* note 22 at 29; Pharand, *supra* note 151 at 70.
179   Pharand, *supra* note 151 at 70.
180   Draft art. 17, *Yearbook of the International Law Commission 1956 Volume II, Documents of the Eighth Session Including the Report of the Commission to the General Assembly, supra* note 73 at 258; Pharand, *supra* note 151 at 69.
181   *Corfu Channel* case, I.C.J. Reports, *supra* note 22 at 29; Pharand, *supra* note 151 at 70.

that the strait would be classified as an international strait.[182] Pharand made an interesting observation in regard to the degree of use required, namely that 'it seems clear that before a strait may be considered international, proof must be made that it has *a history as a useful route for international maritime traffic* similar to that shown to exist in the North Corfu Channel'.[183] In the *Corfu Channel* case there were at least 2,884 crossings made by vessels belonging to seven States over the course of 21 months. The number of vessels crossing a strait can be considered a good starting point when aiming to judge whether a strait is used for international navigation or not.

O'Connell foregrounds the functional significance of straits when he states that '[when ...] a strait in law is a passage of territorial sea linking two areas of high sea this is not to be taken literally, but rather construed as meaning a passage which ordinarily carries the bulk of international traffic not destined for ports on the relevant coastlines. The test of what is a strait, unlike the test of what is a bay, is not so much geographical, therefore, as functional'.[184]

In the 1958 TSC text international straits are only mentioned in Article 16(4). In the 1958 Convention, passage through international straits is only an exception to the general rule of innocent passage. In fact, the 1958 Convention increased the extent of sea area where the right of innocent passage could be applied. This was because the Convention also included straits located between the high seas and territorial seas. Although merely a short contribution, Article 16(4) still constitutes the basis for an autonomous regime for straits.[185] The LOSC, however, contains richer references to straits. Part III of the LOSC concerns straits and a concept of straits that includes the right of overflight for aircraft. According to the LOSC the criterion for the use of straits impacts the Convention's overall definition of what an international strait functions as. If a route through the high seas or a coastal State's EEZ exists, then the rules concerning international straits are not applicable.[186]

The 1958 TSC fulfilled certain objectives related to passage rights, such as freedom of the seas and passage rights through straits. This was principally achieved by incorporating the term 'innocent passage', as well as ultimately prohibiting coastal States from suspending this. The LOSC divides freedom of passage through straits into two categories. When analysing the LOSC,

---

182   Pharand, *supra* note 151 at 69–70.
183   Donat Pharand & Leonard H. Legault, *The Northwest Passage: Arctic Straits* 94 (1984).
184   O'Connell, *supra* note 139 at 497.
185   Maduro, *supra* note 92 at 70–71. The *Corfu Channel* case only concerned straits that connected two parts of the high seas.
186   LOSC art. 36.

'freedom of passage' includes 'innocent passage' but another concept is also prevalent, 'transit passage', which became important as wider territorial seas were introduced. The 1958 TSC limited unimpeded navigation to the concept of 'innocence', which left coastal States wider discretionary powers to determine the nature of passage. The following section now turns to discuss the development of an autonomous legal regime for straits according to the law of the sea.

CHAPTER 4

Navigational Rights

1 Transit Passage

1.1 *The Regime of Transit Passage*

During the Third UN Law of the Sea Conference it became clear that in addition to common interests in international trade, States are also interested in straits because of their strategic value. By controlling these, a State can hinder or completely prohibit traffic. Therefore, it is easy to understand why the United States and the Soviet Union were especially interested in securing free transit rights through straits during the Conference to such an extent that the success of the Convention very much depended on this issue being resolved.[1]

The 1958 TSC provided foreign vessels a right to non-suspendable innocent passage in straits used for international navigation.[2] The rules laid out by the Convention covered territorial seas and did not differ according to whether a territorial sea was a whole or part of a strait. Strait States opposed the extension of transit rights because they hoped that straits would have the same legal status as territorial seas. Hence, since territorial seas and straits share the same legal status, with the same rules and regulations, passage of foreign vessels through straits would not be free and unimpeded. States bordering straits only approved the former rule on innocent passage and wanted to have more discretionary power to regulate passage through straits.[3] To balance the competing interests of the international community, the LOSC created the concept of transit passage.[4]

Article 37 of the LOSC covers the straits where the right of transit passage is applied. The scope of the regime of transit passage is limited 'to straits used

---

1 Brüel in Chapter 3 note 8 at 25; Manner in Chapter 2 note 88 at 120; Kleemola-Juntunen in Chapter 1 note 2 at 25–26.

2 Overflight is prohibited above straits; also submarines must navigate on the surface in straits, which is the procedure for passage through territorial seas.

3 Third United Nations Conference on the Law of the Sea, Volume III: Documents in Chapter 3 note 116 at 189, 192.; UN Doc. A/CONF.62/C.2/L. 11 (17 July 1974), UN Doc. A/CONF.62/C.2/L.16 (22 July 1974); Maduro in Chapter 3 note 92 at 69; S.H. Amin, *The Regime of International Straits: Legal Implications for The Strait of Hormuz*, 12 J. Marit. Law Commer. 387–405, 391 (1981).

4 Hugo Caminos & Vincent P. Cogliati-Bantz, *The Legal Regime of Straits: Contemporary Challenges and Solutions* 38 (2014).

© KONINKLIJKE BRILL NV, LEIDEN, 2019 | DOI:10.1163/9789004364189_005

for international navigation between one part of the high seas or an exclusive economic zone and another part of the high seas or exclusive economic zone' However the LOSC does not define the term 'straits used for international navigation' as the Conference could not agree on the meaning of the term.[5]

Therefore, when striving to provide a definition for the term 'used for international navigation' one must return to the *Corfu Channel* case, which uses a different description of a strait: 'useful routes for international navigation'.[6] A great number of straits may be classed as 'useful routes for international navigation', and consequently a question arises as we wonder whether this term today applies to transit passage or non-suspendable innocent passage. This sort of question seems connected to other questions related to the widths of straits. When a strait is so narrow that it overlaps with a territorial sea, problems may arise. Problems related to passage through straits can be settled by using geographical analyses. If a strait connects 'one part of the high seas or an exclusive economic zone and another part of the high seas or an exclusive economic zone' then the transit passage regime will be the most likely means of regulation and provisions from Part III of the LOSC will apply. While straits connecting territorial seas to high seas or an exclusive economic zone are regulated by a regime of non-suspendable innocent passage, the same regime is applied to straits that are formed by an island belonging to a State bordering the strait if there exists seaward of the island a route through the high seas or through an exclusive economic zone of similar convenience.[7]

1.2   *The Right of Transit Passage*

Article 38 of the LOSC defines the right of unimpeded transit passage in straits referred to in Article 37. The right of transit passage applies to all ships and aircraft; it does not make distinction between their nationality or ownership or legal status (merchant ship or warship, civil or State aircraft). Moreover, the article stipulates that passage is only exercised for the purpose of continuous and expeditious transit. The only exception to the rule of continuous and expeditious transit is when 'entering, leaving or returning from a State bordering a strait, subject to the conditions of entry to that State' (i.e. the Singapore clause, discussed below).[8]

---

5 *Corfu Channel* case, I.C.J. Reports in Chapter 3 note 22 at 28; Caminos in Chapter 3 note 8 at 142–143.
6 *Corfu Channel* case, I.C.J. Reports in Chapter 3 note 22 at 28.
7 LOSC arts. 37, 38, 45; Pharand in Chapter 3 note 151 at 66; Caminos in Chapter 3 note 8 at 143.
8 LOSC art. 38(2), Caminos in Chapter 3 note 8 at 143–144.; Caminos and Cogliati-Bantz, *supra* note 4 at 210.

The wording of the Article does not give to a coastal State a possibility to require prior authorisation or prior notification when vessels undertake passage through the strait locating in their territorial seas.[9] The expression 'freedom of navigation and overflight' links passage through straits to navigation in the high seas; the term is also used in the Geneva Convention on the High Seas.[10]

The change within the legal regime of straits used for international navigation is significant because the concept of transit passage focuses on the territorial seas as it is applied to straits that do not include a route through the EEZs or the high seas. Previously, if a strait was located in the territorial seas of States bordering straits, passage was subject to the regime of non-suspendable innocent passage and there was no right of submerged passage or right of overflight above straits.[11] In straits like these, coastal States were given the discretion to consider whether passage is non-innocent and a possibility to suspend passage. With the widening of territorial seas came the expansion of coastal State jurisdiction and the right of innocent passage was deemed unacceptable by maritime powers. As result coastal States' jurisdiction was reduced in straits used for international navigation because in these types of straits the right of transit passage is applied instead of the right of innocent passage.

The Åland Strait could have also been classified as a strait where the right of transit passage applies without the declaration of Finland and Sweden when they signed and ratified the LOSC. Finland and Sweden stated that Article 35(c) covers the 1921 Åland Convention as an exception to the right of transit passage. The route through the Åland Strait is located on the Swedish side of the Strait. Thus, at the time before the LOSC, passage through the Åland Strait was governed by the right of innocent passage as a rule of international customary law, because Sweden was not party to the 1958 TSC.

The high seas term emphasizes the difference between the regimes of transit passage and innocent passage through the territorial seas and archipelagic waters.[12] It is also noteworthy that the regime of passage through straits used for international navigation does not affect the legal status of the waters forming straits nor prejudice sovereignty or jurisdiction of States bordering straits with respect to activities unrelated to passage and remain subject to other applicable provisions of the Convention. Both the first and the second paragraph of Article 34 of the LOSC refer to the sovereignty and jurisdiction and establish

---

9   Caminos in Chapter 3 note 8 at 144; Caminos and Cogliati-Bantz, *supra* note 4 at 167.

10   Art. 2, Convention on the High Seas, 450 UNTS 11; Finnish Treaty Series 6–7/1965.

11   R.B. McNees, *Freedom of Transit through International Straits*, 6 J. Marit. Law Commer. 175–211, 185–186 (1974).

12   Yturriaga in Chapter 3 note 140 at 167.

the legal limits of a coastal State's sovereign jurisdiction if they share their borders with international straits. State sovereignty and jurisdiction is regulated by the provisions of Part III and other rules of international law. Therefore, any activities that are unrelated to passage remain subject to other applicable provisions of the LOSC. Provisions on the right of transit passage are not applicable to internal waters of coastal States that are connected to straits. However, an exception to this rule is made for sea areas that had never previously been considered as internal waters.[13]

If the width of a strait is more than 24 nautical miles or if States bordering straits have not extended their territorial seas sufficiently then there will be a corridor through the strait which falls within the jurisdiction (but not sovereignty) of States bordering the strait. In that case the application of the regime of transit passage is addressed in Article 36, which applies to straits that include routes passing through high seas or EEZs. The Article also has the effect in the cases in which the width of strait is more than 24 nautical miles and the high sea or EEZ route is not suitable, the right of transit passage is applied in this kind of strait. Although the term 'similar convenience' can be determined by such factors as time, distance, safety the state of the sea, visibility depth of water and ease of fixing a vessel's position, it may have multiple meanings depending on who interprets it. Thus, a vessel's flag State may find that a particular route in the high seas is not navigable for certain categories of vessels, whereas States bordering a strait may consider the route navigable for all vessels, or vice versa.[14]

The application of rules regulating passage through territorial seas or archipelagic waters in straits used for international navigation is excluded by incorporating the phrase 'this Part' in Article 34(2).[15] Manner suggests that the regime of transit passage does not require an extension of coastal State territorial waters in the strait. Also in cases where States bordering straits are not tempted or able to widen their territorial waters beyond their earlier limits, the right of transit passage exists if straits are otherwise covered by provisions found in Articles 34, 35(a), 38 and 39. If a strait used for international navigation consists of parts of a coastal State's territorial sea or EEZ, as well as of the high seas without a general rule of transit passage, freedom of navigation would only apply to routes through EEZs and high seas. Consequently, acts of

---

13   Manner in Chapter 2 note 88 at 121; Nordquist in Chapter 3 note 94 at 298; Kleemola-Juntunen in Chapter 1 note 2 at 31.

14   Yturriaga, in Chapter 3 note 140 at 168; Nordquist in Chapter 3 note 94 at 299, 314; Pharand in Chapter 3 note 151 at 81.

15   Nordquist in Chapter 3 note 94 at 299.

passage through territorial seas that are also a part of straits would be covered by existing rules of innocent passage as well as governed by the sovereign jurisdiction of States bordering straits.[16] Thus, passage through straits that include a high seas corridor or an EEZ falls within the scope of the doctrine of freedom of navigation, whereas passage through straits previously governed by provisions relating to innocent passage falls within the scope of the regime of transit passage. In some straits, however, foreign vessels' rights are enforced at the expense of States' sovereign jurisdiction. Although the initial purpose of the regime of transit passage was to retain freedom of navigation through straits where high sea routes disappear as territorial seas expand, during the negotiation process of the Third Law of the Sea Conference it also emerged that the right of transit passage would cover straits where previous high sea routes had not existed.

Vessels and aircraft do not need any other reason to navigate in international straits other than that they simply travel between one part of the high seas or EEZ to another part of the high seas or EEZ. According to Article 38(2) foreign vessels have a right of transit passage through territorial waters of States bordering straits if such vessels are in the process of entering or leaving territorial waters. This right is important in circumstances where a strait is long and provides the only entry to harbours belonging to strait States. During the Third Law of the Sea Conference this clause was known as the 'Singapore clause' because the Straits of Malacca and Singapore, and the Strait of Johore provided the only means of entrance to ports in Singapore. Without this clause, passage to ports located within straits could not be considered 'continuous and expeditious' because visits to ports break passage and take time. Moreover, vessels and aircraft have no right to transit passage but are given a right of innocent passage instead, whereas aircraft must obtain prior permission before entering air space. Paragraph 2 also provides that entry, exit or return to harbours or airports in strait States must be conducted in accord with the conditions of entry that pertain to that particular State.[17]

1.3   *Duties of Ships and Aircraft during Transit Passage*

The 1982 Law of the Sea Convention lists activities that are prohibited during innocent passage but in other similar provisions such a list cannot be found to regulate transit passage. Paragraph 3 of Article 38 only loosely states how 'any

---

16   Manner in Chapter 2 note 88 at 120–121.

17   Pharand in Chapter 3 note 151 at 82–83; Nordquist in Chapter 3 note 94 at 330; Myron H. Nordquist, *United Nations Convention on the Law of the Sea 1982: A Commentary, Volume 4, Articles 192 to 278, Final Act, Annex VI* 388 (1991).

activity which is not the exercise of the right of transit passage through a strait remains subject to the applicable provisions of this Convention'.[18] Article 39 includes rules on what kind of activities are acceptable for ships and aircraft in transit or any other activities that are outside the scope of the transit passage regime. These provisions link transit passage to the protection and preservation of the marine environment, which is dealt with in Part XII of the Convention and Article 42 as well. What is also noteworthy is that Article 39(1)(b) includes the duty of foreign vessels to refrain from posing a threat during transit passage. Exactly the same duty exists for foreign vessels during innocent passage.[19]

The concept of freedom of navigation in the high seas means that there are almost no limitations or qualifications exist apart from a 'reasonableness' obligation. But the concept of freedom of navigation does not mean the same thing in the context of transit passage. Article 39 establishes common duties for vessels and aircraft exercising the right of transit passage. Paragraph 1(a) says that passage is to proceed 'without delay and through or over the strait'. The same thing is expressed in Article 38, 'solely for the purpose of continuous and expeditious transit'. Articles 38 and 39 elaborate on the idea that ships and aircraft do not enjoy other rights of freedom of navigation and overflight but are only provided free and unimpeded passage through and above straits.[20] Nevertheless, when it is 'rendered necessary' due to circumstances of force majeure or distress a vessel may deviate from the activities incidental to the normal modes of continuous and expeditious transit. Thus, a vessel would be allowed to stop and anchor in distress or for purposes of rendering assistance to persons, vessels or aircraft in danger or distress.[21]

During transit passage through straits ships and aircraft are required to 'refrain from any threat or use of force against the sovereignty, territorial integrity or political independence of a State bordering a strait'. Article 39(1)(b) builds upon general principles of international peace and security, which are expressed in the United Nations Charter Article 2(4), to cover the regime of transit passage. Article 19 also contains principles of international law concerning innocent passage through territorial seas. Therefore, duties associated with vessels and aircraft exercising the right of transit passage are likewise linked to other duties that have been established for vessels exercising the right of

---

18   Pharand in Chapter 3 note 151 at 82.
19   *Id.* at 83; Caminos in Chapter 3 note 8 at 144–145.
20   W. Michael Reisman, *The Regime of Straits and National Security: an Appraisal of International Law-making,* 74 Am. J. Int. Law 48–76, 69–70 (1980); Yturriaga in Chapter 3 note 140 at 168.
21   LOSC art. 39(1)(c); Caminos in Chapter 3 note 8 at 148.

innocent passage through territorial seas. However, it is noteworthy that 'innocence' is not the criterion from the regime of transit passage that needs to be fulfilled.[22]

Another interpretation of the regime of transit passage has typically been that it may also be regarded to be the same thing as freedom of navigation.[23] Reisman criticised this way of thinking and he claims that the 'freedom of navigation' in the context of 'transit passage' is not the same as freedom of navigation in the high seas. The phrasing of Article 38(2) restricts freedom of navigation for the purpose of continuous and expeditious transit. Paragraph 3 says that activities that are not related to passage must remain subject to other applicable provisions of the Convention. Many other aspects relating to freedom of navigation, such as military exercises, weapons testing, surveillance and intelligence gathering are likewise prohibited during transit through straits. However, these types of activities would not be included in a vessel's 'normal mode' of passage because they are not incidental to transit, regardless of whether provisions on transit passage mention the operational rights of seaborne forces by name.[24] However, within the context of transit passage a vessel's 'normal mode' of passage may be open to various interpretations. Furthermore, passage rights and freedoms are protected in straits by means of applying the term 'normal mode'. Hence, a vessel's 'normal mode' is uncertain and greatly depends on how the term 'freedom of navigation and overflight' is interpreted.[25]

An interesting vessel from the point of view of transit passage is an aircraft carrier because its 'normal mode' of passage includes aircraft landing and rising up from its flight deck. On the other hand, transit passage provides that vessels and aircraft refrain from posing any threat to the sovereignty, territorial integrity, or political independence of States bordering straits.[26] An aircraft

---

22   *Id.* at 148–149.

23   Reisman, *supra* note 20 at 70–72; Natalie Klein, *Maritime Security and the Law of the Sea* 34 (2011).

24   Reisman, *supra* note 20 at 72; Charles E. Pirtle, *Military Uses of Ocean Space and the Law of the Sea in the New Millenium*, 31 Ocean Dev. Int. Law 7–45, 18 (2000). A.V. Lowe, *The Commander's Handbook on the Naval Operations and the Contemporary Law of the Sea*, in *International Law Studies, Volume 64, The Law of Naval Operations, U.S. Naval College* 109–147, 122 (Horace B. Robertson Jr. ed., 1991). Lowe considers that the right of overflight does not seem sufficient to warrant aircraft landing and rising from an aircraft carrier's flight deck in straits used for international navigation.

25   Klein, *supra* note 23 at 33–34. See also Yturriaga in Chapter 3 note 140 at 224–225; Pirtle, *supra* note 24 at 18.

26   LOSC art. 39(1)(b); George Galdorisi, *An Operational Perspective on the Law of the Sea*, 29 Ocean Dev. Int. Law 73–84, 79 (1998).

carrier can be noted to comply with many criteria of transit passage, which include continuous and expeditious transit proceeding without delay.[27] Hence, as long as aircraft carrier activities are not negatively focussed on the actual States that border the straits then the military character of a vessel cannot be the lone reason for denying transit passage.

1.4   Duties of Strait States

The key difference between transit passage and innocent passage relates to the varying degrees of State jurisdiction or control over passage through straits. A strait State has a right to prevent non-innocent passage, which is determined by twelve criteria listed in Article 19(2) of the LOSC.[28] The evaluation of innocent passage does not entirely fall within the free discretion of States bordering straits because States are obliged to adhere to the criteria outlined in Article 19(2). However, the regime of transit passage has a different type of criterion for 'innocence', which is not applicable to vessels and cannot restrict passage on grounds related to national security.[29] Pharand points out that provisions relating to transit passage do not refer to 'other rules of international law', while provisions relating to innocent passage do. States bordering straits

---

27   John Astley III & Michael N. Schmitt, *The Law of the Sea and Naval Operations*, 42 Air Force Law Rev. 119–156, 133 (1997); Klein, *supra* note 23 at 33–34.

28   LOSC art. 19(2):
Passage of a foreign ship shall be considered to be prejudicial to the peace, good order or security of the coastal State if in the territorial sea it engages in any of the following activities:
(a) any threat or use of force against the sovereignty, territorial integrity or political independence of the coastal State, or in any other manner in violation of the principles of international law embodied in the Charter of the United Nations;
(b) any exercise or practice with weapons of any kind;
(c) any act aimed at collecting information to the prejudice of the defence or security of the coastal State;
(d) any act of propaganda aimed at affecting the defence or security of the coastal State;
(e) the launching, landing or taking on board of any aircraft;
(f) the launching, landing or taking on board of any military device;
(g) the loading or unloading of any commodity, currency or person contrary to the customs, fiscal, immigration or sanitary laws and regulations of the coastal State;
(h) any act of wilful and serious pollution contrary to this Convention;
(i) any fishing activities;
(j) the carrying out of research or survey activities;
(k) any act aimed at interfering with any systems of communication or any other facilities or installations of the coastal State;
(l) any other activity not having a direct bearing on passage.

29   Maduro in Chapter 3 note 92 at 72.

are therefore only allowed to take measures that are explicitly mentioned by the Convention.[30]

The sovereign jurisdiction of States bordering straits is managed by Article 42, which entitles States to enact laws and regulations relating to transit passage. The first paragraph contains four sub-paragraphs that list circumstances where States are allowed to enact such laws and regulations, which limits their sovereign jurisdiction significantly.[31] Article 42 also states that the flag State is held accountable for losses or damage to States bordering straits if their vessels or aircraft act contrary to the laws, regulations, or any other provision concerning straits used for international navigation. The sovereign jurisdiction of States bordering straits are quite limited in the sense that such States have no real enforcement measures to punish or effectively prevent violations of 'laws and regulations'. Only Article 233 lists cases where States bordering straits may take appropriate enforcement measures. Nevertheless, the Article is not comprehensive enough, as it only relates to environmental matters and damage must be significant. Thus, the Article requires that vessels violating the laws and regulations of strait States must be causing or threatening major damage to the strait's marine environment. The interpretation of the concept 'major' is challenging, because most releases from oil tankers result from routine discharges during operations.[32]

Article 42 is linked to Article 41.[33] A comparison made between provisions concerning the jurisdiction of coastal States when regulating innocent passage through territorial seas and provisions concerning the jurisdiction of States bordering straits when regulating passage shows that the jurisdiction of States bordering straits is more restricted.[34] Article 41(4) states that

> [b]efore designating or substituting sea lanes or prescribing or substituting traffic separation schemes, States bordering straits shall refer

---

30   Pharand in Chapter 3 note 151 at 83–84.

31   In making these laws and regulations, States have to take in the consideration that they do not discriminate in form or in fact among foreign ships or have any practical effect of denying, hampering or impairing the right of transit passage.

32   Maduro in Chapter 3 note 92 at 72–73; John Norton Moore, *The Regime of Straits and the Third United Nations Conference on the Law of the Sea*, 74 Am. J. Int. Law 77–121, 109 (1980); Kari Hakapää, *Marine Pollution in International Law: Material Obligations and Jurisdiction: With Special Reference to the Third United Nations Conference on the Law of the Sea* 203–205 (1981); Yturriaga in Chapter 3 note 140 at 171; Roach and Smith in Chapter 3 note 164 at 279–281; Donald R. Rothwell & Tim Stephens, *The International Law of the Sea* 243 (2010).

33   LOSC art. 42(1).

34   LOSC arts. 21–22, 41–42.

proposals to the competent international organisation with a view to their adoption. The organisation may adopt only such sea lanes and traffic separation schemes as may be agreed with the States bordering the straits, after which the States may designate, prescribe or substitute them.

It is difficult to imagine that the organisation mentioned in the above-mentioned paragraph could be any other than the International Maritime Organization (IMO). The provision also requires that States bordering straits cooperate with each other when discussing sea lanes and traffic separation schemes that include territorial seas belonging to two or more States. The Article notes that sea lanes and traffic separation schemes must also conform to generally accepted international regulations.[35] An international organisation may only adopt sea lanes and traffic separation schemes that are agreed upon by States bordering straits. Moreover, due to the Article's regulations, cooperation between States bordering straits and international organisations has been successful and long lasting, which is often the case with cooperation between States and the IMO.[36]

But is it possible that States bordering straits can deem transit passage of vessels to not be 'continuous and expeditious', which would then allow States to apply Article 38(3) and its stricter provisions on innocent passage. In the 1958 TSC, States bordering straits were entitled to exclusive jurisdiction when considering whether passage was innocent or not. The wide discretion of States bordering straits was seen to be a weakness of the Convention, which was regarded as something to be avoided in the new Convention.[37] During the Third Law of the Sea Conference many felt that any extensive form of discretion for States bordering straits could be avoided by including provisions that limited discretion. Article 38(1), for example, particularly mentions that transit passage 'shall not be impeded'. According to Article 42(2), States are allowed to enact laws and regulations to regulate transit passage through straits, but such laws and regulations are not allowed to practically deny, hamper or impair the right of transit passage.[38] The Convention also includes duties for States bordering straits. For instance, Article 44 states that States bordering straits 'shall not hamper transit passage' and also declares that '[t]here shall be no

---

35   LOSC art. 41(3).
36   Moore, *supra* note 32 at 105; Yturriaga in Chapter 3 note 140 at 173–175; Nordquist in Chapter 3 note 94 at 363–365.
37   *Report of the Committee on the Peaceful Uses of the Sea-Bed Committee and the Ocean Floor Beyond the Limits of National Jurisdiction, Official Records, 28th Session, Supplement No. 21 (A/9021), Volume I* in Chapter 3 note 99 at 50.
38   Caminos in Chapter 3 note 8 at 146–147.

suspension of transit passage'. As regards warships and other vessels that are entitled to sovereign immunity, the Convention prescribes that coastal States do not interfere with or take enforcement action against them.[39]

1.5   Non-compliance with Obligations Related to the Right of Transit Passage

While exercising the right of transit passage all vessels and aircraft are obliged to refrain from posing a threat or using force against States bordering straits.[40] This provision clearly obliges vessels and aircraft to behave in a self-disciplinary and responsible way. Nevertheless, it does not create any such condition for transit passage that could allow States bordering straits a right to prohibit transit passage.[41] Furthermore, vessels and aircraft are given a further obligation to refrain from any activities that might be considered alternative to their normal modes of continuous and expeditious transit unless completely necessary – i.e. due to circumstances of force majeure or distress.[42] Nevertheless, in circumstances where vessels or aircraft violate this obligation, their activities remain subject to the applicable provisions of the Convention.[43] Hence, other provisions relating to the right of innocent passage are also applicable, which is why the passage of vessels can be prohibited on grounds that their activities are deemed to be non-innocent. This similarly applies to overflight of aircraft above straits, which can likewise be denied since the right of innocent passage does not refer to overflight at all.

However, the prohibition of passage requires that a vessel engages in any of the activities mentioned in Article 19(2) concerning non-innocent passage. If this is not the case, the only legal option available for States bordering straits seems to be the right to pursue the matter related to passage as a breach of international law through diplomatic channels and other dispute settlement procedures.[44] Therefore, transit passage differs completely from provisions concerning innocent passage through territorial seas. According to Article 25 a coastal State has the right 'to prevent passage which is not innocent'. The provision is also applicable in straits where the right of innocent passage is

---

39   LOSC arts. 31, 32, 42(5), 236; Caminos in Chapter 3 note 8 at 147.
40   LOSC art. 39(1)(b).
41   R.R. Churchill & A.V. Lowe, *The Law of the Sea* 107 (1999); Caminos in Chapter 3 note 8 at 150.
42   LOSC art. 39(1)(c).
43   LOSC art. 38(3).
44   If the obligations listed in Article 39 are violated by the transiting vessel the flag State has jurisdiction, not the State bordering the strait. Caminos in Chapter 3 note 8 at 150; Churchill and Lowe, *supra* note 41 at 107.

applied instead of transit passage because according to Article 45, '[t]here shall be no suspension of innocent passage through such straits'. Accordingly, passage through straits used for international navigation can be suspended only if it is considered non-innocent.

Articles 38 and 39 create separate rights and obligations. Any violation of duties of vessels and aircraft included in Article 39 does not mean that a vessel forfeits its right to transit passage. These Articles need to be read with Articles 42(2) and 44, which state that bordering straits shall not impede or interfere with the right of transit passage in any way whatsoever.[45] Because no provisions exist to determine the meaning of 'transit passage', unlike 'innocent passage' a difference between transit passage and innocent passage also appear with State's security issues. Coastal States have no similar right to take measures against foreign vessels undertaking transit passage, whereas in comparison they are allowed to take action if a vessel's passage is considered non-innocent.[46] However, it is noteworthy that the right of transit passage might not exclude the right of self-defence.[47] Thus, it seems that there is a clear difference between the jurisdiction of different States bordering straits depending on the type of passage rights that are used, transit or innocent passage.[48]

Article 39 includes duties that are only applicable to vessels and aircraft. Vessels in transit must comply with generally accepted international regulations, procedures and practices for safety at sea, including the International Regulations for Preventing Collisions at Sea, and must also comply with similar international regulations, procedures and practices for the prevention, reduction and control of pollution at sea. By referring to the obligation of coastal States to comply with generally accepted international regulations, procedures and practices, it was intended that this kind of legal regime would guarantee uniformity and predictability among foreign vessels. The phrasing of Article 39(2) allows for an extensive interpretation covering both rules of customary international law and treaty provisions that are generally accepted.[49] Without such a provision in place, States bordering straits could have inconsistent regulations,

---

45   Caminos in Chapter 3 note 8 at 150.

46   LOSC arts. 19 (2) and 44; Churchill and Lowe, *supra* note 41 at 107; Mahmoudi in Chapter 3 note 106.

47   I.C.J. Reports, *Military and Paramilitary Activities in and against Nicaragua (Nicaragua v. United States of America)*, *14*, 102–104, 110–111 (1986); Churchill and Lowe, *supra* note 41 at 107; J. Hargrove, *The Nicaragua Judgment and the Future of the Law of Force and Self-Defense*, 81 Am. J. Int. Law 135–143, 135–143 (1987).

48   Kleemola-Juntunen in Chapter 1 note 2 at 29.

49   Hakapää, *supra* note 32 at 205.

which would be highly difficult for foreign vessels to comply with.[50] In the LOSC the 'generally accepted international regulations' refer to regulations particularly provided by the IMO, which is the head coordinating body for the development of international standards, regulations and practices for the prevention of pollution and safety at sea. The IMO has a significant role in generating a series of obligations which, due to their general acceptance, are applicable to all vessels in transit. These obligations are applicable to vessels in transit, regardless of whether a flag State is party to the particular convention or is a member of the relevant organisation.[51]

1.6   *Submerged Transit*

There is no precise mention in Article 39 of submarines and other underwater vehicles. However, in cases of innocent passage, submarines and other underwater vehicles are required to navigate on the surface and show their flag. This requirement therefore mirrors the 1958 TSC, which includes a similar provision. However, there is no precise mention that the submerged passage of submarines and other underwater vehicles falls within the scope of transit passage.[52]

Major naval Powers have traditionally considered submerged passage to be vital to them because submarines can navigate between oceans undetected. Therefore, it is hard to imagine that they would have given up their insistence upon it. According to Article 38 transit passage regards 'all ships'. Submerged passage is the typical mode of transit for submarines. There is no restriction on submarines that would require them to navigate on the surface. If this kind of restriction were intended, it would have been specifically mentioned in Article 38. Transit passage through international straits is linked to freedom of navigation and overflight, which is normally enjoyed above high seas and exclusive economic zones. In comparison, transit passage was meant to remove any hindrances to the implementation of that freedom. Limitations to transit passage

---

50   *Id.* at 205; Caminos in Chapter 3 note 8 at 151.

51   Caminos in Chapter 3 note 8 at 151; J. Ashley Roach, *Enforcement of International Rules and Standards of Navigational Safety in the Malacca and Singapore Straits*, 3 Singapore J. Int. Comp. Law 323–336, 324 (1999); Caminos and Cogliati-Bantz, *supra* note 4 at 312. See also Caminos in Chapter 3 note 8 at 151. Examples of these kinds of conventions are COLREGS, SOLAS, and MARPOL. The International Law Association has discussed the purpose and meaning of the concepts of 'generally accepted international rules and standards' and 'applicable international rules and standards', see International Law Association, *Final Report of the Committee on Coastal State Jurisdiction Relating to Marine Pollution*, ILA Report 473–492 (2000).

52   Pharand in Chapter 3 note 151 at 85.

do exist, of course, but these are mentioned in Articles and there is no reason to insert limitations on that freedom in addition to those to be found in the Articles themselves.[53]

The right of submerged transit is not expressly mentioned in Section 2 of the LOSC, which has prompted discussion about whether submarines have a right to submerged transit. It is noteworthy that Article 87 of Part VII Section 1 does not explicitly mention submerged passage. The term 'freedom of navigation' refers to submerged navigation and is included in Article 2 of the 1958 Convention on the High Seas. The observance, application and interpretation of international treaties are regulated in Part III of the Vienna Convention on the Law of Treaties. The general rules of interpretation for treaties are found in Section 3 of Article 31 of the Vienna Convention: that is, treaties 'shall be interpreted in good faith in accordance with the ordinary meaning to be given to the terms of the treaty in their context and in the light of its object and purpose'. Furthermore, Article 32 sets out supplementary means of interpretation and accepts that interpretations can also be based on preparatory works. Supplementary means of interpretation can be used in order to confirm the meaning of Article 31 or to determine the extent of ambiguity left open to interpretation by the Article.[54]

If rules of interpretation of the Vienna Convention were to be applied then the right of submerged passage would form an essential part of the regime of transit passage. This type of interpretation of submerged passage seems to have been agreed on by most commentators. Indeed, Reisman asserts that Article 38 does not explicitly require submarines to navigate on the surface. Moore's opinion relies on different reasoning as he states that if one were to analyse the LOSC's text it then becomes obvious that the concept of transit passage includes rights of submerged transit through straits. The section on transit passage includes a list of vessels' duties during passage, which is extensive and goes on to state that vessels must 'comply with other relevant provisions' regulating passage through straits used for international navigation. The section on innocent passage expressly states that submarines are 'to navigate on the surface and to show their flag', which shows how this type of requirement is not applicable to the transit passage section. Thus, it seems that if submarines were required to navigate on the surface this would have been explicitly mentioned in the LOSC.[55]

---

53   *Id.* at 85–86.
54   Caminos in Chapter 3 note 8 at 154.
55   Moore, *supra* note 32 at 92, 95–96; Caminos in Chapter 3 note 8 at 154; Burke in Chapter 3 note 91 at 193.225; Reisman, *supra* note 20 at 67–76; Robertson Jr in Chapter 3 note 101

Article 39(1)(c) of the LOSC requires that ships and aircraft in transit 'refrain from any activities other than those incidental to their normal modes of continuous and expeditious transit'. Many of those who have commented on this particular provision have interpreted it so literally that submarines and other underwater vehicles have a right to submerged passage. However, it is worth questioning what sort of activities a 'normal mode' of transit may include. Moore writes that transit passage includes a right of transit in the 'normal mode of continuous and expeditious transit', which for a modern submarine is submerged passage. Caminos considers 'normal' passage to imply flight at normal speed and altitude for aircraft, surface navigation for surface vessels, foilborne or airborne navigation for hovercraft, and submerged navigation for submarines.[56]

When provisions concerning transit passage are compared with provisions concerning innocent passage the difference between the two becomes obvious. Article 20 of Part II of the LOSC specifically requires submarines and other underwater vehicles to navigate on the surface and show their flag. An equivalent provision is found in Article 14(6) of the 1958 TSC. The LOSC the term 'other underwater vehicles', which is not used in the 1958 Convention. The difference between the regimes of transit passage and innocent passage is intentional, because States had preferred that parts of their territorial seas that are not regulated by provisions on transit passage should require vessels to navigate on the surface while allowing submerged transit through straits used for international navigation. Of course, submarines should also be able to navigate on the surface in straits because although they have a right to submerged passage it does not mean that they must always navigate in this mode, and the choice of the mode of passage for submarines is up to the discretion of the flag State in question and not the coastal State.[57]

Part VII of the LOSC handling the high seas is silent on the issue of submerged passage but this does not mean that the right is excluded from the high seas regime. Article 2 of the 1958 Geneva Convention on the High Seas[58] uses

---

at 843–846; Kheng Lian Koh, *Straits in International Navigation: Contemporary Issues* 151 (1982); O'Connell and Shearer in Chapter 3 note 13 at 333; Churchill and Lowe, *supra* note 41 at 109.

56 Burke in Chapter 3 note 91 at 212–214; Moore, *supra* note 32 at 96; Caminos in Chapter 3 note 8 at 154. O'Connell states a submarine is defined as an underwater vehicle, which is why its 'normal mode'of the operation is submerged passage, O'Connell and Shearer in Chapter 3 note 13 at 333. For a different opinion see Reisman, *supra* note 20 at 71–75.

57 Burke, *supra* note 214 at 213–214; Robertson Jr in Chapter 3 note 101 at 844; Caminos in Chapter 3 note 8 at 155.

58 Convention on the High Seas, adopted 29 April 1958, entered into force 30 September 1962, 450 UNTS 11.

the term 'freedom of navigation', which includes submerged navigation and has been used in Article 87 of the LOSC. In Article 38(2), the same term has been subsumed within the transit passage regime so that a right of submerged passage through straits exists and is used for international navigation. The term 'freedom of navigation' has its roots in Article 87 of the LOSC and Article 2 of the 1958 Convention on the High Seas. Thus, any derogation of 'freedom of navigation' should have been correctly explained in the Convention's text. It is also questionable why 'freedom of navigation' is mentioned in the Article if the intention was to limit rights of submerged transit and other freedoms of transit.[59]

The other argument in support of the right of submerged passage, which is mentioned in Article 38(2) is that '[t]ransit passage means the exercise in accordance with this Part of the freedom of navigation'. Thus, this sort of restriction indicates that there is no cross-reference to other parts of the LOSC and passage through international straits is only subject to conditions of transit passage described in Part III of the Convention. Furthermore, Article 45 of Part III clearly establishes specific provisions on innocent passage that require surface navigation. If some kind of cross-reference from these specific provisions were intended to be applied to transit passage they would have been specified in the Convention.[60] The practice of cross-referencing is not unusual in the LOSC. When it is expected that provisions fall outside the scope of the legal regime of straits, regulated in Part III, the provision involves a cross-reference. For instance, Article 233 of Part XII dealing with the protection and preservation of the marine environment refers to straits used for international navigation.[61]

When the negotiations of the Third Law of the Sea Conference first began there was no agreement on the breadth of territorial seas. The 1958 and 1960 Law of the Sea Conferences failed to reach an agreement on this particular issue, as many coastal States claimed territorial seas of twelve miles and a few States even made claims for up to 200 miles. Such claims raised concerns for passage through straits as a result of 12-mile territorial seas becoming a rule of customary international law. It was clear to many that an extension of territorial sea breadths would have an impact on the legal status of international straits. In straits that would be 24 miles wide or less no high sea routes would exist. Passage that would have previously been based on the freedom of navigation would be dependent on the right of innocent passage.[62]

---

59   Moore, *supra* note 32 at 96; Caminos in Chapter 3 note 8 at 155.
60   Caminos in Chapter 3 note 8 at 155.
61   Moore, *supra* note 32 at 93; Caminos in Chapter 3 note 8 at 156.
62   Burke in Chapter 3 note 91 at 195–196.

Questions regarding the legal status of straits were very important to some States, especially for military reasons. The 1958 TSC gave coastal States wide discretionary powers to decide whether passage was innocent or not. There was a possibility that States' decisions might not be objective, which could lead to their interference with inoffensive passage. Another important point to make is that aircraft did not enjoy a right of innocent passage and submarines had to navigate on the surface when exercising their right of innocent passage.[63]

The United States and the Soviet Union both considered it vital to their national interests that submarines should not be obliged to navigate on the surface through international straits. Submarines are characteristically undetectable and not vulnerable to attack but surface navigation would weaken their effect. During negotiations those States in possession of significant navies emphasised the importance of freedom of navigation and linked this to their national security interests. Consequently, questions regarding straits were very important for them.[64]

During the Conference there was a great deal of discussion on the concept of 'freedom of navigation'. Many States generally agreed that the term referred to passage of vessels in high seas, whereby vessels were thought to be entitled to wide-ranging operations and manoeuvres. There is no doubt that freedom of navigation in the high seas also includes the right of submerged passage. Many States shared the opinion that although freedom of navigation is mentioned in the Convention's text it does not imply the same meaning as transit passage through international straits. The justification for the different meaning was that so many qualifications and restrictions exist that it was never deemed necessary to include submerged passage exclusively. Transit passage must be exercised 'solely for the purpose of continuous and expeditious transit' and other articles of the Convention impose obligations on vessels and aircraft during transit. Thus, provisions only set limits for navigation that were not applicable in high seas. Submerged passage was not specifically mentioned in the Convention because the provisions could be interpreted to mean that submerged passage is not permitted.[65] However, as argued by others the provisions can also be interpreted in a way that freedom of seas is recognised as a general concept that includes freedom of action, which is only intended to restrict expressly mentioned cases. In other words, submerged passage is

---

63   *Id.* at 196.
64   *Id.* at 197.
65   *Id.* at 200–202.

excluded from the Convention's text and therefore submarines are not obliged to navigate on the surface. The restrictions implied by the term 'continuous and expeditious passage' do not exclude submerged passage because a submarine's submerged mode of passage can be as 'continuous and expeditious' as surface movement.[66]

The United States and the Soviet Union had both clearly expressed how it would be within their best interests if the right of passage through straits would also be secured for warships and that submarines would have the right to submerged navigation. Both had wanted to retain their existing potential to navigate through straits consisting of high sea routes and to increase the scope of their right of navigation through straits within territorial seas. By expanding their territorial seas to 12 nautical miles, States bordering straits could extend the scope of their jurisdiction to cover the entire area of the strait if the strait's width was 24 nautical miles or less. However, transit passage through straits with widths of 6 nautical miles or less would include the same rules concerning submerged passage. It was understandable that States bordering narrow straits were concerned about their own security. However, one may as well ask the following question: does submerged transit or overflight comprise a prohibited use or threat of force or coercion against the sovereignty, territorial integrity or political independence of States bordering straits? The possibility of a threat cannot arise from passage alone but requires other activities. States bordering straits are not allowed to suspend transit passage or innocent passage through straits, but coastal States may temporarily suspend innocent passage in other areas of territorial seas. Coastal States may only deny passage through straits on grounds of 'cause', which implies vessels do not fulfil the requirements of innocence or meet the conditions of transit passage.[67]

During the work of the Sea-Bed Committee, the United States and the Soviet Union clearly indicated that they would not accept a convention that functioned in a way that is prejudicial to their right of navigation through international straits. The United States and the Soviet Union wanted to preserve the global movement of new submarines that had long-range weapons capacity and could stay submerged for long periods of time.[68] This opinion was voiced

66   *Id.* at 207–208; Moore, *supra* note 32 at 92 (fn 27); Robertson Jr, in Chapter 3 note 101 at 844–845.

67   Burke in Chpater 3 note 91 at 207–208; Said Mahmoudi, *Customary international law and transit passage*, 20 Ocean Dev. Int. Law 157–174, 165 (1989).

68   Caminos in Chapter 3 note 8 at 156. For more on the significance of transit rights through straits see Booth in Chapter 3 note 86 at 101–103.

during the 1974 Caracas Session, which Stevenson and Oxman summarised as an important period in history where unimpeded passage became of 'vital importance' to the United States and others.[69]

By 1975, States had expressed their opinions on submerged passage through straits used for international navigation. A proposal made by Fiji in 1974 in Caracas did not seek to guarantee a right of submerged navigation through territorial seas, because coastal States were able to order submarines to navigate on the surface and show their flags. In contrast, the Soviet and British proposals left no doubt that transit passage should be included in the right of submerged navigation.[70] Burke concluded that

> [s]tatements by Sri Lanka, Egypt, Peru and Spain, in commenting both on the United Kingdom proposal and the United States intervention on the subject, are especially revealing of the contemporary understanding of freedom of navigation in this context. Each of these delegations questioned the need for, and desirability of, submerged passage for submarines. The comments, questions and proposals advanced by these delegations are virtually impossible to explain unless they understood that submerged passage was intended to be included in the concept of 'freedom of navigation' in straits.[71]

Spain and Greece proposed amendments to the articles, according to which submarines and other underwater vehicles needed to navigate on the surface and show their flag if coastal States had not given their authorisation. This proposal did not gain full support from other States.[72] Oxman comments on these proposed amendments and notes that '[e]arlier attempts to impose a requirement that submarines navigate on the surface failed and were not revived'.[73] It is clear that the right of submerged navigation is an integral part of the regime of transit passage, which is validated by both a textual and contextual interpretation of the LOSC.[74] In his article Robertson also concludes that

---

69 John R. Stevenson & Bernard H. Oxman, *The Third United Nations Conference on the Law of the Sea: The 1974 Caracas Session*, 69 Am. J. Int. Law 1–30, 1, 15 (1975).

70 *Third United Nations Conference on the Law of the Sea, Volume III: Documents* in Chapter 3 note 116 at 183–186, 189–190, 196–198; Caminos in Chapter 3 note 3 at 156.

71 Burke in Chapter 3 note 91 at 205.

72 Caminos in Chapter 3 note 8 at 157 (fn 362).

73 See Bernard H. Oxman, *The Third United Nation's Conference on the Law of the Sea: The 1977 New York Session*, 72 Am. J. Int. Law 57–83, 64 (1978).

74 Caminos in Chapter 3 note 8 at 158.

[t]he two basic elements which the proponents of free transit or transit passage sought to include in the treaty which were not already included in the concept of innocent passage were the right of overflight and submerged transit. To eliminate either of these two key elements from the concept of transit passage would reduce the articles to virtual meaninglessness.[75]

This kind of interpretation is relevant to the Åland Strait. If the regime of transit passage were to have been applied to the Åland Strait, submarines would have been able to navigate submerged through the Strait towards the Gulf of Bothnia, as well as through the northern strait called Kvarken (in Finnish: *Merenkurkku*) where the freedom of navigation and overflight is applied in the Finnish EEZ. Therefore, foreign submarines could navigate and also foreign aircraft fly continuously through the Baltic Sea until reaching the Gulf of Bothnia while being submerged. If this were to have happened it would have highly likely affected the military balance in the Baltic Region, especially since during the time when the Convention was signed the region was greatly influenced by two military blocs.

1.7 The Right of Overflight through Straits Used for International Navigation

Article 38(1) and (2) of the LOSC state that 'all ships and aircraft enjoy the right of transit' as well as 'freedom of navigation and overflight'. These terms indicate that vessels and aircraft exercising a right of transit passage enjoy the same rights. With regard to the passage of aircraft, this seems to signify a great difference from the regime of innocent passage, which is not applied to overflight above territorial seas. No rule has ever existed in customary international law that grants foreign aircraft a right of overflight above territorial seas. The right of transit passage covers overflight of military aircraft above territorial seas that are a part of straits used for international navigation. Article 38(1) and (2) clearly state that military aircraft enjoy the same rights of transit passage through straits as warships do by stating that 'all ships and aircraft enjoy the right of transit passage' and also enjoy 'freedom of navigation and overflight'.[76]

Nevertheless, Article 38(3) includes a limit to the passage of aircraft in the sense that the provision only applies in a particular way. For instance, Article 38(3) says that 'any activity which is not an exercise of the right of transit passage through a strait remains subject to the other applicable provisions of the

---

75   Robertson Jr in Chapter 3 note 101 at 845.
76   Caminos in Chaper 3 note 8 at 158; Rothwell and Stephens, *supra* note 32 at 282.

Convention'. With regard to vessels, other applicable provisions may include those covering the right of innocent passage, whereas aircraft do not enjoy a right of innocent passage above the territorial seas of foreign States. This further implies that if an aircraft were to undertake measures that were not covered by transit passage then they would need the consent of relevant States bordering straits because no rule exists to secure rights of innocent passage or non-transit passage for aircraft. Therefore, it seems that the right of transit passage for aircraft seems stricter than the right of transit passage for vessels.[77]

Although vessels and aircraft both enjoy a similar right of transit their duties are not the same. Article 39(3) covers aircraft and refers to the rules of the air established by the International Civil Aviation Organization (ICAO), which apply to civil aircraft. The Article alludes to an expectation that all aircraft will normally comply with ICAO safety measures and should pay attention to the general safety of navigation, which also applies to State aircraft. Furthermore, State aircraft must at all times monitor the radio frequency assigned them by the competent internationally designated air traffic control authority or the appropriate international distress radio frequency.[78]

A reference made in the Article to the 'Rules of the Air' aims to enact the ICAO's aviation code in such a way that it may be applied with respect to the activities of civil aircraft. Hence, the provision also rules out any application of a coastal State's national legislation with regard to flight and manoeuvring of aircraft. As regards State aircraft, which includes military, customs and police services, ICAO safety standards are not automatically applicable. The meaning of the word 'normally' is ambiguous and leaves a significant amount of discretion to each State in order to deviate from the Rules of the Air. Due to the fact that a coastal State cannot fill the gap because of the rules of the transit passage regime, State aircraft are allowed to follow their own rules with regard to flight and manoeuvring of aircraft.[79] Spain objected to Article 3(3) and proposed that the word 'normally' should be deleted. However, when voted on the proposal did not receive much support: 21 votes in favour, 55 against, and 60

---

77   P. De Vries Lentsch, *The Right of Overflight over Strait States and Archipelagic States: Developments and Prospects*, 14 Netherlands Yearb. Int. Law 165–225, 205 (1983); Caminos in Chapter 3 note 8 at 158; Mahmoudi in Chapter 3 note 106.

78   Rothwell and Stephens, *supra* note 32 at 282–283.

79   Kay Hailbronner, *Freedom of the Air and the Convention on the Law of the Sea*, 77 Am. J. Int. Law 490–520, 501 (1983).

abstentions.[80] Upon signature and ratification[81] of the LOSC, Spain declared that a coastal State should be permitted to apply its own air regulations in its airspace provided that transit passage is not impeded.[82]

1.8   Sea Lanes and Traffic Separation Schemes

There had already been many proposals submitted to the Sea-Bed Committee suggesting that States bordering straits would be allowed to designate sea lanes and impose traffic regulation schemes in straits used for international navigation. The contents of each proposal were almost identical and the only notable difference between them related to the implementation of the traffic regulation schemes. Many proposals raised alternative points of view and scenarios where States have the power to unilaterally enforce traffic regulation schemes. However, even when given the freedom to enforce these kinds of traffic regulations States must consult each other and cooperate with international organisations. Article 41 of the LOSC is formulated in a way that obliges States bordering straits to submit proposals for traffic separation schemes to competent international organisations. The purpose of this obligation was to avoid any situation where the rights of coastal States could be abused and to give greater weight to coastal State sovereignty, particularly with respect to protecting its territory by adopting and implementing traffic separation schemes.[83]

The most competent international organisation is the IMO, which is the leading authority on international shipping despite this not being clearly mentioned in Article 41.[84] When it was first established in 1959, the principal task of the IMO was to contribute to the safety of navigation. The desire to establish sea lanes and traffic separation schemes is linked to the safety of navigation. At times the volume of vessels navigating particular straits may be so large that in order to maintain a good level of security, States bordering straits are obliged to take measures such as introducing sea lanes or traffic separation schemes.[85]

---

80   *Third United Nations Conference on the Law of the Sea, Volume XVI: Eleventh Session* 132, 223, http://legal.un.org/diplomaticconferences/1973_los/vol16.shtml [last access 24.3.2018].

81   https://treaties.un.org/doc/Publication/UNTS/Volume%201962/volume-1962-A-31363 -English.pdf [last access 24.3.2018].

82   See more Yturriaga in Chapter 3 note 140 at 227–232.

83   Caminos in Chapter 3 note 8 at 164 (fn 382).

84   Churchill and Lowe, *supra* note 41 at 108; R. Douglas Brubaker, *The Russian Arctic Straits* 128 (2005); S.N. Nandan, *An Introduction to the Regime of Passage Through Straits Used for International Navigation and Through Archipelagic Waters*, in *Freedom of Seas, Passage Rights and the 1982 Law of the Sea Convention* 57–75, 59 (Myron H. Nordquist, T.B. Koh, & J.N. Moore eds., 2009); Rothwell and Stephens, *supra* note 32 at 242.

85   http://www.imo.org [last access 24.3.2018].

Article 42 allows States bordering straits regulatory power with respect to a number of specified activities. However, Article 42 is just as prescriptive as Article 39. In cases where a vessel violates the laws enacted by a strait State, the strait State in question would still not be allowed to deny the right of transit passage. Therefore, in such circumstances the only option available for strait States is to recourse in legal proceedings against the vessels or their flag States. However, warships and other vessels entitled to sovereign immunity are even more difficult to prosecute for violating coastal State laws. As regards vessels that are not entitled to sovereign immunity, coastal States lack enforcement jurisdiction because safeguard regulations are not comprehensive. Some see the violation of regulations enacted for the safety of navigation or the prevention, reduction and control of pollution to be a major cause of damage to the marine environment in straits. According to Article 233 of Part XII, States bordering straits can take 'appropriate enforcement measures' against vessels. However, the laws and regulations concerning the prevention, reduction and control of pollution adopted by strait States can only be exercised by 'giving effect to applicable international regulations'. Article 39(2) is one such example among many of applicable international regulations that stem from the IMO.[86]

Article 42 includes duties for strait States and vessels in transit. States bordering straits must give relevant publicity to their laws and regulations imposed under their jurisdiction, while foreign vessels are required to conform to these laws and regulations. Paragraph 4 links the duties of vessels and aircraft to Article 39(1), which requires vessels 'to comply with other relevant provisions of this [p]art'.[87]

Finland and Sweden both proposed the establishment of traffic separation schemes north and south of the Åland Islands. In 2008 the IMO adopted a resolution on the establishment of Traffic Separation Scheme 'Åland Sea', which entered into force on 1st January 2010. The system includes two-way routes with traffic lanes for traffic moving in opposite directions, traffic separation schemes (TSS), new precautionary areas, and amended Deep Water Routes (DW routes). The main reason for establishing these routes was to ensure a higher degree of maritime safety. For instance, east-west passenger vessel traffic in the region comes into frequent contact with north-south cargo vessel traffic.[88]

---

86   LOSC arts. 42(1)(a)(b), 233; Caminos in Chapter 3 note 8 at 168–169.
87   LOSC arts. 42(3)–(4), 39(1); Caminos in Chapter 3 note 8 at 169.
88   International Maritime Organization, *IMO Document COLREG.2/Circ.60, 10 December 2008, New and Amended Existing Traffic Separation Schemes*; Anne Oikkonen, *Vuosaaren väylä aukeaa ja Ahvenanmeri saa reittijakojärjestelmän*, Meriväylä 12–13, 13 (2008). Number of

1.9   Enforcement of Laws and Regulations of Strait States

Although the regime of transit passage restricts State jurisdiction within straits, the LOSC grants States bordering straits a right to enforce laws and regulations in order to govern transit passage. States bordering straits may regulate traffic by prescribing sea lanes and traffic separation schemes, but they need to be adopted by the IMO. Also the laws and regulations of strait States relating to pollution must comply with generally accepted regulations.[89] The duty of States to comply with international safety and pollution standards ensures that there are no differing or possibly inconsistent regulations when sailing around the world.[90] Internationally agreed upon standards and requirements are not derived from the legislation of coastal States. For strait States it seems that the advantage of implementing international standards is that they become directly enforceable by their own national authorities. Furthermore, any legal action as a breach of these kinds of obligations would not be left solely in the hands of the flag State alone.[91] As regards research and survey activities, while undertaking passage foreign vessels have a duty to refrain from carrying out research and survey activities unless prior authorisation has been given and approved by all coastal States involved. Moreover, States bordering straits may adopt rules and regulations that are applicable to vessels passing through straits but only in relation to specific maritime issues.[92] Strait States have unrestricted jurisdiction but due to the fact that their laws and regulations must comply with international standards they may not discriminate against foreign vessels and cannot 'have the practical effect of denying, hampering or impairing the right of transit passage'.[93]

As regards the actual fulfilment of this requirement to not deny, hamper or impair the right of transit passage, it is also challenging for States bordering

---

vessel crossings in Åland West was 14433 and Åland East 1397 in 2013, Helsinki Commission (HELCOM), *Annual Report on Shipping Accidents in the Baltic Sea in 2013* 7 (2014).

89   LOSC art. 42 (1).

90   Churchill and Lowe, *supra* note 41 at 108; S.N. Nandan, *Legal Regime for Straits Used for International Navigation*, in *The Proceedings of the Symposium on the Straits Used for International Navigation, 16–17 November 2002, Ataköy Marina, Istanbul, Turkey* 1–11, 6 (Bayram Öztürk & Reşat Özkan eds., 2002).

91   Churchill and Lowe, *supra* note 41 at 108; Nandan, *supra* note 90 at 6.

92   Matters concerning fishing, loading and unloading commodities, currency or persons in contravention of customs, fiscal, immigration or sanitary regulations. Mahmoudi, *supra* note 67 at 165.

93   Churchill and Lowe, *supra* note 41 at 108; Nandan, *supra* note 90 at 6; Karin M. Burke & Deborah A. DeLeo, *Innocent Passage and Transit Passage in the United Nations Convention on the Law of the Sea*, 9 Yale J. Int. Law 389-408, 405 (1983). LOSC art. 42(1)(c)–(d).

straits because they have criminal jurisdiction with regard to merchant ships. Article 34 states that the regime of passage through straits is used for international navigation and does not affect the legal status of a strait's waters. For example, as regards jurisdiction of States bordering straits the criminal jurisdiction of States bordering straits extends to cover territorial seas of straits and may extend to cover enforcement actions on the basis of Article 27[94] of the LOSC. With respect to criminal jurisdiction, the enforcement actions of States bordering straits may also extend to cover the transit passage of foreign vessels. Nevertheless, a State advocating its position would have to prove that a crime had been committed on board while the ship was within its territorial sea area.[95]

Furthermore, according to Article 44, strait States may not hamper transit passage, thus strait States must refrain from enforcing laws and regulations that might cause a disturbance to transit passage. However, the Convention does not give any information or guidelines on how to actually do so. Overall, it seems that restrictions imposed in Article 44, do not leave much authority to strait States to interfere with passage, as they may not hamper or suspend transit passage. When comparing the jurisdiction of States bordering straits on matters concerning transit passage with matters concerning innocent passage it would appear that State competencies in relation to transit passage are significantly limited.[96]

Measures to prevent pollution that are mentioned in Article 233 are exceptions to the general rule. According to these provisions, if a vessel is not entitled to sovereign immunity and violates laws or regulations on pollution or

---

94   LOSC art. 27(1):

       The criminal jurisdiction of the coastal State should not be exercised on board a foreign ship passing through the territorial sea to arrest any person or to conduct any investigation in connection with any crime committed on board the ship during its passage, save only in the following cases:
       (a) if the consequences of the crime extend to the coastal State;
       (b) if the crime is of a kind to disturb the peace of the country or the good order of the territorial sea;
       (c) if the assistance of the local authorities has been requested by the master of the ship or by a diplomatic agent or consular officer of the flag State; or
       (d) if such measures are necessary for the suppression of illicit traffic in narcotic drugs or psychotropic substances.

95   Hakapää, *supra* note 32 at 197–198; Churchill and Lowe, *supra* note 41 at 98; Rüdiger Wolfrum, *Freedom of Navigation: New Challenges*, in *Freedom of Seas, Passage Rights and the 1982 Law of the Sea Convention* 79–102, 91 (Myron H. Nordquist, Tommy T.B. Koh, & John Norton Moore eds., 2009); Rothwell and Stephens, *supra* note 32 at 243.

96   Nordquist in Chapter 3 note 94 at 375, 388; Churchill and Lowe, *supra* note 41 at 108; Nandan, *supra* note 90 at 6; Rothwell and Stephens, *supra* note 32 at 243.

threatens major damage to the marine environment while undertaking transit passage then it may be subject to 'appropriate enforcement measures', which would be administered by the relevant State. Therefore, States bordering straits are justified when taking enforcement measures against vessels in transit in this situation.[97]

1.10   *Innocent Passage through Straits Used for International Navigation*
The regime of innocent passage is applied in straits that do not comply with Article 38(1) and its applications concerning transit passage, as well as other straits that are located between a part of the high seas or an EEZ and a territorial sea of a foreign coastal State.[98] As regards the suspension of innocent passage the LOSC follows the 1958 TSC in the sense that it also prohibits States from interfering with passage.[99] Nevertheless, such a prohibition does not imply that passage is completely free because States bordering straits have a right to deny passage if it is deemed to be non-innocent.[100]

Article 14(4) of the TSC prescribes that passage is innocent so long as it is not prejudicial to the peace, good order or security of the coastal State.[101] The term 'prejudicial to the peace, good order or security of the coastal State' opened up possibilities for various interpretations of non-innocent passage because only fishing vessels' activities and the mode of passage of submarines are explicitly mentioned in the text. Foreign fishing vessels must obey the laws

---

97   Hakapää, *supra* note 32 at 205; Erik Jaap Molenaar, *Coastal State Jurisdiction over Vessel-Source Pollution* 295–298 (1998); Nandan, *supra* note 90 at 6; Rothwell and Stephens, *supra* note 32 at 243. Caminos analyses Article 233 and its relationship to Article 41 and 42. He concludes that Article 233 seems to mean that the only exception to the general rule of unimpeded transit passage. When considering the sheer importance of unimpeded transit passage, then, it seems essential that a narrower interpretation of this Article 233 could be made. It can be applied only in cases where a breach of regulations on safety of navigation or maritime traffic or prevention, reduction and control of pollution, approved in accordance with Articles 41 and 42 together with the competent specialised international organisation, causes or threatens major damage to the marine environment. In such cases, a strait State would be allowed to take appropriate enforcement measures that may directly influence a vessel's general right of unimpeded transit passage, Caminos in Chapter 3 note 8 at 174–177. De Yturriaga has expressed his concern about other ways to pollute, other than those existing in 42(1)(b) such as dumping, because the regulations adopted by strait States may only cover 'discharge of oil, oily wastes and other noxious substances in the strait'. De Yturriaga has also a different interpretation of 42(1)(c), though he comes to the same conclusion as Caminos, Yturriaga in Chapter 3 note 140 at 174–178.

98   LOSC arts. 38, 45; Koh, *supra* note 55 at 164.

99   TSC art. 16(4).

100   Maduro in Chapter 3 note 92 at 75.

101   TSC art. 14(4).

and regulations of coastal States that prevent fishing in their respective territorial seas. Other more coherently phrased provisions suggest that non-innocent passage refers to submarines refraining from navigating on the surface
and stopping and anchoring during passage, which are not related to ordinary
navigation, force majeure or distress. Hence, the nature of passage was widely
left to the discretion of coastal States when considering whether passage is innocent or not.[102]

The LOSC contains a similar provision on innocent passage, providing more
detail about what kinds of activities are considered prejudicial to the peace,
good order or security of the coastal State. If a foreign vessel commits 'non-
innocent' activities listed in Article 19(2), the legal status of its passage will be
compromised. If a foreign vessel's passage is compromised in this way then
the coastal State in question has a right to take necessary steps to prevent
passage.[103]

As noted above, Article 19(2) enumerates activities considered to be prejudicial to the peace, good order or security of the coastal State. Nevertheless, the list
found in Article 19(2) is not a comprehensive one, because the last item forbids
any activity that is not applicable to passage.[104] This Convention also includes
a specific rule for submarines regarding innocent passage.[105] Many of the activities mentioned are linked to military activities,[106] which is understandable
because navigation through straits is very important to naval powers. On the
other hand, however, States bordering straits have been concerned about their
own national security. Nowadays the growing size of ships and heavy sea traffic
will probably encourage international support for environmental security, as
mentioned in Article 19(2)(h). Thus, the discretion of coastal States to decide
whether passage is innocent or not tends to focus on merchant vessels. When
compared with the 1958 TSC, the formulation of Article 19(2) includes quite a
few more rules and gives States bordering straits less discretionary power to
decide whether passage is innocent or not.

Duties of vessels and aircraft undertaking transit passage are included in
Article 39 but there is no mention of this in Section 3 of Part II, which focuses on the duties of vessels during innocent passage. Duties of vessels are

---

102   TSC art. 14(3), (5), (6); Maduro in Chapter 3 note 92 at 77.
103   LOSC art. 25.
104   Pharand in Chapter 3 note 151 at 77.
105   According to Article 20 submarines and other underwater vehicles are required to navi-
       gate on the surface and to show their flag.
106   Koh, *supra* note 55 at 165.

primarily related to the concept of 'innocent passage' but are more specifically mentioned in Articles 21 and 22, which declare that coastal States may adopt laws and regulations relating to innocent passage in territorial seas.[107]

In light of innocent passage, the *Corfu Channel* case seems important because the Court had ruled that the character of passage was the determining factor, not the character of the vessel. The Court added that the main thing to consider was whether passage could be deemed consistent with the principle of innocent passage.[108] Nevertheless, during the Third Law of the Sea Conference, States argued that in spite of the Court's decision it was still uncertain whether warships have a right of innocent passage. Some States strongly opposed the right of innocent passage for warships.

2   Straits Governed in Whole or in Part by Long-Standing
       International Conventions in Force

Article 35 of the LOSC states from the beginning that '[n]othing in this [p]art affects: [...] the legal régime in straits in which passage is regulated in whole or in part by long-standing international conventions in force specifically relating to such straits'. Consequently Article 35(c) creates a special status for straits that are governed 'in whole or in part' by long-standing international conventions in force. This is a significant exception which means that passage rights in these straits are governed by legal instruments existing prior to the LOSC entering into force. Consequently, the legal regime of these straits does not change.[109] During the Third Law of the Sea Conference, a great deal of discussion on Danish Straits took place because of the Conventions agreed upon in the year 1857[110] concerning the Sound Dues.[111] Besides the Danish Straits, the Conference also focused on issues regarding the Turkish Straits, the Strait of

---

107   *Id.* at 165.

108   *Corfu Channel* case, I.C.J. Reports in Chapter 3 note 22 at 228, 30.

109   Donald R. Rothwell, *International Straits*, in *The Oxford Handbook of the Law of the Sea* 114–133, 127 (Donald Rothwell et al. eds., 2015).

110   See Treaty between Great Britain, Austria, Belgium, France, Hanover, Mecklenburg-Schwerin, the Netherlands, Oldenburg, Prussia, Russia and Sweden, and Norway and the Hansa Towns, on the One Part, and Denmark on the Other Part, for the Redemption of the Sound Dues signed at Copenhagen and Convention between United States of America and Denmark for the Discontinuance of the Sound Dues, 116 PCTS 357, 465.

111   William. L. Jr. Schachte & J. Peter A. Bernhardt, *International Straits and Navigational Freedoms*, 33 VA. J. Int. Law 527–556, 544 (1993).

Magellan, and the Åland Strait since these straits regulated passage 'by [means of] long standing international conventions in force'.[112]

Article 35(c) has its roots in the late 1960s, when idea of the Third Law of the Sea Conference was in its formative stages. Navigation through international straits was on the agenda in the negotiations between the superpowers and the discussion also touched straits with a special regime. The negotiations between the United States and the Soviet Union show that although it was important for them to retain the freedom of navigation and overflight through international straits, they also shared a view that the provisions of the new convention did not affect the legal status of particular straits where passage is regulated by existing international agreements specifically relating to those straits.[113] During the Third Law of the Sea Conference, the negotiations continued and the ground for the interpretation of Article 35(c) lies in the negotiations between the United States, the Soviet Union and Finland and Sweden in the Conference. It was the goal of Finland and Sweden that the legal status of the Åland Strait would not change.[114]

While signing the LOSC Finland issued the following Declaration:

> [i]t is the understanding of the Government of Finland that the exception from the transit passage regime in straits provided for in article 35 (c) of the Convention is applicable to the strait between Finland (the Åland Islands) and Sweden. Since in that strait the passage is regulated in part by a long-standing international convention in force, the present legal regime in that strait will remain unchanged after the entry into force of the Convention.

Sweden gave a corresponding Declaration.[115] The wording of Article 35(c) is interesting as it uses the term, 'in whole or in part', which can be interpreted

---

112   C. John Colombos, *The International Law of the Sea* 197–200 (1967); Manner in Chapter 2 note 88 at 126; Caminos and Cogliati-Bantz, *supra* note 4 at 71.

113   Finnish Ministry for Foreign Affairs Archives, Documents relating to the Third Law of the Sea Conference, Documents 11.1.1968 to P.M.

114   Finnish Ministry for Foreign Affairs Archives, *Documents on the Negotiations in the Third United Nations Conference on the Law of the Sea.*

115   http://www.un.org/depts/los/convention_agreements/convention_declarations.htm# Sweden%20Upon%20signature [last access 24.3.2018]. 'It is the understanding of the Government of Sweden that the exception from the transit passage régime in straits, provided for in Article 35 (c) of the Convention is applicable to the strait between Sweden and Denmark (Oresund) as well as to the strait between Sweden and Finland (the Aland islands). Since in both those straits the passage is regulated in whole or in part by long-standing

in several ways. Schachte and Bernhardt suggest that transit passage is not applicable if a convention governs a given strait but only according to certain circumstances, for instance with regard to merchant vessels but not aeroplanes, because if the regime of transit passage is not applied then straits must be regulated by other rules of customary international law.[116] Schachte and Bernhardt do not mention the 1958 TSC although it includes regulations on passage through international straits and also mentions in Article 25 that provisions of the TSC do 'not affect conventions or other international agreements already in force, as between States Parties to them'. However, if a convention were to govern a strait partly, the right of transit passage, as a normal regime, would apply in the part not regulated by the Convention.[117] Consequently according to Schachte and Bernhard, the character of a vessel, e.g. a warship

---

international conventions in force, the present legal régime in the two straits will remain unchanged'.

However, Erik Castrén argues in his statement in 1959 that the legal status of the Åland Strait is not that of a strait used for international navigation. He contests that as regards foreign warships, the Åland Strait is not an important strait used for international navigation because warships do not need this route for navigating between home ports and oceans. Therefore, sailing to the Gulf of Bothnia is not necessary for them. If the Åland Strait would not have been a strait 'used for international navigation' it would have excluded non-suspendable innocent passage in the Strait. Had this been the case, the Sea area would have been treated as a territorial sea and the relevant coastal State would have had a right to suspend innocent passage temporarily. According to Castrén, any interpretation to deny innocent passage of warships on grounds that they did not enjoy the right of innocent passage would apply to the Åland Strait. See Castrén, Statement 23.10.1959 for the Ministry for Foreign Affairs, part of the statement is available in Komulainen in Chapter 2 note 1 at 305–310, liite 6. The original statement is not available in the Archives of the Ministry for Foreign Affairs.

Consequently, it seems that Castren's statement does not pay attention to the *Corfu Channel* case in which the Court stated that the amount of traffic and the significance of the strait in regard to international navigation are not decisive factors. The Court refers that it is adequate that the strait is useful for international navigation. Thus, according to *Corfu Channel* case the significance of the Åland Strait for navigation of warships was irrelevant. On both coasts of the Gulf of Bothnia several important import and export ports are located and transportation to these ports passes through the Åland Strait. Therefore, the Åland Strait it is useful for international navigation. On the other hand, the Åland Strait is also useful to the Finnish navy when its vessels navigate between the Gulf of Finland and the Gulf of Bothnia so there is no doubt that the Åland Strait can be considered to be 'used for international navigation'. *Corfu Channel* case, I.C.J. Reports in Chapter 3 note 22 at 28–29. See also Rotkirch in Chapter 1 note 2 at 372; Manner in Chapter 2 note 88 at 128–129.

116   See art. 35(c); Schachte and Bernhardt, *supra* note 111 at 544.

117   *Id.* at 544–545.

or a merchant ship, plays the determinant role in terms of its legal status within the strait and with its navigational rights in certain straits regulated by long-standing Conventions. This might cause confusion between applicable Conventions and therefore it is unlikely that States had intended for certain straits a dual legal regime that varies according to types of vessels or other factors like geography. On the contrary it is likely that States had intended for long-standing Conventions to be sufficient enough when seeking to regulate different straits.[118]

As noted above, on the basis of the discussions that took place during the Third Law of the Sea Conference, the Danish Straits, the Turkish Straits, the Strait of Magellan, and the Åland Strait are exceptions to the regime of transit passage. Each of these straits have unique regimes governed by 'long-standing conventions in force'. It is noteworthy that one requirement for straits governed by Article 35(c) is that its status must be accepted by the international community. It is considered sine qua non that contracting parties to the Convention should have the relevant competencies to determine the territorial status. However, it does not mean that third-party States are obliged to respect this sort of status. Schachte and Bernhardt believe that all States cannot be expected to become parties to these conventions. On the contrary, it is adequate that third-party States comply with the regulations imposed by the conventions. An objective regime would imply that third-party States are bound by the Conventions and therefore expected to respect not only the written rules and regulations but also the unwritten context surrounding them.

An interesting set of questions hinge on the possibility of altering the convention, which is something that may only be managed by the parties. The convention includes certain rights that affect not only its parties but also non-parties. The general principle is that amendments to the convention bind parties but do not bind non-parties. However, an objective regime indicates that the special regimes of these straits may not be amended without their consent.[119] Making amendments is therefore a complicated issue, especially when considering the Åland Strait, which is partly regulated by the 1921 Åland Convention. The demilitarisation and neutralisation of the Åland Islands has attained a regional customary law status in the Baltic Sea region and has been referred to as a European regional customary 'norm' by many academics.

---

118   Kleemola-Juntunen in Chapter 1 note 2 at 41.
119   Schachte and Bernhardt, *supra* note 111 at 545; Caminos and Cogliati-Bantz, *supra* note 4 at 73–74.

All States have an obligation to respect the rules of customary law, which is why the legal status of the Åland Islands might have become a permanent settlement by international treaty arrangements and practices since the Second World War.[120] Therefore, it is possible that in the event that the 1921 Åland Convention were amended a revaluation of passage rights would be necessary.

---

120   Hannikainen in Chapter 2 note 88 at 625–626.

CHAPTER 5

The Legal Regime of the Åland Strait

1 Baselines

The outer limits of a territorial sea and other coastal State zones are measured from a line referred to as a 'baseline'. Internal waters are located landwards from a baseline, while a State's territorial sea continues seawards. Baselines often mark differences between areas where States either do or do not have general rights and are also useful when drawing up maritime boundaries. For example, if two neighbouring States agree that the boundary between their maritime zones is to be a line equidistant from them, equidistance is calculated from the baselines of each respective State.[1]

Coastal States' territorial sovereignty over their internal waters is linked to the land domain and is therefore subject to the same legal regime. A baseline acts as a dividing line between maritime zones and internal waters where foreign States have no general rights.[2] However, despite the fact that coastal States

---

1 Churchill and Lowe in Chapter 4 note 41 at 31; Kari Hakapää, *Uusi kansainvälinen oikeus* 383–384 (2010).

2 Judge Huber made 'some general marks on *sovereignty in its relation to territory*' during the Island of Palmas case, 1928, Reports of International Arbitral Awards, *Island of Palmas Case (or Miangas) (United States of America v. the Netherlands), Volume II*, 838–839 (1928).

> Sovereignty with regard to relations between States signifies independence. Independence with regard to a portion of the globe is the right to exercise functions of a State regardless of any other State interests. The development of the national organisation of States during the last few centuries and, as a corollary, the development of international law, have established the principle of exclusive competence of a State in regard to its own territory in such a way as to make it the point of departure when settling most questions that concern international relations.

> Territorial sovereignty...involves the exclusive right to display the activities of a State. This right has a corollary duty: the obligation to protect within the territory the rights of other States, in particular their right to integrity and inviolability in peace and in war, together with rights that each State may claim for its nationals in a foreign territory. Without manifesting its territorial sovereignty in a manner corresponding to its circumstances a State cannot fulfil this duty. Territorial sovereignty cannot limit itself to its negative side, i.e. to exclude activities of other States; for it serves to divide among nations a space from which human activities are employed, in order to assure the minimum protection according to international law which acts as a guardian.

See also Rainer Lagoni, *Internal Waters*, 11 Encycl. Public Int. Law 153–155, 153 (1989); Churchill and Lowe in Chapter 4 note 41 at 31, 60–61; Klein in Chapter 2 note 119 at 264; Hakapää, *supra* note 1 at 386.

© KONINKLIJKE BRILL NV, LEIDEN, 2019 | DOI:10.1163/9789004364189_006

enjoy a legal right to mark their territorial boundaries, the international influence on sovereignty is not avoidable because conventions on the law of the sea set the rules for drawing baselines.[3] The difference between the legal status of internal waters and territorial seas is substantial, as foreign ships do not enjoy a general right of innocent passage through internal waters. Furthermore, a coastal State's jurisdiction over foreign ships differs within different maritime zones. However, this rule is not without some exceptions based on treaty law. For example, after establishing straight baselines, sea areas may be thereafter considered internal waters although the right of innocent passage still remains through those waters.[4]

As a general rule, a coastal State may enact laws and apply them to foreign ships within its internal waters, which is permissible according to international law. These obligations may also be enforced by international treaties or customary international law as the Permanent Court of International Justice stated in its Judgement in the 1923 *S.S. 'Wimbledon'* case.[5] On the other hand, a coastal State has an obligation to disallow any activities from happening within its internal waters contrary to the rights of other States. This could relate to, for instance, the integrity and safety of foreign ships.[6]

1.1   *Normal Baseline*

According to Article 5 of the LOSC, 'the normal baseline for measuring the breadth of the territorial sea is the low-water line along the coast as marked on large-scale charts officially recognised by the coastal State'. The wording is identical to Article 3 of the TSC. By choosing the low-water line instead of the high-tide line, the outer limit of a territorial sea and other maritime zones

---

3 Lagoni, *supra* note 2 at 155. This was pointed out by the ICJ in the 1951 *Fisheries* case.

4 TSC art. 5 (2); LOSC arts. 8 (2), 35(a).

5 Permanent Court of International Justice, *S.S. Wimbledon (Britain et al. v. Germany)* 24 (1923), www.icj-cij.org/pcij/series-a.php?p1=9&p2=1. The Court stated: 'The Court declines to see in the conclusion of any Treaty by which a State undertakes to perform or refrain from performing a particular act an abandonment of its sovereignty. No doubt any convention creating an obligation of this kind places a restriction upon the exercise of the sovereign rights of the State, in the sense that it requires them to be exercised in a certain way. But the right of entering into international engagements is an attribute of State sovereignty'. E.D. Brown, *The International Law of the Sea, Volume I: Introductory Manual* 38 (1994); Haijiang Yang, *Jurisdiction of the Coastal State over Foreign Merchant Ships in Internal Waters and the Territorial Sea* 48 (2006).

6 See *Corfu Channel* case, I.C.J. Reports in Chapter 3 note 22 at 22. The Court stated coastal States' obligations in regard to their territorial waters: 'every State's obligation not to allow knowingly its territory to be used for acts contrary to the rights of other States'.

seawards is extended further, especially when concerning coasts that have a wider tidal range.[7]

Articles 3 and 5 were drafted with relatively straight and unintended coasts in mind. In both the 1958 TSC and the LOSC the low-water line is described as 'the normal baseline'. Both conventions include provisions for cases in which the low-water line is not suitable as a baseline because of the variety of geographical circumstances. Specific rules concerning special geographical conditions according to the conventions are: 1) reefs; 2) straight baselines for coasts deeply indented or fringed with islands; 3) river mouths; 4) bays; 5) permanent harbour works; 6) low-tide elevations; and 7) islands.[8]

Coastal States enjoy discretion when choosing alternative low-water lines, as there is no standardised State practice when determining this line. The normal baseline method is the general rule. However, a normal baseline may cause problems for States when determining the outer limits of their territorial sea if their coastline consists of groups of islands. Currently, most States apply a straight baseline method as decribed below.[9]

1.2   Straight Baselines

Norway is a State which has had the most influence over the rules concerning straight baselines. The Norwegian coastline is penetrated by fjords and fringed by numerous islands, islets, rocks and reefs. There is no restriction in drawing up low-water lines across this type of coast. However, due to the fjords, islands and rocks, collectively known as the skjærgaard, it would not be an easy task to discern the outer limit of Norway's territorial sea. Consequently, since the mid-nineteenth century onwards, Norway has used a series of straight lines connecting the outermost points of the skjærgaard as a baseline. By using this method, the outer limit of Norway's territorial sea was extended further seaward than it would have been if applying a low-water mark. The first dispute occurred in 1911 when a British fishing vessel was seized and condemned for having engaged in fishing activities within Norwegian coastal waters without

---

7   Brown, *supra* note 5 at 23; Churchill and Lowe in Chapter 4 note 41 at 33; Klein in Chapter 2 note 119 at 266. For various possibilities when defining a low-water line, see O'Connell and Shearer in Chapter 3 note 13 at 171–185.

8   These rules are laid down in the TSC Section 2 and LOSC Section 2 relating to limits of the Territorial Sea. Churchill and Lowe in Chapter 4 note 41 at 33.

9   *Third United Nations Conference on the Law of the Sea, Volume II: Summary Records (1st, 2nd and 3rd Committee)* in Chapter 3 note 121 at 115, 117; Hakapää in Chapter 3 note 162 at 35–36; Nordquist in Chapter 3 note 94 at 89; Brown, *supra* note 5 at 23.

permission. Norway and the United Kingdom then held negotiations in regard to these incidents.[10]

However, in spite of numerous warnings and arrests British trawlers continued to appear west of North Cape until 1932. Eventually the United Kingdom sent a memorandum to Norway in 1933, which declared that Norwegian methods used to demarcate its territorial waters were contrary to international law. The UK's motives pertained to British fishing vessels, which would have enjoyed a larger portion of the high seas area if Norway had applied the low-water line method. Norway established its fisheries zone by a Decree in July 1935. Negotiations between Norway and the UK continued, although the two States still had not reached any form of agreement in 1948. As a result, disputes became much more frequent. In its 1949 Application to the International Court of Justice, the UK asked for the principles of international law to be made clearer when determining baselines. The UK also made a reference to Norway, in regard to how it should delineate its fisheries zone.[11]

In its judgement on the 1951 *Anglo-Norwegian Fisheries* case, the Court stated that the Norwegian coastline did not constitute a clear dividing line between land and sea, and that the outer limit of skjærgaard constituted the real dividing line. The court stated that 'three methods have been contemplated to effect the application of the low-water mark rule', namely 1) tracé paralléle, drawing the outer limit of the belt of territorial sea by following the coast in all its sinuosities; 2) the courbe tangente (envelopes of arcs of circles), drawing arcs of circles from points along the low-water line with the aim being to ensure that the belt of territorial waters follows the coastline; and 3) straight baselines (previously mentioned above). According to the Court, if a coast is deeply indented or fringed by islands, neither the tracé paralléle nor the courbe tangente methods are appropriate. The Court stated that 'the baseline becomes independent of the low-water mark, and can only be determined by means of a geometric construction'. Such a geometric construction was a straight baseline and several States have deemed it necessary to follow this method without objections from other States.[12] The Court agreed overall that the straight baseline method, as established by Norwegian long-standing practice, was not contrary to international law.[13] Moreover, the Court stated that '[t]here is one

---

10   *Fisheries* case, I.C.J. Reports in Chapter 3 note 144 at 118, 124–125; Brown, *supra* note 5 at 24–25; Churchill and Lowe in Chapter 4 note 41 at 33–34.

11   *Fisheries* case, I.C.J. Reports in Chapter 3 note 144 at 118, 124–125; Brown, *supra* note 5 at 24–25; Churchill and Lowe in Chapter 4 note 41 at 33–34.

12   *Fisheries* case, I.C.J. Reports in Chapter 3 note 144 at 128–129.

13   *Id.* at 139.

consideration not to be overlooked, the scope of which extends beyond purely geographical factors: that of certain economic interests peculiar to a region, the reality and importance of which are clearly evidenced by a long usage'.[14]

The rules outlined within the Court's judgement on the *Anglo-Norwegian Fisheries* case were followed up by the ILC as it prepared the First Law of the Sea Conference. Hence, the formulation of Article 4 of the 1958 TSC has a direct connection to the Court's judgement. However, the 1958 TSC and the LOSC consider straight baselines as a distinct method of construction, contrary to the Court's viewpoint which suggests that they are a special variation of a low-water line when constructing baselines.[15] According to both of the Conventions' provisions, States may use the straight baselines method 'in localities where the coast line is deeply indented and cut into, or if there is a fringe of islands along the coast in its immediate vicinity'.[16] The wording indicates that a State has a choice as to whether it uses straight baselines or not, even if entitled to do so. It is beneficial, however, for States to apply a straight baseline because the outer limits of their different maritime zones could be placed further seawards than when using other methods of drawing baselines.[17]

Both the 1958 TSC and the LOSC include provisions on conditions where straight baselines may be drawn. The influence of the *Anglo-Norwegian Fisheries* case is evident in Article 7(3) for straight baselines, which suggests that they 'must not depart to any appreciable extent from the general direction of the coast, and the sea areas lying within the lines must be sufficiently closely linked to the land domain to be subject to the regime of internal waters'.[18]

The Conventions prohibit drawing straight baselines to or from low-tide elevations, unless lighthouses or similar installations that are permanently above sea level have been built on them; or, as the LOSC states, 'except in instances where the drawing of baselines to and from such elevations has received general international recognition'.[19] This provision endeavoured to restrict baselines from being drawn too far seawards from the coast.[20] A State is not allowed to apply a straight baseline method in such a manner as to separate another State's territorial sea from the high seas or its respective exclusive economic

---

14   *Id.* at 133.
15   *Id.* at 133; *Yearbook of The International Law Commission 1952 Volume I, Summary Records of the Fourth Session 4 June–8 August 1952* 143–144, 147–148, 155, 166; Brown, *supra* note 5 at 26; Churchill and Lowe in Chapter 4 note 41 at 35.
16   TSC art. 4 (1); LOSC art. 7 (1).
17   Hakapää in Chapter 3 note 162 at 36; Churchill and Lowe in Chapter 4 note 41 at 35.
18   *Fisheries* case, I.C.J. Reports in Chapter 3 note 144 at 129, 133. TSC art. 4(2); LOSC art. 7(3).
19   TSC art. 4 (3); LOSC art. 7 (4).
20   Hakapää in Chapter 3 note 162 at 36; Churchill and Lowe in Chapter 4 note 41 at 37.

zone (EEZ).[21] This Article covers situations where a smaller territory is embedded in a larger territory or where small islands belonging to one State are located near to the coast of another State.[22] If a State is to draw straight baselines, these must be shown on charts to which 'due publicity' must also be given.[23]

Both conventions take into account State and non-State actors' economic interests 'in determining particular baselines, of economic interests peculiar to the region concerned, the reality and the importance of which are clearly evidenced by a long usage'.[24] This reasoning stems from the *Anglo-Norwegian Fisheries* case, in which fishing was of obvious concern. This particular case still influences decision-making when agreeing to the length of individual baselines because the Conventions are silent on this matter. In the *Anglo-Norwegian Fisheries* case the Court upheld that the forty-four mile long baseline was valid.[25] Yet in spite of the guidance provided from the *Anglo-Norwegian Fisheries* case, States have interpreted their obligations under customary law of the sea and the LOSC quite flexibly, and have determined baseline lengths independently by themselves.[26]

2   Finnish National Legislation

In 1995, Finland extended the breadth of its territorial sea from four nautical miles to 12 nautical miles.[27] However, there are some exceptions in the Gulf of Finland, the Åland Sea and the Gulf of Bothnia areas. Finland began using

---

21   TSC art. 4 (5); the EEZ is added to LOSC art. 7 (6).
22   Churchill and Lowe in Chapter 4 note 41 at 37.
23   TSC art. 4 (6); LOSC art. 16.
24   TSC art. 4 (4); LOSC art. 7 (5).
25   *Fisheries* case, I.C.J. Reports in Chapter 3 note 144 at 131.
26   Brown, *supra* note 5 at 26–27; J.R.V. Prescott, *Political Frontiers and Boundaries* 146 (1987). Prescott notes that States such as 'Canada, Chile, Finland and Yugoslavia have drawn straight baselines which are models of propriety and beyond criticism'.
      The LOSC includes a geographical situation which does not exist in the 1958 TSC. In Article 7 (2) it is provided that
      'Where because of the presence of a delta and other natural conditions the coastline is highly unstable, the appropriate points may be selected along the furthest seaward extent of the low-water line'. See more about the interpretation and application of the provision in Churchill and Lowe in Chapter 4 note 41 at 38.
27   Act on the Delimitation of the Territorial Waters of Finland 18th August 1956, Statutes of Finland 463/1956, amended on 5th March 1965, Statutes of Finland 144/1965, 25th March 1966, Statutes of Finland 332/1966, 5th December 1969, Statutes of Finland 781/1969, 3rd March 1995, Statutes of Finland 981/1995 entered into force on 30th July 1995 as enacted by the Decree of 17th July 1995, Statutes of Finland 982/1995.

the straight baselines method in 1956, but the breadth of territorial waters was not changed; the breadth remained as four nautical miles. According to previous legislation, the maximum distance between basepoints was eight nautical miles as basepoints were not allowed to exceed twice the breadth of the territorial sea. Nonetheless, when Act on the Delimitation of the Territorial Waters of Finland was changed, this kind of special limitation was not deemed necessary. Although the 1958 TSC nor the LOSC limit the distance between basepoints, Finland had to take into account its agreements made with other States before expanding the breadth of its territorial sea. For instance, the Åland Sea was one of these special maritime areas and Finland began negotiations with Sweden regarding the maritime boundary pertaining to the Åland Sea and the northern part of the Baltic Sea while it was preparing to widen its territorial sea. The Agreement Concerning the Delimitation in the Åland Sea and the Northern Part of the Baltic Sea of the Finnish Continental Shelf and Fishing Zone and the Swedish Economic Zone was made in consideration of the Decree on the Application of the Act on the Delimitation of the Territorial Waters of Finland, which stipulates that Finland's outer boundary within the Åland Sea area does not, in any instance cross into Sweden's EEZ.[28]

3   The Maritime Boundary between Finland and Sweden

Finland and Sweden share a common maritime boundary in the Gulf of Bothnia, the Åland Sea and the northern part of the Baltic Sea. In 1972 Finland and Sweden concluded the Agreement between Finland and Sweden Concerning the Delimitation of the Continental Shelf at the Gulf of Bothnia, The Åland Sea and the Northernmost Part of the Baltic Sea.[29] This agreement only delimited

---

28   Section 5a(2), Statutes of Finland 981/1995; Government Proposal 114/1994; see also Spiliopoulou Åkermark, Heinikoski, and Kleemola-Juntunen in Chapter 1 note 2 at 49–50.
        For the first time ever, the inner limits of internal waters had been defined. The reason for defining inner limits of internal waters was due to a change in scope of the 1992 Convention on the Protection of the Marine Environment of the Baltic Sea Area, which entered into force on 17th January 2000. The Convention is applied to the Baltic Sea area which, according to Article 1, which 'includes the internal waters, i.e., for the purpose of this Convention waters on the landward side of the base lines from which the breadth of the territorial sea is measured up to the landward limit according to the designation by the Contracting Parties'. Section 3, Statutes of Finland 981/1995; Government Proposal HE 114/1994.
29   Agreement between Finland and Sweden concerning the Delimitation of the Continental Shelf at the Gulf of Bothnia, The Åland Sea and the Northernmost Part of the Baltic

the continental shelf boundary between Finland and Sweden because the fisheries were not considered important. However, when fishery zones were established in the 1970s it soon became obvious that a continental shelf boundary would suffice when ruling fishery jurisdiction west and south of the Åland Islands.[30]

After fishery zones were introduced in the 1970s, Finland established a fishing zone boundary in 1975. Sweden developed its own zone later in 1978. The breadth of Finland's fishing zone was mainly 8 nautical miles while Sweden's went beyond 12 nautical miles.[31] Finland amended its legislation on its fishery zone after an exchange of notes with Sweden in 1977, after which time Finnish legislation followed the Swedish legal system with respect to coordinates and delimitation principles. Fishing zone boundaries were established by national legislation and were based on an equidistant line that crosses the continental shelf boundary line, back and forth, between several points; thus forming so-called 'fishery pockets'. It seems that both Finland and Sweden considered the 1921 Åland Convention to be insufficient when delimiting fisheries jurisdiction in this region.[32] It was inherently clear that such a discrepancy had to be settled, one way or another, between the two neighbouring States.

The problem was partly resolved in 1977 when Finland and Sweden concluded an agreement concerning the outer fishery limit north of the Åland Strait, which is the northernmost entrance to the Åland Sea. For fishery purposes, the continental shelf boundary line was suitable for both States. Therefore, the outer limit of Sweden's fishing zone follows the continental shelf boundary line north of the Åland Strait, as concluded by the 1972 Agreement. Nevertheless, there still remained two delimitation lines west and south of the Åland Islands; one existing for the sake of demarcating the continental shelf; the other for fishery purposes. The fishery pockets created areas where States with fishery jurisdiction had no jurisdiction with respect to continental shelves. The fishery boundary was an equidistant line drawn up between the parties' respective

---

Sea, adopted 29 September 1972 entered into force 15 January 1973, Finnish Treaty Series 7/1973.

30   Erik Franckx, *Finland – Sweden, Report Number 10 – 3*, in *International Maritime Boundaries, Volume II* 1945–1957, 1947 (J.I. Charney & L .M. Alexander eds., 1993); Erik Franckx, *Finland-Sweden Delimitation Agreement*, 11 Int. J. Mar. Coast. Law 394–398 (1996).

31   Act of 15th November 1974, On the Extent of the Finnish Fishing Zone, Statutes of Finland 839/1974, Decree of 11th August 1977, On the Extent of the Swedish Fishing Zone, Svensk Författningssamling, 1977: 642.

32   See Franckx, *supra* note 30 at 1945–1957.

straight baselines, whereas the continental shelf boundary line seemed to be
dependent upon historic events like the Peace Treaty of Fredrikshamn.[33]

Finland and Sweden started negotiations on a new delimitation agreement
in 1989.[34] Both Finland and Sweden wanted to discuss sea areas with respect to
where their fishery zone limits differed from the 1972 continental shelf boundary.[35] Negotiations were suspended in 1991 for two years because of the dissolution of the Soviet Union. During this period, Finland was allowed to arrange
its boundary relations with the Russian Federation and Estonia, both of which
were new coastal States within the Gulf of Finland. There were also changes
to Swedish legislation in relation to its maritime boundaries when Sweden established its EEZ on 1st January 1993.[36] For many years the former Soviet Union
was the only State claiming an economic zone in the Baltic Sea.[37] At present all
Baltic Sea States have established an exclusive economic zone.

Section 1 of the Act on the Economic Zone of Sweden stipulates that Sweden's economic zone includes the marine area outside of the territorial boundary prescribed by the Government. However, this zone may not extend beyond
the demarcation line agreed upon with other States. Nor can it, in the absence
of such an agreement, extend beyond the equidistance line. Sweden concluded
numerous agreements concerning its maritime boundaries with neighbouring

---

33   The Agreement referred to established boundary lines. On the one hand, according to an
      earlier topographic description drawn up in 1811, the frontier drawn up after the Peace of
      Fredrikshamn (Hamina) and the 1921 Åland Convention; see Article 1 of the Agreement
      between Sweden and Finland concerning the Delimitation of the Continental Shelf in
      the Gulf of Bothnia, the Åland Sea and the Northernmost Part of the Baltic Sea, Finnish
      Treaty Series 7/1973; Erik Franckx, *Finland–Sweden, Report Number 10 – 13*, in *International
      Maritime Boundaries, Volume III* 2539–2555, 2546 (J.I. Charney & L.M. Alexander eds.,
      1998).

34   In the previous year Sweden concluded difficult negotiations on the maritime delimi-
      tation with the former Soviet Union. These negotiations had been ongoing for approx-
      imately 20 years. Finland had concluded an agreement with the Soviet Union in 1985.
      Agreement between the Government of the Republic of Finland and the Government of
      the Union of Soviet Socialist Republics regarding the Delimitation of the Economic zone,
      the Fishery Zone and the Continental Shelf in the Gulf of Finland and the North-Eastern
      Part of the Baltic Sea, Finnish Treaty Series 88/1986; Agreement on the Delimitation of
      the Continental Shelf and of the Swedish Fishing zone and the Soviet Economic zone in
      the Baltic, 27 ILM 295; Agreement regarding the Delimitation of the Areas of Finnish and
      Soviet Jurisdiction in the Field of Fishing in the Gulf of Finland and the North-Eastern
      Part of the Baltic Sea, Finnish Treaty Series 43/1980; Erik Franckx, *Finland and Sweden
      Complete Their Maritime Boundary in the Baltic Sea*, 27 Ocean Dev. Int. Law 291–314, 299
      (1996).

35   Franckx, *supra* note 34 at 291–314.

36   Act on Sweden's Economic Zone, Svensk författningssamling 1992: 1226.

37   Franckx, *supra* note 34 at 291–314.

States. It was noted that Sweden's EEZ boundary could be established through Exchanges of Notes with neighbouring States that were in a position to confirm their own existing continental shelf and fishing zone boundaries.[38]

A bilateral Agreement on Finland's and Sweden's maritime boundaries, signed in 1972, was completed with an agreement and additional protocol attached to it. The Agreement between Finland and Sweden Concerning the Delimitation in the Åland Sea and the Northern Part of the Baltic Sea of the Finnish Continental Shelf and Fishing Zone and Swedish Economic Zone was signed on 2nd June 1994 and entered into force on 30th July 1995.[39] According to the annexed protocol, the border between Finland's fishing zone and Sweden's economic zone follows the continental shelf border north of Märket, as established by the 1972 Agreement, until both parties agree to a technical revision of the boundary in question.[40] The protocol is still valid at this point in time, since Finland and Sweden have not yet carried out a technical revision of the boundary.[41]

It seems that both Finland and Sweden, as contracting parties to the 1921 Åland Convention, had bypassed the 1921 Åland Convention as an irrelevant issue, preferring the equidistant line in their national legislation to demarcate the fishery zone. The 1994 Agreement brings back the significance of the 1921 Åland Convention, since it partially relies on the Convention when establishing fishery boundaries. This highlights the fact that historical considerations have influenced the boundary line and for this reason equidistance is not a governing principle of this Agreement either. In fact, both parties established their outer fishery zone limits on the basis of an equidistant line between their respective baselines, which was the topic of renewed negotiations later on.

Article 2 of the Agreement says that demarcation Points 2, 3 and 4 correspond to Points 15, 14 and 13 respectively from the 1921 Åland Convention. The reference to the 1921 Åland Convention is familiar from the 1972 Agreement between Finland and Sweden concerning the continental shelf. Likewise, Points 13, 15 and 17 of the 1972 Agreement correspond to Points 15, 14 and 13

---

38   Sveriges Ekonomiska Zon, Ds 1990: 41; Alexander Gerard Oude Elferink, *The Law of Maritime Boundary Delimitation: A Case Study of the Russian Federation* 206 (1994).

39   Agreement between Finland and Sweden Concerning the Delimitation in the Åland Sea and the Northern Part of the Baltic Sea of the Finnish Continental Shelf and Fishing Zone and Swedish Economic Zone, adopted 2 June 1994 entered into force 30 July 1995, Finnish Treaty Series 39/1995.

40   Finnish Treaty Series 39/1995; Decree of 17th July 1995, Statutes of Finland 983/1995.

41   On 1st May 2010 an agreement concerning boundaries between Finland and Sweden entered into force. However, this agreement only covers land territory, Finnish Treaty Series 35/2010, Presidential decree of 9th April 2010.

respectively from the Åland Convention. The new segment between points 4 and 5 represents nearly 40 percent of the total boundary line length. This segment has no relation to the 1921 Åland Convention. The islets of Bogskär[42] must have influenced this new segment, but it is not known to what extent this is true since Finland and Sweden stressed different elements in this respect. It is noteworthy that the system of geographic coordinates used in the 1994 Agreement is not the same as the system used in the 1921 Åland Convention. This suggests that a slight inconsistency exists between coordinates because the positions of the points in the Agreement have been determined with reference to geographical longitude and latitude marks established by the 'World Geodetic System 1984'.[43]

4   Internal Waters in the Åland Strait

In the second paragraph of Article 2, the 1921 Åland Convention defines the method to be used when demarcating the Åland Islands' territorial waters. This sea area is measured according to a low-water mark, which is then extended by a distance of three nautical miles from islands, islets and reefs that are not permanently submerged. The low-water line as it is mentioned in the second paragraph, however, defines the system by which this demilitarised and neutralised sea area is to be measured and the legal status of maritime zones. Navigational rights mentioned in the 1921 Åland Convention focus on the territorial sea and are applied at the extent of three nautical miles from the low-water line. At the time Finland had four nautical mile territorial sea but it is understandable that at the time the four-mile limit, Finland's suggestion in the 1921 Conference, was not acceptable for non-Scandinavian Parties to the 1921 Åland Convention

---

42 Bogskär, is a distant, uninhabited place and is located approximately 24 nautical miles from the nearest main island of the Åland Islands, and exists outside of the straight baselines system. Finland's territorial sea to the south of Bogskär does not extend beyond 3 nautical miles.

43 The 1921 Åland Convention refers to the British Admiralty map N°2297, dated 1872 (corrected up to August 1921). However, the position of Points 1–11 are taken from the following maps, Finnish maps No. 32, 1921, No. 29, 1920, and Russian map No. 742, 1916 (corrected in March 1916); Franckx, *supra* note 33 at 2543, 2548, 2550. The Ministry for Foreign Affairs of Finland asked the National Land Survey in 2012 to perform the technical delimitation of the areas defined by the Åland Convention. The changes were made according to the ETRS89 system and 17 geographical points mentioned in the Åland Convention were transferred into the Finnish version of this system called EUREF-FIN. Technical Delimitation of the Areas Defined by the Åland Convention, Finnish Treaty Series 31/2013.

since they would avoid the possibility of allowing wider territorial seas.[44] The Convention also includes the right of innocent passage for foreign warships when navigating territorial waters, which also relates to the area of the Åland Strait as straits did not have a separate legal status at the time.

Nevertheless, the 1921 Åland Convention does not set the correct method Finland should use when defining its internal and external waters in general,[45] which is why Finland chose to draw baselines using the straight baseline method in 1956. More interestingly, however, is the fact that, according to the law of the sea, the sea area surrounding the Åland Islands may be regarded as either internal waters or a territorial sea, depending on how Finland defines its maritime boundaries.[46] At present the Act on the Delimitation of the Territorial Waters of Finland defines Finland's territorial sea as a zone immediately adjacent to its internal waters with a breadth of 12 nautical miles from the outer limits of internal waters.[47]

Although applying the straight baseline method in 1956 did not widen the demilitarised and neutralised area, it did extend the size of Finland's internal waters. By doing so, Finland also diminished its territorial sea in the Åland Strait and decreased the range of sea area where the right of innocent passage applied, eastwards of Märket Reef the right of innocent passage ceased to exist as it became internal waters.

It is important to remember, however, that the Baltic region was a theatre of war throughout the nineteenth century and the First World War. The object and purpose of the 1921 Åland Convention was to ensure that a military

---

44   Secrétariat permanent Société des Nations, *Conference relative a la non-fortification et a la neutralisation des Iles d'Aland, tenue a Geneve, du 10 au 20 octobre 1921 : actes de la conference*, 30 (1921).

45   *Id.* at 30–31; Erich in Chapter 2 note 34 at 175; Söderhjelm in Chapter 2 note 2 at 247; S.R. Björksten, *Kansainvälinen oikeus* 108 (1937).

46   Act on the Delimitation of the Territorial Waters of Finland as amended by Act No 144/1965, Act No 332/1966 and Act No 981/1995:
      The internal waters shall mean that part of the territorial waters the landward limits of which consist of the mean water line along the coast and, at river mouths, of a straight line across the mouth between the limit points situated on the mean water line of the banks, and the seaward outer limits of which consist of straight baselines, the points of which are located on the outermost landmarks, either on the mainland or on islands, rocks or low-water elevations. (Section 3)
      The base points referred to in Section 3 above shall be selected from among points located above the mean water level at a certain epoch, designated on the basis of long-term water level measurements. Even points below the said level may be used as base points, provided that they are at least periodically within sight and a lighthouse or other installation permanently above the sea level has been built on them. (Section 4.)

47   The waters surrounding Bogskär are three nautical miles, which is an exception.

presence within the area would not become a threat to the Baltic coastal States. If only the land areas had been considered to be part of the demilitarised and neutralised area, the Åland Islands' surrounding sea area would have been part of Finnish territorial waters without any special status. Had this been the case, Finland would have had a similar right to naval operations within the archipelago as it would have enjoyed within other parts of its territorial sea and internal waters.[48] This would have particularly impacted Finland's jurisdiction over parts of its internal waters that presently belong to the Åland Islands' territorial waters. This kind of scenario was rejected by defining the sea area around the archipelago as a demilitarised and neutralised zone. This highlights the Åland Islands' independent status. Warfare methods and techniques today differ from the relevant security issues that existed when the 1921 Convention was being negotiated. Military technological developments might influence interpretations of the Convention's text with regard to exceptional circumstances, as well as the meaning of the term, 'temporarily'.

4.1   The Legal Status of Internal Waters

When discussing internal waters in international law, the delimitation of the outer limit has more relevance than the inner limit.[49]

In regard to its internal waters, a coastal State's sovereignty is not restricted by a general obligation to grant the right of innocent passage to foreign vessels. In this regard, a comparison can be drawn between access to a State's internal waters and access to its territory. There is no right of innocent passage through internal waters, although customary international law may establish limitations upon coastal State sovereignty. Restrictions to coastal State sovereignty particularly arise in connection to foreign vessels' rights to navigate internal waters and enter ports. Nevertheless, the breadth of territorial seas is measured from the outer limit of a State's internal waters. Therefore, the breadth of internal waters has an international aspect because it affects the range of territorial seas and other maritime zones.[50]

Treaty law includes provisions that regulate the practice of establishing internal waters. However, treaties do not influence norms practised within internal waters. For this reason, a treaty provision that retains transit rights in situations where the establishment of straight baselines enclose seas as

---

48   Spiliopoulou Åkermark, Heinikoski, and Kleemola-Juntunen in Chapter 1 note 2 at 58.

49   Kaare Bangert, *Belts and Sund*, in *Max Planck Encyclopedia of Public International Law* [MPEPIL] (2013), http://opil.ouplaw.com/view/10.1093/law:epil/9780199231690/law -9780199231690-e1145?rskey=FfoVsh&result=1&prd=EPIL.

50   Lagoni, *supra* note 2 at 155; Brown, *supra* note 5 at 38.

internal waters, even though such areas had previously not been considered internal waters such as Article 5(2) of the TSC and Articles 8(2) and 35(a) of the LOSC, is exceptional. These provisions are extraordinary when considering State sovereignty, since the legal status of internal waters is linked to territorial sovereignty. One might deduce that internal waters are not independent from treaty law because according to some cases an overlap between treaty and customary law exists.[51]

A comparison can be made between a State's jurisdiction over its internal waters and its land territory because a State has an exclusive right to establish a boundary line on land, whereas according to international law it must have a valid territorial claim over its waters. If the boundary line is established between two or more States then different kinds of options exist. For example, States have the opportunity to conclude an agreement, enact corresponding unilateral acts with neighbour States, or to adopt a single act that could come into effect through recognition or acquiescence. Furthermore, there is no general rule according to international law that concerns the delimitation of different kinds of internal waters, such as rivers. In particular regard to different kinds of internal waters, then, solution can only be provided vis-à-vis State practice because methods for the delimitation of internal waters are subject to modification by treaties. However, States may also choose to create bilateral agreements concerning the rights of passage through their internal waters.[52]

As the 1921 Åland Convention sets up limitations concerning navigation within the territorial waters of the Åland Island, it also sets up limitations concerning navigation within the Åland Strait. As a consequence, the Convention simultaneously establishes limitations within Finland's internal waters in the Strait. The Convention restricts Finland's right to grant access to foreign vessels within the Åland Islands' territorial waters and also limits the access of Finnish warships within these waters. With this understanding of the abovementioned limitations imposed by the 1921 Åland Convention in mind, it is clear that Finnish sovereignty is also limited in the Åland Strait by the international convention. Furthermore, the 1921 Åland Convention denies Finland's right to seek bilateral agreements, for example, which could allow the passage of foreign warships through internal waters situated within the demilitarised and neutralised zone.[53]

---

51   Lagoni, *supra* note 2 at 153, 155; Brown, *supra* note 5 at 38; Bangert, *supra* note 49.

52   Lagoni, *supra* note 2 at 154;

53   Spiliopoulou Åkermark, Heinikoski, and Kleemola-Juntunen in Chapter 1 note 2 at 59.

4.2   Passage Rights and the Use of Straight Baselines

The 1951 *Anglo-Norwegian Fisheries* case showed how the ICJ had concluded that a coastal State may be allowed to use straight base lines when connecting their outermost parts, including islands, to their coastline. Moreover, the ICJ noted the importance of relationships between land and sea, further emphasising that certain sea areas are 'sufficiently closely linked to the land domain to be subject to the regime of internal waters'. Besides special geographical conditions, such as those pertaining to Norway's skjærgaard, the ICJ also considered economic interests to be relevant. According to the ICJ, 'certain economic interests [are] peculiar to a region, the reality and importance of which are clearly evidenced by a long usage'. During the *Anglo-Norwegian Fisheries* case a number of geographical, historical, and economic interests were perceived to be worthy of consideration. The judgement made at the time does not elaborate on a few issues, such as whether there was some sort of hierarchy in regard to different interests, or on what grounds the comparison of interests is made, or whether it is adequate if only one of the criteria is fulfilled.[54]

The *Anglo-Norwegian Fisheries* case had an influence on law of the sea convention provisions. The ILC could not ignore the ICJ's judgement. There was a need to reconcile the use of straight baselines with the right of innocent passage. In 1956 the ILC added a new paragraph to a draft version of Article 5, in which the right of innocent passage was retained in parts of internal waters that had previously been considered as a part of territorial sea or high seas. However, the provision was only applied to all areas of water where international traffic would have normally occurred, suggesting that there were intentions to preserve the right of international navigation within traditional routes.[55] The right of navigation would have been substantially restricted without the addition of paragraph 3. The preservation of transit rights was crucial to international trade, since longer voyages meant an increase in costs. Furthermore, States with larger naval forces would have had to plan their navigation routes all over again.

The First Law of the Sea Conference in 1958 adopted the use of straight baselines as an alternative method to normal baselines. However, a modified version of the draft article prepared by the ILC was adopted at the Conference. Previous requirements regarding the use of international traffic were excised

---

54   *Fisheries* case, I.C.J. Reports in Chapter 3 note 144 at 133; Hakapää, *supra* note 1 at 383–384; Bangert, *supra* note 49.

55   *Yearbook of the International Law Commission 1956 Volume II, Documents of the Eighth Session Including the Report of the Commission to the General Assembly* in Chapter 3 note 73 at 267–268.

from the text and Article 5, which referred solely to waters that were previously considered to be part of territorial sea or high seas, was adopted in their place. Provisions referring to straight baselines in both the TSC and the LOSC include similar elements but are not identical. First, Article 8 of the LOSC excludes archipelagic waters because they are regulated according to Part IV of the Convention, which gives them a distinct legal status. Secondly, the Article replaces territorial sea and high seas with a more ambiguous expression: 'areas which had not previously been considered as such'. When looking at the Convention more closely, one sees that there have been intentions to cover territorial sea, high seas, contiguous zones, and newly established exclusive economic zones.[56]

Thirdly, paragraph 2 refers to instances where straight baselines can be used by stating that, 'in accordance with the method set forth in article 7', all baselines established under the circumstances and conditions set out in Article 7 fall within the scope of the LOSC. It is worth mentioning that States had used the straight baseline method prior to the 1958 Law of the Sea Conference. For instance, Finland had already been applying the straight baseline method before the 1958 TSC. By applying this method, coastal States stood to gain larger internal waters than by using a normal baseline, which is the main rule. As a result, most States have tended to use the method considered most advantageous to them despite requirements established by conventions. In the absence of any restrictions on passage rights through internal waters, one consequence of the tendency of coastal States to expand their internal waters would appear to be to restrict the freedom of maritime communication on the part of other States. The right of innocent passage through internal waters also covers straits used for international navigation and those areas that are enclosed as internal waters by established straight baselines.[57] According to Article 45(2) there should be no suspension of innocent passage through straits used for international navigation. This provision also covers those parts of a strait belonging to the internal waters of coastal States. From this it follows that a coastal State has limited jurisdiction over straits that are also a part of their internal waters. This limits coastal State sovereignty in areas where the legal regime is linked to the land domain.

Nevertheless, States bordering straits have the right to prohibit non-innocent passage. Article 35(a) on the application of the straight baseline method in cases of transit passage rights, however, goes further. When the establishment

56   Nordquist in Chapter 3 note 94 at 106–107.
57   Hakapää in Chapter 3 note 162 at 103; Lagoni, *supra* note 2 at 154; Nordquist in Chapter 3 note 94 at 107–108; Hakapää, *supra* note 1 at 383–384.

of strait baselines has an effect of enclosing as internal waters areas that were never previously considered as such, transit passage rights are preserved. The transit passage regime follows provisions belonging to the regime of innocent passage as regards the effects of establishing straight baselines. Ships and air-craft both enjoy transit passage rights, which cannot be compromised. Such provisions explicitly mention that coastal States cannot interfere with oth-ers' passage rights by simply expanding their internal waters. States bordering straits where transit passage rights exist have more restrictions to their juris-diction than when compared to rights of innocent passage in straits. A coastal State's limited jurisdiction is extended to include its internal waters, which is an area that would have otherwise remained outside of the Convention. In both cases the establishment of straight baselines does not change the legal status of a strait being used for international navigation.

The right of innocent passage varies depending on what kind of method to demarcate its borders a coastal State chooses to use. If a State applies a low-water line method, then no right of innocent passage exists through its inter-nal waters. On the other hand, if a state uses a straight baseline method and fulfils requirements concerning the right of innocent passage, then a question remains as to whether parts of the States' internal waters are individually af-fected by the right of innocent passage. Has a coastal State the right to deter-mine the areas of territorial waters through which foreign vessels have a right of innocent passage? Or may it only determine the routes that foreign vessels must navigate in the case of innocent passage as well?

Writers have had different opinions regarding Article 8(2) of the LOSC and its application. For example, Peters suggests that a coastal State is bound to respect foreign States' right of innocent passage within its internal waters. However, he goes on to say that this only applies if the waters in question have become a part of the coastal States' internal waters after the LOSC had en-tered into force.[58] It is noteworthy that some kind of limitations on the use of straight baselines had already been mentioned in the 1958 TSC. However, trea-ty provisions went further than customary international law because although the ICJ had considered the right to use straight baselines as a rule of customary international law, it did not contain an obligation to retain innocent passage through those waters.[59]

In the event that a State would have established straight baselines and pre-viously defined the breadth of its territorial sea by applying a low-water line

---

58   Christian H. Peters, *Innere Gewässer im Neuen Seerecht: Aspekte der fortschreitenden Ent-wicklung im Staats-, Europa – und Völkerrecht* 87 (1999).
59   *Fisheries* case, I.C.J. Reports in Chapter 3 note 144 at 116.

the internal waters of a State would have been divided into two parts. The first section would be the sea area located between straight baselines and low-water lines, along the coast, or the closing lines across river mouths and bays or ports. This would be drawn according to rules established by Articles 9, 10, and 11 of the LOSC and would then be regarded as the internal waters of the State in question, in which the right of innocent passage or transit passage would be retained if other criteria were to be fulfilled. The second section of sea area is located between the low-water line and the land territory. Within this sea area no rights of navigation are applied because their legal status has not changed.[60]

Due to different criteria to those mentioned in Article 7 of the LOSC, coastal States have also claimed that the provisions relating to the straight baselines method are not applied to them. Moreover, the phrase 'had not previously been considered as such' is problematic because, due to the lack of public knowledge, it may be difficult for foreigners to make sure that navigable sea areas had never previously been a part of a State's internal waters.[61]

By including Article 35(a), the LOSC in fact excludes internal waters from the general regime of straits. Provisions pertaining to the regime of transit passage would be only applied in sea areas that were previously considered a part of the high seas or territorial seas but had since been enclosed by straight baselines. As regards the preservation of passage rights, transit passage and innocent passage are interpreted in the same way. The eastern side of the Åland Strait became a part of Finland's internal waters in 1956 when Finland established straight baselines. Straight baselines were established according to customary international rules and practice, which had previously been applied by the ICJ during the *Anglo-Norwegian Fisheries* case[62] in 1951. However, the Court did not mention the continuation of the right of innocent passage when the establishment of straight baselines has the effect of enclosing as internal waters areas which had not previously been considered as such. Before the 1958 TSC, the position of the ICJ was unclear on matters relating to innocent passage. Whereas after the 1958 TSC and the LOSC, it became clear that the right of innocent passage would not be affected if a sea area were to become a part of a coastal States' internal waters. Before the 1958 TSC, for example, most States believed that rules of customary international law were vague. Moreover, at this point in time the retroactive effect would not favour coastal States that employed straight baselines because the right of innocent passage does not

60   Yang, *supra* note 5 at 73.
61   Peters, *supra* note 58 at 87; Yang, *supra* note 5 at 73.
62   See *Fisheries* case, Judgment of 18th December 1951, I.C.J. Reports in Chapter 3 note 144.

continue to exist. In conclusion, the right of innocent passage does not seem to exist in the eastern part of the Åland Strait because this part of the Strait has belonged Finland's internal waters from the mid-1950s. This kind of interpretation would also apply to the right of transit passage.

5   The Åland Strait and Article 35(c)

Article 35(c) of the LOSC was the result of a compromise. The article says that '[n]othing in this Part affects [...] the legal regime in straits in which passage is regulated in whole or in part by long-standing international conventions in force specifically relating to such straits'.

Article 35(c) requires that passage in the strait is governed by the long-standing conventions. In terms of passage rights the 'long-standing conventions' relevant to Finland were the 1856 Convention on the Demilitarisation of the Åland Islands, the 1921 Geneva Convention relating to the Non-fortification and Neutralisation of the Åland Islands, and the 1940 Treaty between Finland and Soviet Union regarding the Åland Islands. The Åland Strait extends in the east towards Finland and west towards Sweden, and its borderline is drawn through Märket Reef. With respect to the Åland Strait, the main question has typically related to geography because the treaty arrangements relating to the demilitarisation and neutralisation only cover the Finnish part of the Strait and the treaties established a three nautical mile territorial sea around the Åland Islands.[63] These treaty arrangements have internationalised and made neutral the Finnish part of the Åland Strait. Due to the Strait's international status and provisions of the 1921 Åland Convention, certain limitations on the entry of Finnish as well as foreign warships into the zone have been set and overflight of foreign military aircraft has been prohibited. In addition, the 1921 Åland Convention grants the right of innocent passage for foreign warships. Furthermore, when taking into consideration the fact that these limitations focus partly on Finland as a coastal State there seems to be no doubt that treaty arrangements of the Åland Islands regulate passage through the Åland Strait in the meaning of Article 35 (c).[64]

As mentioned above only the Finnish part of the Strait is covered by the abovementioned conventions. Article 35 (c) refers to a strait 'regulated in whole or in part' but it does not elaborate further the meaning 'in part' in the

---

63   Roach and Smith in Chapter 3 note 164 at 282.
64   Söderhjelm in Chapter 2 note 2 at 251; Manner in Chapter 2 note 88 at 128–129; Kleemola-Juntunen in Chapter 1 note 2 at 42.

text. In other words, the Article does not set any requirements for a part of a Strait that is covered by long-standing conventions. During the Conference Finland and Sweden firmly held the view the Åland Strait falls under Article 35(c) as it is adequate that long-standing international convention covers the Finnish part of the Strait.[65] Finland and Sweden voiced their opinion in Declarations made on the signature and ratification of the LOSC.[66] The main sea route through the Strait passes through the territorial sea of Sweden. However, nothing prevents Finland to establish a route through the Finnish part of the Strait. In this kind of situation passage should be undertaken according to the provisions of 1921 Åland Convention in place of the right of transit passage.

The rationale behind the concept of transit passage was to retain freedom of passage and overflight in straits where high sea routes would disappear because of the introduction of 12-nautical-mile territorial seas. Thus, it was clear from the origin of the concept of transit passage that this new regime was going to change the legal regime of international straits, as it would enable foreign submarines to navigate submerged through the straits and allow overflight foreign aircraft. The presence of a great number of naval vessels until the beginning of the 1990s of both NATO and the Warsaw Pact engaging in a number of intensive naval activities within the Baltic Sea would have certainly had an influence on the political and military status quo.[67] It is obvious that if the concept of transit passage had been applied to passage through the Åland Strait, Finland and Sweden would have been even more restricted in their efforts to follow and control foreign military activities in the Åland Strait and Gulf of Bothnia.[68]

---

65   Rotkirch in Chapter 1 note 2 at 372; Manner in Chapter 2 note 88 at 126–127.

66   'It is the understanding of the government of the Kingdom of Sweden that the exception from the transit passage regime in straits, provided for in article 35(c) of the Convention is applicable to the strait between Sweden and Denmark (Öresund), as well as to the strait between Sweden and Finland (the Åland Islands). Since in both those straits the passage is regulated in whole or in part by long-standing international conventions in force, the present legal regime in the two straits will remain unchanged'. There is similar declaration made by Denmark in 2004: '[t]he Kingdom of Denmark makes the following declaration: It is the position of the Government of the Kingdom of Denmark that the exception from the transit passage regime provided for in article 35 (c) of the Convention applies to the specific regime in the Danish straits (the Great Belt, the Little Belt and the Danish part of the Sound), which has developed on the basis of the Copenhagen Treaty of 1857. The present legal regime of the Danish straits will therefore remain unchanged'. http://treaties. un.org/pages/ViewDetailsIII.aspx?&src=UNTSONLINE&mtdsg_no=XXI~6&chapter=21& Temp=mtdsg3&lang=en#EndDec [last access 24.3.2018].

67   Johnson Theutenberg in Chapter 2 note 89 at 198.

68   Both Finland and Sweden have EEZs in the Gulf of Bothnia. Finland established its EEZ in 2005. The Act on the Exclusive Economic Zone of Finland Act on the Exclusive Economic

At the time of the negotiations of the Third Law of the Sea Conference both Finland and Sweden required prior notification from foreign warships. This requirement, however, did not prevent several unlawful intrusions that reached also the Gulf of Bothnia. Today, incidents by submarines spying in Swedish and Finnish waters continue most recent are reported from the years 2014 and 2015.[69] Furthermore, as it was accepted in the Conference that this new regime of transit passage would also cover straits where the right of innocent passage had previously applied, Finland and Sweden had valid grounds during the negotiations to bring out their security concerns relating to this new regime and their requirements to retain the right of innocent passage in the Åland Strait, which is its narrowest point is no more than six nautical miles wide.[70] Otherwise all vessels and aircraft would have enjoyed passage through the Åland Strait in a large portion of the sea that would have extended to the most northern part of the Gulf of Bothnia. Submarines would have been allowed to navigate submerged through the strait, military aircraft would have had a right of overflight, and aircraft carriers could have exercised their activities unrestrictedly.

However, different interpretations have not been avoidable as Article 35(c) does not mention those strait that are governed by long-standing international conventions. Although the Finnish archive documents relating to the negotiations in the conference clearly show that the Åland Strait belongs to the category of straits 'in which passage is regulated in whole or in part by long-standing international conventions in force', in some publications this interpretation has been argued.

In addition to the US Department of State, it has also been stated by some writers that the Åland Strait does not belong to any category that exists outside of the regime of transit passage. Roach and Smith as well as Heintschel von

Zone of Finland Statutes of Finland, 25th November 2004, Statutes of Finland 1058/2004, entered into force on 1st February 2005, amended on 22nd December 2009, Statutes of Finland 1385/2009, 29th December 2009, Statutes of Finland 1682/2009, 11th March 2011, Statutes of Finland 236/2011, 25th March 2011, Statutes of Finland 275/2011, 27th May 2011, Statutes of Finland 591/2011, 10th June 2011, Statutes of Finland 629/2011, 22nd July 2011, Statutes of Finland 854/2011 and Decree on the Exclusive Economic Zone of Finland, 2nd December 2004, entered into force on 1st February 2005, Statutes of Finland 1073/2004.

69   Manner in Chapter 2 note 88 at 124–125; Johnson Theutenberg in Chapter 2 note 89 at 381–384; Gordon H. McCormick, *Stranger than Fiction. Soviet Submarine Operations in Swedish Waters* 11 (1990); James Kraska, *Putting Your Head in the Tiger's Mouth: Submarine Espionage in Territorial Waters*, 54 Columbia J. Transnatl. Law 164–247, 166–169, 193–195, 198–199 (2015). For more on the numerous unlawful intrusions and so called 'submarine incidents' see Johnson Theutenberg, McCormick and Kraska.

70   Johnson Theutenberg in Chapter 2 note 89 at 198.

Heinegg share the same view, according to which the special regime of sea area surrounding the Åland Islands is not applicable to all of the waters comprising the Åland Strait. They conclude that the territorial sea of the Åland Islands extends out to three nautical miles from the low-water mark and therefore does not extend beyond the outer limits of the straight-line segments established by the 1921 Åland Convention. For this reason the Convention does not have effect in the remaining sea area that forms the international strait.[71] Caminos and Cogliati-Bantz also come to conclusion that the 1921 Åland Convention does not have spatial effects in the Strait. Rauch's argument rests in Article 5 of the 1921 Åland Convention that does not restrict the right of innocent passage of warships through the demilitarised and neutralised zone, which means that such passage remains subject to existing international rules and usages and thereby there is no special regime of passage.[72]

The negotiation history based on the Finnish documents in the archives of the Finnish Ministry for Foreign Affairs does not seem to support the above-mentioned views. It is also noteworthy that Moore in his writing refers several times to the negotiations in the Conference, but he only mentions the Turkish Straits, Strait of Magellan and Danish Straits as those straits falling within Article 35(c), not the Åland Strait, although the Åland Strait was in the focus in the same negotiations as the Danish Straits.[73] It seems that they interpret the expression 'whole or in part' to mean classification of ships to warships or merchant ships in the treaties. However, during the negotiations in the Conference no State opposed the Finnish and Swedish interpretations that it was also a strait, which is geographically partly covered by the convention under Article 35(c).[74] Some writers conclude that only the treaty regulating the Turkish Strait is clearly covered by Article 35(c). It is noteworthy that Turkey is not party to the LOSC and neither is the United States. Neither Finnish nor Swedish declarations within the signature and ratification of the LOSC have been opposed by the other parties to the Convention. The LOSC is a 'package deal', and the adoption of the convention by States has been depended on this deal, and Article 35(c) is a part of this deal. The preservation of the legal regime in

---

71   US Department of State in Chapter 3 note 165 at 66–67: 'The United States, which is not a party to this Convention, has never recognized this international strait as falling within the Article 35(c) exception'. Heintschel von Heinegg in Chapter 3 note 164 at 279; Roach and Smith in Chapter 3 note 164 at 284; Kleemola-Juntunen in Chapter 1 note 2 at 41–42.

72   Rauch in Chapter 3 note 164 at 52; Caminos and Cogliati-Bantz in Chapter 4 note 4 at 106; Kleemola-Juntunen in Chapter 1 note 2 at 41–42.

73   Moore in Chapter 4 note 32. Finnish Ministry for Foreign Affairs Archives, Documents relating to the Third Law of the Sea Conference.

74   Caminos in Chapter 3 note 8 at 192–195.

the Åland Strait is one part of this 'package deal'. Should there be some kind of joint interpretation about the Article 35(c) as is from the Article 19 regulating the right of innocent passage between the United States and the former Soviet Union?

In terms of navigational rights, it seems that the 1921 Åland Convention has effects outside the geographical scope of the Convention, but in fact it is the core issue of the 1921 Åland Convention. The object and purpose of the Convention is to secure that the area of the Åland Islands shall never become a threat to Baltic Sea States, especially to Sweden, which is an immediate neighbour of this regime. From the Swedish national security point of view, it was vital that the Åland Islands regime extends to the Swedish side of the Åland Strait as such a historical regime as is referred to in Article 35(c) and the right of the innocent passage is retained in the Åland Strait.[75]

The 1921 Åland Convention does not particularly only relate to the Åland Strait but it refers to passage by stipulating that the right of innocent passage through Åland's territorial waters is not restricted and restricting access of Finnish warships to the zone. Furthermore, the Convention prohibits overflight of foreign military aircraft over the zone. The right of innocent passage is specifically mentioned in Article 5, whereby the phrasing of the Article refers to the prohibition of warships entering and remaining in the zone, which is not restricted by freedom of innocent passage. The 1921 Åland Convention keeps the balance in the area, regulating among others passage in the surrounding sea areas of the Åland Islands and thereby also partly in the Åland Strait. It has to be borne in mind that the legal status of the Åland Islands was created with the best interests of European States in mind and therefore the provisions of the Convention were part of 'European law' and have attained a regional customary law status.[76] Thereby although only part of the Åland Strait by virtue of the treaties demilitarising and neutralising the Åland Islands with surrounding sea area is under the special regime, the influence of the regime created by the Convention extends to the Swedish side of the strait, because phrasing of Article 35(c) excludes the transit passage regime from the whole strait, when the strait meets the requirements set by the provision. The aim and purpose of Article 35(c) was to avoid any attempt to change the existing situation in these special straits regulated by the long-standing international conventions, which

---

75   Marie Jacobsson, *Sweden and the Law of the Sea*, in *The Law of the Sea The European Union and Its Member States* 495–520, 502 (Tullio Treves & Laura Pineschi eds., 1997). Finland and Sweden required foreign warships to give prior notification to innocent passage through their territorial seas until mid-1990s.

76   Manner in Chapter 2 note 88 at 1927–128; Hannikainen in Chapter 2 note 88 at 619–620.

in the case of the Åland Strait means that non-suspendable innocent passage continues to apply to passage of foreign vessels.

Currently the main sea route through the Åland Strait is located within the territorial waters of Sweden. Therefore, passage is regulated by Swedish legislation that does not contain similar separate provisions for passage through the Åland Strait as it does relating to the passage through the Sound. Thus, all foreign vessels have a right of innocent passage through the Åland Strait covered by the Swedish territorial sea.[77] However, east of Märket Reef the Strait belongs to the demilitarised and neutralised area and also belongs to Finland's internal waters where passage of foreign vessels has needed the consent from Finland since 1950's. Today the contemporary dilemma is that what has changed and why after the Conference where the naval powers on the one hand and delegations of Finland and Sweden on the other reached a consensus about the content of Article 35(c). It is also noteworthy that the other parties to the LOSC have not challenged Finnish and Swedish interpretations of the scope of Article 35(c) expressed in their declarations.

---

77   Foreign state ships have a right of passage through the Swedish territorial sea. Passage may not be prejudicial to the peace, good order or security of Sweden and must be continuous and expeditious. Tillträdesförordning, Svensk författningssamling 1992: 118. In the Sound, the passage regime is more liberal than innocent passage but more strict than the transit passage. See Ove Bring, *Nordic Rules of Neutrality, Commentary*, in *The Law of Naval Warfare: A Collection of Agreements and Documents with Commentaries* 839–843, 841 (Natalino Ronzitti ed., 1988).

CHAPTER 6

Some Observations on the Times of War

1   General Remarks

Both the 1958 TSC and the LOSC grant passage rights through international straits, the right of non-suspendable innocent passage or transit passage. However, neither of these conventions clearly refer to times of war.[1] For example the preamble of the LOSC says that matters not regulated by the LOSC continue to be governed by the rules and principles of international law. There are treaties relating to naval operations and armed conflicts at sea such as 1856 Paris Declaration,[2] 1907 Hague Conventions,[3] and the 1936 Submarine Protocol.[4] However, today the rules governing naval warfare mainly consist of customary international law.[5] In addition, there are San Remo Manual on International Law Applicable to Armed Conflicts at Sea prepared by International Institute of International Humanitarian Law and Helsinki Principles on the Law of Maritime Neutrality prepared by International Law Association, which declare the current law of naval warfare and maritime neutrality.[6] Further, although there are important straits that are governed by long-standing international conventions, these conventions do not deal in detail with the law of war.[7] The 1857 treaty arrangements applicable to the Danish Straits[8] do not contain specific

---

1   Natalino Ronzitti, *The Law of Naval Warfare: A Collection of Agreements and Documents with Commentaries* 14–15 (1988).
2   Declaration Respecting Maritime Law. Paris, adopted 16 April 1856, available at https://ihl -databases.icrc.org/applic/ihl/ihl.nsf/Treaty.xsp?action=openDocument&documentId=1020 7465E7477D90C12563CD002D65A3 [last access 24.3.2018].
3   Second Peace Conference at The Hague, adopted 18 October 1907 entered into force 26 January 1910. The 1907 Hague Conventions are available at https://ihl-databases.icrc.org/ihl/ INTRO/240?OpenDocument [last access 24.3.2018].
4   Procés-verbal concernant les règles de la guerre sous-marine prévues par la partie IV du traité de Londres du 22 Avril 1930. Signé a Londres le 6 Novembre 1936, 173 LNTS 353.
5   Caminos and Cogliati-Bantz in Chapter 4 note 4 at 12–13, 19–20; J. Ashley Roach, *The Law of Naval Warfare at the Turn of Two Centuries*, 94 Am. J. Int. Law 64–77, 64–65 (2000).
6   Wolff Heintschel von Heinegg, *War Zones,* in *Max Planck Encyclopedia of Public International Law* [MPEPIL] (2015), http://opil.ouplaw.com/view/10.1093/law:epil/9780199231690/law -9780199231690-e436?rskey=mVFwWq&result=2&prd=EPIL [last access 24.3.2018].
7   Caminos and Cogliati-Bantz in Chapter 4 note 4 at 15.
8   Treaty between Great Britain, Austria, Belgium, France, Hanover, Mecklenburg-Schwerin, the Netherlands, Oldenburg, Prussia, Russia and Sweden, and Norway and the Hansa Towns,

provisions regarding war. The 1938 Montreux Convention[9] contains provisions dealing with passage rights of foreign vessels during in time of war but no provision dealing with restrictions of Turkish warships. When Turkey is a belligerent State, passage of foreign warships is left to the discretion of the Turkish government, consequently, instead of special treaty regime, the same rules apply as in international straits.[10]

As far as special regime of other straits governed by 'longstanding international conventions' the Strait of Magellan is neutralised for ever by the treaty between Argentina and Chile, which grants free passage to the flags of all nations.[11] The 1921 Åland Convention grants neutrality to the Finnish part of the Åland Strait, prohibiting military, naval or air forces from entering or remaining within the zone[12] but does 'not prejudice the freedom of innocent passage though the territorial waters'.[13] However, neutrality does not prevent a State from exercising its sovereignty and carrying out defensive military action if there is a need to protect its territory from an invasion. It is obvious that the point of demilitarisation and neutralisation is to make it clear that a particular territory is completely outside of armed conflict. Were a foreign State to invade or otherwise threaten to undermine the status of another sovereign territory, the State under attack would be allowed to defend its territory by armed means, even within the neutral zone.[14]

It would surely be an odd security paradox if a State exercising sovereignty over its demilitarised and neutralised territory were to be denied the right to use military force within the zone in order to protect it. For instance, Russia had fortified the Åland Islands during the First World War but expressly stated

---

on the One Part, and Denmark on the Other Part, for the Redemption of the Sound Dues signed at Copenhagen, adopted 14 March 185 entered into force 1 April 1857, 116 Parry Consolidated Treaty Series 357. Convention between United States of America and Denmark for the Discontinuance of the Sound Dues adopted 11 April 1857 entered into force 12 January 1858, 116 Parry Consolidated Treaty Series 465.

9   Convention Regarding the Regime of the Straits, Montreux, adopted 20 July 1936 entered into force 9 November 1936, 173 LNTS 213.

10   Heintschel von Heinegg in Chapter 3 note 164 at 264; Caminos and Cogliati-Bantz in Chapter 4 note 4 at 16. The Montreux Convention art. 20.

11   Treaty between Argentine Republic and Chile, Establishing the Neutrality of Straits of Magellan, 3 Am. J. Int. Law, Suppl. Off. Doc. 121–122 (1903), adopted 23 July 1881 Buenos Aires entered into force 22 October 1881.

12   Art. 4; The Convention also prohibits the manufacture, import, transport and re-export of arms and implements of war in this demilitarised and neutralised zone.

13   Art. 5.

14   Söderhjelm in Chapter 2 note 2 at 1–19, 215–239; Björkholm and Rosas, in Chapter 2 note 47 at 16–17; Christer Ahlström, *Demilitarised and Neutralised Territories in Europe* 21 (2004); Hannikainen in Chapter 2 note 88 at 616. See also Bring, *supra* note 109 at 26–32.

that there was a danger that Germany could threaten to occupy the Islands. During 1918 Sweden occupied the Åland Islands, and then Germany did so thereafter.[15] The next military occupation of the Islands took place when Finland decided to fortify the Åland Islands and lay mines in the Åland Strait during the Second World War, in order to guarantee the neutrality of its territory. The Soviet Union and Germany also had plans to occupy the Islands, yet there were no attempts ever made.

2   State Practice

The Hague Convention XIII and the San Remo Manuals as well as the decision of the Permanent Court of International Justice (PCIJ) in the *Wimbledon* case established that mere transit passage of belligerents in the strait does not prejudice the neutrality of the state bordering an international state.[16] The state practice seems to endorse this position. According to Brüel Denmark and Sweden–Norway left Danish straits open to both warships and merchant ships of the belligerents during the Crimean war as well as during the Franco–German war in 1871 and during the Russo–Japanese war in 1904–1905. The Danish and Swedish Royal decrees of 1912 illustrate their policy in case of war, being neutral, they leave the straits open to warships of belligerent states.[17]

The passage of foreign vessels through the Danish Straits was conditional on the use of so-called 'sound dues', which lasted for more than four hundred years. The Danish Straits connect the Baltic Sea to the North Sea. The three main straits are the Sound, the Little Belt and the Great Belts. Sound dues were originally enforced by King Erik Pomerania in the 1420s, which were first applied to the Sound and later to both of the Belts as well. The dues were criticised by other States but were nonetheless recognised as legitimate. International commerce and shipping increased during the 1820s and '30s, which gave rise to many protestations from States who felt that the dues were a great impediment to freedom of navigation. Nevertheless, protests against the Sound dues were mostly founded on common disdain for their mode of collection and rates of payment, rather than the actual lawfulness of the dues.[18] The matter of the lawfulness of the dues was brought up by the United States when it started

---

15   Rotkirch in Chapter 1 note 2 at 362; Hannikainen in Chapter 2 note 88 at 617–618.
16   Ronzitti, *supra* note 1 at 15–16.
17   Brüel in Chapter 3 note 8 at 111.
18   *Id.* at 103.

its world-wide campaign against trade barriers. As a result of this campaign the dues were abolished according to a treaty[19] drawn up on 14th March 1857.[20]

As warships did not pay Sound Dues, the 1857 Treaty did not go into detail about warship passage through straits. Therefore, passage of warships through the Danish straits was decided on by means of reference to existing general rules of international law.[21] A lack of clarity on the right of passage for warships gave Denmark an opportunity to incorporate a policy on prior authorisation for warships as they navigated through Danish territorial waters that were part of straits. During the 1910s, however, Denmark liberalised its regulations so that warships were able to navigate through straits without notification in times of peace.[22] In effect, Denmark left the straits open to all ships in times of war.[23] During the First Word War Sweden did not close the Swedish side of the Sound.[24]

Although Japan had opened some of its ports to foreign ships it still prohibited passage of foreign ships through Japanese straits. The Netherlands and other States ignored this prohibition in the case of the Shimonoseki Strait. Japan responded to their disobedience by closing the strait and also declaring that passage was prohibited by means of force. In 1864 England, France, the Netherlands, and the United States protested against Japan closing the strait in a Joint Note which claimed that Japan had violated international law.[25] Influential and powerful maritime powers stated in the Note that international law had been violated when Japan closed and refused to open the strait, which then urged other States to force Japan to open it again by engaging in a common

---

19   Treaty between Great Britain, Austria, Belgium, France, Hanover, Mecklenburg-Schwerin, the Netherlands, Oldenburg, Prussia, Russia and Sweden, and Norway and the Hansa Towns, on the One Part, and Denmark on the Other Part, for the Redemption of the Sound Dues signed at Copenhagen, adopted 14 March 185 entered into force 1 April 1857, 116 PCTS 357.

20   Further to the Treaty, the United States and Denmark signed a special straits convention in Washington in 1857, Convention between United States of America and Denmark for the Discontinuance of the Sound Dues, adopted 11 April 1857 entered into force 12 January 1858, 116 PCTS 465. Brüel in Chapter 3 note 8 at 103–104.

21   Gunnar Alexandersson, *The Baltic Straits* 75 (1982).

22   Brüel in Chapter 3 note 88 at 54–55.

23   *Id.* at 55–56. The Straits were left open during the Crimean War of 1854–1856, the Franco-German War of 1871, and the Russo-Japanese War of 1904–1905.

24   Brüel in Chapter 3 note 8 at 120; Ronzitti, *supra* note 1 at 17.

25   Brüel in Chapter 3 note 8 at 104–105; Nihan Ünlü, *The Legal Regime of the Turkish Straits* 24 (2002). Protest of States took shape in a memorandum, dated 27th July 1864, available at British and Foreign State Papers, Volume 62, p. 933 cited in Brüel in Chapter 3 note 8 at 105 (n 1); Ünlü, *supra* note 25 at 24 (n 91).

movement. In hindsight this event seems to suggest two things: first, that maritime powers did not properly recognise the exclusive jurisdiction of a coastal State; and second, that straits are of particular value to maritime States.[26] The outcome of this event might have also had an effect on the Tsugaru Strait, which was left open for neutral merchant vessels during the 1904–1905 Russo-Japanese war. By leaving the Tsugaru Strait open to neutral merchant vessels, Japan as a belligerent State can be considered a good example when looking at the limited extent of jurisdiction coastal States may have when attempting to prohibit shipping or passage through territorial waters that are also part of international straits.[27]

Maritime powers' interests were also voiced in 1881 during negotiations concerning the Strait of Magellan, which is located between Chile and Argentina. The Unites States made its position clear when claiming that it would not tolerate any exclusive claims from other States whenever the Strait of Magellan was concerned.[28] Brüel holds that the statement given by the United States is applicable to the passage of warships in times of peace, as well as neutral warships' passage during wartime.[29] During the First World War, Chile allowed passage of warships. However, Italy had a different position when it as a neutral State closed the Strait of Messina during the First World War.[30]

Turkey prohibited the passage of foreign ships through Turkish Straits for hundreds of years. Nonetheless, there were several exceptions to this main rule, which was based on bilateral treaties and gave foreign merchant vessels a right to navigate through the straits. Although the 1805 Treaty of Alliance closed off the Straits from foreign warships in peacetime, the Treaty also opened the straits to Russian warships.[31]

When reflecting on the rules of passage through the Turkish Straits, it is noteworthy that such rules had been determined on the basis of changing political contingencies. Indeed, as a result of the Turco–Egyptian war in 1841, the multilateral London Convention was signed by Austria, Great Britain, France, the Ottoman Empire, Prussia, and Russia, which aimed at prohibiting foreign

---

26   Brüel in Chapter 3 note 8 at 105.

27   Brüel in Chapter 3 note 8 at 109–110; Ünlü, *supra* note 25 at 24. Tsugaru Strait was open only in daytime and vessels were subject to Japanese pilotage.

28   Brüel in Chapter 3 note 8 at 105.

29   *Id.* at 106.

30   R.R. Baxter & Jan F. Triska, *The Law of International Waterways: With Particular Regard to Interoceanic Canals* 191,194 (1964); Ronzitti, *supra* note 1 at 16; Caminos and Cogliati-Bantz in Chapter 4 note 4 at 32.

31   A similar effect was noticeable a few decades later as a result of the Hünkar Iskelesi Treaty in 1833. Brüel in Chapter 3 note 88 at 276–278, 281; Ünlü, *supra* note 25 at 28–29.

warships from entering the Turkish Straits. This Treaty differed from the general tendency of States to allow merchant vessels and warships a right of passage through Straits but did seem to reflect the interests of great naval powers at the time.[32] However, the Treaty rule prohibiting the passage of warships was sustained in principle until the 1923 Lausanne Convention,[33] which was itself restored to some extent by the 1936 Montreux Convention establishes the present regime which is applicable to transit through the Turkish Straits during peace and wartime.[34]

State practice suggests that neutral merchant ships have a long history of enjoying a right of passage through international straits, regardless of whether peace or conflict was prevalent. On the contrary, when a coastal State whose territorial sea touched upon a strait was not itself belligerent, it had no right whatsoever to deny the passage of belligerent or neutral merchant vessels. More importantly, belligerent warships enjoyed a right of passage through these straits, although in comparison with merchant vessels their status during peacetime was somewhat less certain at the time. With respect to warships' rights of passage through straits during peacetime, however, State practice did not change and new rules of international law were not established. However, the tendency of legal developments regarding passage of warships through straits seemed to show increasing liberality before the First World War.[35]

3 Some Remarks on the Åland Strait during the Times of War

The 1921 Åland Convention regulates the demilitarised and neutralised sea area both in the time of peace and the time of war. Article 6 of the Convention covers the time of war and neutralises the zone. 'Neutralisation' refers to a total nonexistence of military activity within a neutral territory, even during times of armed conflict. The aim of neutralisation is to ensure that under no circumstances whatsoever does a specific area become a theatre of war.

---

32 Ünlü, *supra* note 25 at 29–30.

33 The Lausanne Convention contained liberal rules for the passage of merchant vessels and also gave warships freedom of passage through straits during wartime. Nevertheless, the Convention did impose some restrictions upon warships' freedom of navigation. The Lausanne Convention (Treaty of Peace with Turkey the Convention Respecting the Regime of the Straits and Other Instruments), available at http://wwi.lib.byu.edu/index .php/Treaty_of_Lausanne [last access 24.3.2018].

34 Convention Regarding the Regime of the Straits; Rozakis and Stagos in Chapter 3 note 3 at 81.

35 Ünlü, *supra* note 25 at 23–24.

Article 6(1) says that 'In time of war, the zone described in Article 2 shall be considered as a neutral zone and shall not, directly or indirectly, be used for any purpose connected with military operations'. Nonetheless, according to Article 6(2), Finland has the right to lay mines if the Baltic Sea temporarily if ever involved in a war as the second paragraph permits Finland 'temporarily to lay mines in its territorial waters, and for this purpose to take such measures of a maritime nature as are strictly necessary'. The right to lay mines is an exception to neutralisation and it also covers eastern side of the strait belonging to the demilitarised and neutralised zone.

The 1921 Åland Convention expressly refers to the time of war unlike the law of the sea conventions. The meaning of war has changed from the gunfire between surface warships, control of maritime commerce, and shore bombardment to a multilevel framework of complex concepts, methods, and military technology. This multilevel framework is regulated by the rules of international law. There are treaties relating to naval operations and armed conflicts at sea but there is no comprehensive treaty governing naval warfare. As mentioned above the Finnish side of the Åland Strait (east of the Märket Reef) is a neutralised area on the basis of the 1921 Åland Convention. The status of the western side of the Strait varies whether Sweden is a neutral or belligerent strait State.

The Naval warfare was regulated during the First World War by the treaties such as Convention for the Adaptation to Maritime Warfare of the Principles of the 1864 Geneva Convention that was adopted in 1899 in the First Hague Peace Conference and the results of the second Hague Peace Conference in 1907; seven treaties relating to naval operations, and customary laws of naval war. International rules regulating naval war were also on the agenda of the international learned societies and in 1913 the Institute of International Law adopted a manual, 'The Law of Naval War Governing the Relations between Belligerents'.[36]

During the First World War demilitarisation of the Åland Islands was regulated by the 1856 Convention, which does not clearly define the territory to which it applies. The 1856 Convention is also silent regarding defence arrangements permitted during times of war. During the First World War, Russia fortified the Åland Islands and used them as a base for military operations against Germany. However, as regards the sea area, it was possible to carry out military operations in the seas surrounding the Åland Islands without infringing on the principle of demilitarisation.[37] Although the demilitarisation of the Åland

---

36   Roach, *supra* note 5 at 65.
37   See Pirjo Kleemola-Juntunen, *The Right of Innocent Passage: The Challenge of the Proliferation Security Initiative and the Implications for the Territorial Waters of the Åland Islands*,

Islands was not respected as Russia fortified the Åland Islands, the Åland Strait was not blocked by the coastal states, Sweden and Russia. In September 1914, three German destroyers and a cruiser were in the southern part of the Gulf of Bothnia and in December a German mine carriers sailed through the Åland Sea and they laid mines in front of Pori and Rauma.[38]

During the Winter War, the situation was different as result of the settlement of the League of Nations in the dispute of the sovereignty of the Åland Islands between Finland as a new independent state and Sweden. First, the coastal states of the Åland Strait were Finland and Sweden and second, as a result of the settlement of the League of Nations, the Åland Islands and its surrounding sea area was demilitarised and neutralised by the multilateral treaty that contained an exception to the neutralisation. allowing to lay mines in the territorial waters of Åland Islands and for this purpose to take such measures of a maritime nature as are strictly necessary. As regards laying mines the necessity of the provision was actualised during the Winter War when both Finland as a belligerent State and Sweden as a neutral State laid mines in the Åland Strait. The Finnish coastal fleet mined sea routes within the Åland area; whilst in regards to the mining of the Åland Strait, this undertaking was carried out jointly by Finland and Sweden.[39] Finland informed the League of Nations and Contracting Parties to the Convention about its actions; all of whom approved of these measures discretely.[40]

Events during the Second World War show that Finland's concern about the suspension of passage was not without justification in the Geneva Conference in 1921. During the negotiations of the 1921 Åland Convention, Finland's concerns were responded to by the reference of the 1907 Hague Convention when Finland brought up its desire to have a right to suspend passage in the special circumstances.[41] It is obvious that Finland was concerned the time of war and navigation of belligerent ships. As mention earlier international straits are considered as highways between the seas and oceans, and therefore closure of a strait is a controversial issue. The 1907 Hague Conventions VIII[42] and XIII[43]

---

in *The Future of the Law of the Sea. Bridging Gaps Between National, Individual and Common Interests* 239–269, 244 (Gemma Andreone ed., 2017).

38   Johnson Theutenberg in Chapter 2 note 89 at 197–198.

39   Gardberg and Törnroos in Chapter 1 note 3 at 14–15; Komulainen in Chapter 2 note 1 at 191–192; Säämänen in Chapter 2 note 65 at 60–64.

40   See Chapter 2 note 56. See also Johnson Theutenberg in Chapter 2 note 89 at 198.

41   Société des Nations in Chapter 5 note 44 at 64.

42   Convention (VIII) relative to the Laying of Automatic Submarine Contact Mines.

43   Convention (XIII) concerning the Rights and Duties of Neutral Powers in Naval War.

speak about territorial waters but are silent about international straits. However, straits were on the agenda in the conference but they did not end up to the convention articles. During the conference it became obvious that the position of international straits is not comparable to the position of territorial seas. Although international straits were left out from the conventions the right to pass in straits was not contested by states.[44] Today, according to San Remo Manual the right of transit passage applicable in international straits in peacetime continues in times of armed conflict in the relations of belligerent and neutral States.[45] Nevertheless, in international straits where passage falls under Article 35(c) exception the pre-existing regulatory regime is preserved.[46] Thus, according to Finnish and Swedish declarations to the LOSC on the application of Article 35(c) in the Åland Strait, non-suspendable innocent passage applies in Swedish side of the Åland Strait when Sweden is a neutral strait State.

---

44   Caminos in Chapter 3 note 8 at 28–29; Caminos and Cogliati-Bantz in Chapter 4 note 4 at 14–15.

45   *San Remo Manual on International Law Applicable to Armed Conflicts at Sea, 12 June 1994,* paras 27–30 (1994).

46   Wolff Heintschel von Heinegg, *Warships,* in *Max Planck Encyclopedia of Public International Law* [MPEPIL] (2015), http://opil.ouplaw.com/view/10.1093/law:epil/9780199231690/law-9780199231690-e443?rskey=mVFwWq&result=3&prd=EPIL [last access 24.3.2018].

CHAPTER 7

Concluding Remarks

The Åland Strait's legal status appears to be totally dependent on Article 35(c). Yet, without including the phrase 'in whole or in part' within the Article, this sea area would have belonged to a category of straits that apply transit passage rights. If this were the case, the transit of foreign warships through the Åland Strait to the Gulf of Bothnia would have been more liberal. In addition, the application of transit passage rights could have introduced rights for the submerged passage of submarines up to the north point of the Gulf of Bothnia, since there is a narrow EEZ area in the northern Strait (Kvarken), as well as allowing aircrafts relatively free overflight. Therefore, had transit passage rights been applied, Finland and Sweden would have lost a great deal of their jurisdiction over the region, and thus would have posed a challenge to their national security policies. Due to their policies on navigation through the Åland Strait, Finland and Sweden have the possibility of controlling maritime activities within their respective EEZs. Transit passage rights would have sufficiently expanded the navigational rights of foreign ships within the Åland Strait. The rationale behind the concept of transit passage was to retain freedom of passage and overflight in straits despite the fact that routes through high seas would disappear because of the extension of territorial seas.

Regardless, it was accepted by States in the Third Law of the Sea Conference that this new regime would also cover straits which had already applied the right of innocent passage. This would have included the Danish Straits as well. During Third Law of the Sea Conference negotiations, Denmark, Finland and Sweden espoused that it was necessary to exclude straits like the Danish Straits and the Åland Strait from the scope of transit passage rights. It was clear from the start that negotiations were to assess the status of the Åland Strait. Hence, treaty arrangements for the Åland Islands extending partly to the Åland Strait fulfil requirements pertaining to Article 35(c) of the LOSC. Passage through the Åland Strait falls within the scope of innocent passage, which Finland and Sweden have officially declared when signing and ratifying the Convention and other parties to the LOSC have not questioned this position during or after the Conference.

Another matter related to the Åland Strait is the establishment of straight baselines. Finland had established its straight baselines before the law of the sea conventions came into force. These straight baselines enclosed the sea area

eastwards of Märket Reef as Finland's internal waters. At the time of their establishment, no rule of customary international law existed that would oblige
coastal States to allow innocent passage in these waters. Accordingly, any passage taking place on the eastern side of Märket Reef could not happen without
Finland's prior consent. Law of the sea conventions did not change this state
of affairs. Thus, because of the establishment of straight baselines in the sea
area, stricter restrictions are imposed upon Finnish and foreign warships. By
this measure the regime of demilitarisation and neutralisation has been made
more effective.

The 1921 Åland Convention is often seen in Finland as an obstacle to exercise sovereign rights. However, in the case of the Åland Strait, the legal status of
this narrow waterway would be different. Without this old convention, which
is still in force, the transit passage regime would be applicable in the Swedish
side of the strait and it would have considerable impact on passage in the large
portion of the Gulf of Bothnia.

Appendix 1

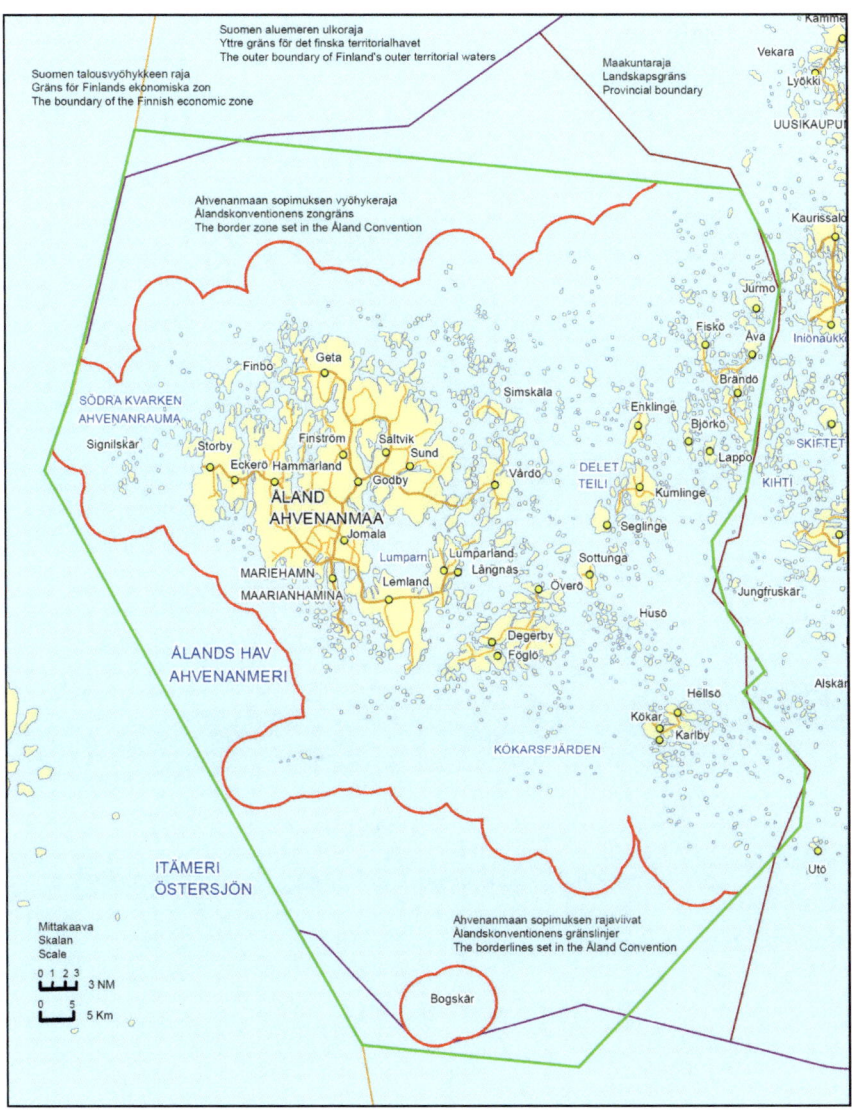

MAP 1   The boundaries of the demilitarised and neutralised zone of the Åland Islands
THE NATIONAL LAND SURVEY AND MINISTRY FOR FOREIGN AFFAIRS OF FINLAND
http://formin.finland.fi/public/default.aspx?nodeid=46371&contentlan=1&culture
=fi-FI (2013)

© KONINKLIJKE BRILL NV, LEIDEN, 2019 | DOI:10.1163/9789004364189_009

Appendix 2

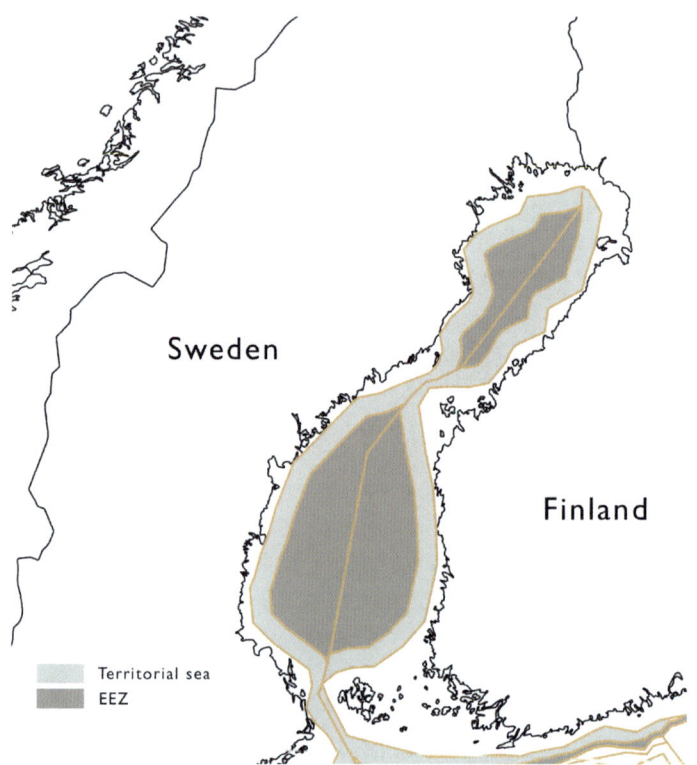

MAP 2   Territorial sea and EEZ boundaries between Finland and Sweden
SOURCE: FINNISH TRANSPORT AGENCY AND THE WEBPAGE OF THE
EUROPEAN ENVIRONMENT AGENCY (EEA),
https://www.eea.europa.eu/data-and-maps/data/maritime-boundaries

© KONINKLIJKE BRILL NV, LEIDEN, 2019 | DOI:10.1163/9789004364189_010

Bibliography

Ahlström, Christer. *Demilitarised and Neutralised Territories in Europe*. Mariehamn: Ålands fredsinstitut, 2004.

Ahlström, Christer. *Demilitarised and Neutralized Zones in a European Perspective, Perspective*, in *Autonomy and Demilitarisation in International Law: The Åland Islands in a Changing Europe*, edited by Lauri Hannikainen and Frank Horn, 41–56. Kluwer Law International, 1997.

Ahvenanmaankysymys: Kansainliiton neuvoston asettaman selostajakomissionin lausunto liitteineen. Ulkoasiainministeriön Julkaisemia Diplomaattisia Asiakirjoja. Helsinki: [Ulkoasiainministeriö], 1921.

Alexander, L.M. *Regional Arrangements in the Oceans*, 71 American Journal of International Law (1977) 84–109.

Alexandersson, Gunnar. *The Baltic Straits*. International Straits of the World; Vol. 6. The Hague: Nijhoff, 1982.

Amin, S.H. *The Regime of International Straits: Legal Implications for The Strait of Hormuz*, 12 Journal of Maritime Law and Commerce (1981) 387–405.

Astley III, John, and Michael N. Schmitt, *The Law of the Sea and Naval Operations*, 42 Air Force Law Review (1997) 119–56.

Bangert, Kaare. *Belts and Sund*, in *Max Planck Encyclopedia of Public International Law* [*MPEPIL*], 2013. http://opil.ouplaw.com/view/10.1093/law:epil/9780199231690/law-9780199231690-e1145?rskey=FfoVsh&result=1&prd=EPIL.

Barclay, Thomas, MM. L. Oppenheim, Theodor Niemeyer, Philip Marshall Brown, and Alejandro Alvarez. *Project de reglement á la mer territoriale en temps de paix Institute of International Law Session de Stockholm – 1928*, 1928. http://www.idi-iil.org/idiF/resolutionsF/1928_stock_03_fr.pdf.

Barros, James. *The Aland Islands Question: Its Settlement by the League of Nations*. New Haven and London: Yale University Press, 1968.

Baxter, R.R., and Jan F. Triska. *The Law of International Waterways: With Particular Regard to Interoceanic Canals*. Cambridge, Mass. : Harvard University Press, 1964.

Björkholm, Mikaela, and Allan Rosas. *Ålandsöarnas demilitarisering och neutralisering*. Åbo: Åbo Akademis förlag, 1990.

Björksten, S.R. *Kansainvälinen oikeus*. Porvoo, 1937.

Boeck, Maximilian. *Die Alandsfrage*. Wuertsburg, 1927.

Booth, Ken. *Law, Force and Diplomacy at Sea*. Routledge Revivals, 2014.

Boursot, Raymond. *La question des Iles d'Aland*. Dijon, 1923.

Bowett, D.W. *The Law of the Sea*. Manchester: Manchester University Press, 1967.

Bring, Ove. *Ålands demilitarisering – alive and kicking!, Åland – fredens öar? Seminarium 19 Oktober 2006, Ålands landskapsregering*. Mariehamn, 2007.

Bring, Ove. *Ålands självstyrelse under 80 År: Erfarenheter och utmaningar*. Mariehamn: Ålands landskapsstyrelse, 2002.

Bring, Ove. *Nedrustningens folkrätt*. Stockholm: Norstedt, 1987.

Bring, Ove. *Nordic Rules of Neutrality, Commentary*, in *The Law of Naval Warfare: A Collection of Agreements and Documents with Commentaries*, edited by Natalino Ronzitti, 839–843, 1988.

Broms, Bengt. *Kansainvälinen oikeus*. Helsinki, 1978.

Brown, E.D. *The International Law of the Sea, Volume I: Introductory Manual*. Aldershot: Dartmouth, 1994.

Brown, Philip Marshall. *The Aaland Islands Question*, 15 American Journal of International Law (1921) 268–272.

Brubaker, R. Douglas. *The Russian Arctic Straits*. Leiden: Martinus Nijhoff Publishers, 2005.

Brüel, Erik. *International Straits, Volume I*. London: Sweet and Maxwell, 1947.

Brüel, Erik. *International Straits, Volume II*. London: Sweet and Maxwell, 1947.

Buntoro, Kresno. *An Analysis of Legal Issues Relating to Navigational Rights and Freedoms through and over Indonesian Waters*, Australian National Centre for Ocean Resources and Security (ANCORS)- Faculty of Law, University of Wollongong, 2010. http://ro.uow.edu.au/theses/3091.

Burke, Karin M., and Deborah A. DeLeo. *Innocent Passage and Transit Passage in the United Nations Convention on the Law of the Sea*, 9 Yale Journal of International Law (1983) 389–408.

Burke, William T. *Submerged Passage through Straits: Interpretation of the Proposed Law of the Sea Treaty Text*, 52 Washington Law Review (1976) 193–225.

Bynkershoek, Cornelius van, Ralph van Deman Magoffin, and James Brown Scott. *De dominio maris dissertatio*. The Classics of International Law; No. 11. Buffalo: William S. Hein & Co, 1995.

Caminos, Hugo. *The Legal Régime of Straits inthe 1982 United Nations Convention on the Law of the Sea*, 205 Recueil Des Cours/ Hague Academy Collected Courses 1987 V (1989) 13–245.

Caminos, Hugo, and Vincent P. Cogliati-Bantz. *The Legal Regime of Straits: Contemporary Challenges and Solutions*, 2014.

Castrén, Erik. *Ahvenanmaan linnoittamattomuus ja neutralisointi*, Lakimies (1939), 255–273.

Castrén, Erik. *Suomen kansainvälinen oikeus*. Porvoo: WSOY, 1959.

Churchill, R.R., and A.V. Lowe. *The Law of the Sea*. Manchester: Manchester University Press, 1999.

Colombos, C. John. *The International Law of the Sea*. London: Longman, 1967.

Darman, R.G. *The Law of the Sea: Rethinking U. S. Interests*, 56 Foreign Affairs (1978) 373–95.

De Vries Lentsch, P. *The Right of Overflight over Strait States and Archipelagic States: Developments and Prospects*, 14 Netherlands Yearbook of International Law (1983) 165–225.

Decision of the Council of the League of Nations on the Åland Islands Including Sweden's Protest, Minutes of the Fourteenth Meeting of the Council, June 24th, League of Nations Official Journal September (1921) 697.

Deuxiéme Conférence Internationale de la Paix, La Haye 15 Jun–18 Octobre 1907, Actes et Documents, Volume I, 1907.

Deuxiéme Conférence Internationale de la Paix, La Haye 15 Jun–18 Octobre 1907, Actes et Documents, Volume III, 1907.

Ekman, Martin. *Det självstyrda och demilitariserade Ålands gränser – historiska, geovetenskapliga och rättsliga synpunkter*. Meddelanden från Ålands högskola, Nr 12. Mariehamn: Ålands högskola, 2000.

Ekman, Per-Olof. *Sjöfront: Sjökrigshändelser i Norra Östersjöområdet 1941–1944*. Helsingfors: Schildt, 1981.

Elferink, Alexander Gerard Oude. *The Law of Maritime Boundary Delimitation: A Case Study of the Russian Federation*. Publications on Ocean Development; Vol. 24. Dordrecht: Nijhoff, 1994.

Erich, Rafael. *Suomen valtio-oikeus I osa*. Helsinki: WSOY, 1924.

Fagerlund, Niklas. *Ålands folkrättsliga status och EG*. Meddelanden från Ålands Högskola, Nr 3. Mariehamn: Ålands högskola, 1993.

Finnish Ministry for Foreign Affairs Archives. *Documents on the Negotiations in the Third United Nations Conference on the Law of the Sea*.

Finnish Ministry of Justice. *En utredning om gränserna för Ålands demilitarisering*. 2006.

Franckx, Erik. *Finland-Sweden Delimitation Agreement*, 11 International Journal of Marine and Coastal Law (1996) 394–398.

Franckx, Erik. *Finland – Sweden, Report Number 10 – 3*, in *International Maritime Boundaries, Volume II*, edited by J.I. Charney and L.M. Alexander, 1945–1957. 1993.

Franckx, Erik. *Finland – Sweden, Report Number 10 – 13*, in *International Maritime Boundaries, Volume III*, edited by J.I. Charney and L.M. Alexander, 2539–55. 1998.

Franckx, *Erik. Finland and Sweden Complete Their Maritime Boundary in the Baltic Sea*, 27 Ocean Development & International Law (1996) 291–314.

Froman, F.D. *Uncharted Waters: Non-innocent Passage of Warships in the Territorial Sea*, 21 San Diego Law Review (1984) 625–689.

Galdorisi, George. *An Operational Perspective on the Law of the Sea*. 29 Ocean Development & International Law (1998) 73–84.

Gardberg, Anders, and Kate Törnroos. *Åland Islands: A Strategic Survey*. Finnish Defence Studies, 8. Helsinki: National Defence College, 1995.

George, Mary. *Transit Passage and Pollution Control in Straits under the 1982 Law of the Sea Convention*, 33 Ocean Development & International Law (2002) 189–205.

Gidel, G. *Le droit international public de la mer: le temps de paix. 3, La mer territoriale et la zone gontigue*. Paris, 1934.

Godey, P. *La mer cotiére*. 1896.

Gregory, Charles Noble. *The Neutralization of the Aaland Islands*, 17 American Journal of International Law (1923) 63–76.

Gross, Leo. *The Geneva Conference on the Law of the Sea and the Right of Innocent Passage through the Gulf of Aqaba*, 53 American Journal of International Law (1959) 564–594.

Grotius, H., Francis W. Kelsey, Arthur E.R. Boak, Henry A. Sanders, Jesse S. Reeves, and Herbert F. Wright. *De Jure Belli Ac Pacis 1625, English Translation*. Lonang Institute, 2005. http://www.lonang.com/exlibris/grotius/index.html.

Gustavsson, Kenneth. *Ålandsöarna – en säkerhetsrisk? Spelet om den demilitariserade zonen 1919–1939*. Mariehamn: PQR-kultur, 2012.

Hailbronner, Kay. *Freedom of the Air and the Convention on the Law of the Sea*, 77 American Journal of International Law (1983) 490–520.

Hakapää, Kari. *Marine Pollution in International Law: Material Obligations and Jurisdiction: With Special Reference to the Third United Nations Conference on the Law of the Sea*. Annales Academiae Scientiarum Fennicae, 28. Helsinki: Suomalainen tiedeakatemia, 1981.

Hakapää, Kari. *Uusi kansainvälinen merioikeus*. Lapin Korkeakoulun Oikeustieteiden Osaston Julkaisuja, 10. Helsinki: Lakimiesliiton kustannus, 1988.

Hakapää, Kari. *Uusi kansainvälinen oikeus*. Helsinki: Talentum, 2010.

Hamburger, R.C.S. *Twee Rechtsvragen aangaande Finland: de demilitarisatie der Alandgroep en de autonomie van Oost-Kareleie*. Utrecht: P. den Boer, 1925.

Hannikainen, Lauri. *Ahvenanmaan itsehallinnon ja ruotsinkielisyyden kansainoikeudelliset perusteet*. Turku: Åbo Akademin ihmisoikeusinstituutti, 1993.

Hannikainen, Lauri. *The Continued Validity of the Demilitarised and Neutralised Status of the Åland Islands*, 54 Zeitschrift für ausländisches öffentliches Recht und Völkerrecht (1994) 614–651.

Hargrove, J. *The Nicaragua Judgment and the Future of the Law of Force and Self-Defense*. 81 American Journal of International Law (1987) 135–143.

Hautefeuille, L.B. *Des droits et des devoirs des nations neutres en temps de guerre maritime*. Paris, 1868.

Heintschel von Heinegg, Wolff. *The Law of Naval Warfare and International Straits*, in *International Law Studies Volume 71, The Law of Armed Conflict: Into Next Millennium*, edited by M.N. Schmitt and L.C. Green, 263–292. 1998.

Heintschel von Heinegg, Wolff. *War Zones*, in *Max Planck Encyclopedia of Public International Law* [MPEPIL], 2015. http://opil.ouplaw.com/view/10.1093/law:epil/9780199231690/law-9780199231690-e436?rskey=mVFwWq&result=2&prd=EPIL.

Heintschel von Heinegg, Wolff. *Warships* in *Max Planck Encyclopedia of Public International Law* [*MPEPIL*], 2015. http://opil.ouplaw.com/view/10.1093/law:epil/9780199231690/law-9780199231690-e443?rskey=mVFwWq&result=3&prd=EPIL.

Helsinki Commission (HELCOM). *Annual Report on Shipping Accidents in the Baltic Sea in 2013.* 2014.

Hill, Charles E. *Le regime international des détroits maritimes*, 45 Recueil Des Cours/ Hague Academy Collected Courses 1933 III (1933).

Holland, T.E. *Studies in International Law*. Oxford: Clarendon Press, 1898. http://archive.org/stream/studiesininternoohollgoog#page/n290/mode/2up.

Holly, Susan K., William B. McAllister, and Edward C. Keefer, eds. *Foreign Relations of the United States, 1969–1976, Volume E–1, Documents on Global Issues, 1969–1972, Document 333*, 2005. http://history.state.gov/historicaldocuments/frus1969-76ve01/d333.

I.C.J. Reports. *Corfu Channel case (United Kingdom v. Albania)*, *4*, (1949).

I.C.J. Reports. *Fisheries case (United Kingdom v. Norway)*, *116*, (1951).

I.C.J. Reports. *International Status of South-West Africa, Advisory Opinion*, (1950).

I.C.J. Reports. *Military and Paramilitary Activities in and against Nicaragua (Nicaragua v. United States of America)*, *14*, (1986).

Institute of International Law (Institut de Droit International). *The 1894 Report of the Institute of International Law: Annuaire Abridgment, Volume III*.

Institute of International Law (Institut de Droit International). *Resolution II "Règles sur la définition et le régime de la mer territoriale", Session de Paris – 1894*, http://www.idi -iil.org.

International Law Association. *Final Report of the Committee on Coastal State Jurisdiction Relating to Marine Pollution, ILA Report*. 2000.

International Law Association. *Report of the Seventeenth Conference*, 1895.

International Law Association. *Report of the Thirty-Third Conference*, 1924.

International Law Association. *Report of the Twenty-Fourth Conference*, 1907.

International Law Association. *Report of the Twenty-Third Conference*, 1906.

International Maritime Organization. *IMO Document COLREG.2/Circ.60, 10 December 2008, New and Amended Existing Traffic Separation Schemes*.

Isaksson, Martin. *Kring Bomarsund*. Ekenäs, 1981.

Isaksson, Martin. *Ryska Positionen Alandskaja. En Översikt av Ålands Militärä Historia Åren 1906–1918*. Ekenäs, 1983.

Jacobsson, Marie. *Sweden and the Law of the Sea*, in *The Law of the Sea The European Union and Its Member States*, edited by Tullio Treves and Laura Pineschi, 495–520. 1997.

Jägerskiöld, Stig, and Kai Kaila. *Mannerheim rauhan vuosina 1920–1939*. Helsinki: Otava, 1973.

Jakobson, Max. *Paasikivi Tukholmassa: J. K. Paasikiven toiminta Suomen lähettiläänä Tukholmassa 1936–39*. Helsinki: Otava, 1978.

Jennings, R.Y. *General Course on Principles of International Law*, 121 Recueil Des Cours/ Hague Academy Collected Courses 1967 (1967) 323–606.

Johnson, Bo. *Kolliderande suverenität*, Tidskrift i Sjöväsendet, no. 5–6 (1973): 172–242.

Johnson Theutenberg, Bo. *Folkrätt och säkerhetspolitik*. Stockholm: Norstedts, 1986.

Kennedy, R.H. *A Brief Geographical and Hydro Graphical Study of Straits Which Constitute Routes for International Traffic, UN Doc. A/CONF.13/6 and Add.1 (1957)*, in *United Nations Conference on the Law of the Sea, Volume I: Preparatory Documents*, 113–164, 1958.

Kleemola-Juntunen, Pirjo. *Straits in the Baltic Sea: What Passage Rights Apply?*, in *Regulatory Gaps in Baltic Sea Governance*, edited by Henrik Ringbom, 21–44. Springer, 2018.

Kleemola-Juntunen, Pirjo. *The Right of Innocent Passage: The Challenge of the Proliferation Security Initiative and the Implications for the Territorial Waters of the Åland Islands*, in *The Future of the Law of the Sea. Bridging Gaps Between National, Individual and Common Interests*, edited by Gemma Andreone, 239–269. Springer, 2017.

Klein, Natalie. *Dispute Settlement in the UN Convention on the Law of the Sea*. Cambridge Studies in International and Comparative Law; 39. Cambridge, UK: Cambridge University Press, 2009.

Klein, Natalie. *Maritime Security and the Law of the Sea*. Oxford: Oxford University Press, 2011.

Koh, Kheng Lian. *Straits in International Navigation: Contemporary Issues*. London: Oceana, 1982.

Komulainen, Arvo. *Taistelu Ahvenanmaasta, Oolannin iäisyyskysymys*. Jyväskylä: Gummerus Kustannus Oy, 2005.

Kosonen, Arto. *Suomen aseviennin oikeudelliset rajoitukset 1*, 80 Lakimies (1982) 205–240.

Kraska, James. *Putting Your Head in the Tiger's Mouth: Submarine Espionage in Territorial Waters*, 54 Columbia Journal of Transnational Law (2015) 164–247.

Lagoni, Rainer. *Internal Waters*, in 11 *Encyclopedia of Public International Law* (1989) 153–155.

Lagoni, Rainer. *Straits Used for International Navigation: Environmental Protection and Maritime Safety in the Danish Straits*, in *The Proceedings of the Symposium on the Straits Used for International Navigation, 16–17 November 2002, Ataköy Marina, Istanbul – Turkey*, edited by Bayram Öztürk and Reşat Özkan, 159–173. 2002.

Lapidoth-Eschelbacher, Ruth. *International Straits of the World: The Red Sea and the Gulf of Aden*. International Straits of the World; 5. Hague: Martinus Nijhoff, 1982.

Lapidoth, Ruth. *Straits, International*, in *Max Planck Encyclopedia of Public International Law* [*MPEPIL*], 2006. http://opil.ouplaw.com.ezproxy.ulapland.fi/view/10.1093/law: epil/9780199231690/law-9780199231690-e1226?rskey=hv3GBT&result=4&prd=EPIL.

Larson, David. *Innocent, Transit, and Archipelagic Sea Lanes Passage*, 18 Ocean Development & International Law (1987) 411–444.

Lehto, Marja. *Itämeren turvallisuusjärjestelmä erityisesti oikeudellisen säännöstön kehityksen kannalta: Aseidenriisunnan neuvottelukunnalle valmistettu raportti.* [Aseidenriisunnan Neuvottelukunta]. Helsinki: Aseidenriisunnan neuvottelukunta (ARNEK), 1986.

Lehto, Marja. *Restrictions on Military Activities in the Baltic Sea – a Basis for a Regional Regime?*, 2 Finnish Yearbook of International Law (1991) 38–65.

Linderfalk, Ulf. *International Legal Hierarchy Revisited – The Status of Obligations Erga Omnes*, 80 Nordic Journal of International Law (2011) 1–23.

Lopez Martin, Ana G. *International Straits: Concept, Classification, and Rules of Passage*. Dordrecht; Springer, 2010.

Lowe, A.V. *The Commander's Handbook on the Naval Operations and the Contemporary Law of the Sea*, in *International Law Studies Volume 64, The Law of Naval Operations, U.S. Naval College*, edited by Horace B. Robertson Jr., 109–147, 1991.

Luntinen, Pertti. *The Imperial Russian Army and Navy in Finland 1808–1918*. Studia Historica, 56. Helsinki: Finnish Historical Society, 1997.

Maduro, Morris F. *Passage through International Straits: The Prospects Emerging from the Third United Nations Conference on the Law of the Sea*, 12 Journal of Maritime Law and Commerce (1980): 65–95.

Mahmoudi, Said. *Customary International Law and Transit Passage*, 20 Ocean Development & International Law 20 (1989): 157–174. DOI:10.1080/00908328909545887.

Mahmoudi, Said. *Transit Passage*, in *Max Planck Encyclopedia of Public International Law* [*MPEPIL*], 2008. http://opil.ouplaw.com.ezproxy.ulapland.fi/view/10.1093/law: epil/9780199231690/law-9780199231690-e1231?rskey=YeKq38&result=4&prd=EPIL.

Manner, E.J. *Some Observations on the Effects and Applications of the New Law of the Sea, with Special Reference to the Baltic*, in *Finnish Branch of the International Law Association*, 114–144. Vammala, 1987.

Manninen, Ohto. *Hanko – "ampumavalmis pistooli" 1940–1941*, Sotilasaikakauslehti, no. 1 (1993) 28–31.

Manninen, Ohto. *Kilpapurjehdus Ahvenanmaalle?*, Sotilasaikakauslehti, no. 3 (1992) 248–250.

Manninen, Ohto. *"Operaatio Tanne" Ahvenanmaan uhkana*, Sotilasaikakauslehti, no. 11 (1994) 61–65.

Mattila, Tapani. *Meri maamme turvana, Suomen meripuolustuksen vaiheita Ruotsin vallan aikana*. Jyväskylä, 1983.

McCormick, Gordon H. *Stranger than Fiction. Soviet Submarine Operations in Swedish Waters*. 1990.

McNair, Arnold Duncan. *The Law of Treaties*. New York: Oxford University Press, 1986.

McNees, R.B. *Freedom of Transit through International Straits*, 6 Journal of Maritime Law and Commerce (1974) 175–211.

Modeen, Tore. *De folksrättliga garantierna för bevarandet av Ålandsöarnas nationella karaktär*. Mariehamn, 1973.

Molenaar, Erik Jaap. *Coastal State Jurisdiction over Vessel-Source Pollution*. International Environmental Law and Policy Series; v. 51. The Hague: Kluwer Law International, 1998.

Moore, John Norton. *The Regime of Straits and the Third United Nations Conference on the Law of the Sea*, 74 American Journal of International Law (1980) 77–121.

Nandan, S.N. *An Introduction to the Regime of Passage Through Straits Used for International Navigation and Through Archipelagic Waters*, in *Freedom of Seas, Passage Rights and the 1982 Law of the Sea Convention*, edited by Myron H. Nordquist, T.B. Koh, and J.N. Moore, 57–75. 2009.

Nandan, S.N. *Legal Regime for Straits Used for International Navigation*, in *The Proceedings of the Symposium on the Straits Used for International Navigation, 16–17 November 2002, Ataköy Marina, Istanbul – Turkey*, edited by Bayram Öztürk and Reşat Özkan, 1–11. 2002.

Ngantcha, Francis. *The Right of Innocent Passage and the Evolution of the International Law of the Sea: The Current Regime of 'Free' Navigation in Coastal Waters of Third States*. London; Pinter Publishers, 1990.

Nordquist, Myron H. *United Nations Convention on the Law of the Sea 1982: A Commentary, Volume 1*. Dordrecht: Martinus Nijhoff, 1985.

Nordquist, Myron H. *United Nations Convention on the Law of the Sea 1982: A Commentary, Volume 2, Articles 1 to 85, Annexes I and II, Final Act, Annex II*. Dordrecht: Martinus Nijhoff Publishers, 1993.

Nordquist, Myron H. *United Nations Convention on the Law of the Sea 1982: A Commentary, Volume 4, Articles 192 to 278, Final Act, Annex VI*. Dordrecht; Martinus Nijhoff, 1991.

O'Connell, David P. *Innocent Passage of Warships, The Law of the Sea (4th Session, September 1976)*, 7 Thesaurus Acroasium (1977) 408–451.

O'Connell, David P. *International Law, Volume 1*. London: Stevens, 1970.

O'Connell, David P., and I.A. Shearer. *The International Law of the Sea, Volume 1*. Oxford, 1982.

Oikkonen, Anne. *Vuosaaren väylä aukeaa ja Ahvenanmeri saa reittijakojärjestelmän*, Meriväylä, no. 3 (2008) 12–13.

Oppenheim, L. *Oppenheim´s International Law, Volume 1*, edited by Robert Jennings and Arthur Watts. 9th ed. 1993.

Oxman, Bernard H. *The Third United Nation's Conference on the Law of the Sea: The 1977 New York Session*, 72 American Journal of International Law (1978) 57–83.

Paasikivi, J.K. *Toimintani Moskovassa ja Suomessa 1939–41: 2, Välirauhan aika*. Porvoo: WSOY, 1958.

Padelford, Norman J., and K .Gosta A. Andersson. *The Aaland Islands Question*, 33 The American Journal of International Law (1939) 465–487. DOI:10.2307/2190793.

Pakaslahti, Aaro. *Talvisodan poliittinen näytelmä: UM:n poliittisen osaston päällikön päiviä ja öitä*. Porvoo: WSOY, 1970.

Peltier, L.C., and G.E. Pearcy. *Military Geography*. D. Van Nostrand Company, 1966.

Pépin, E. *The Law of the Air and Draft Articles Concerning the Law of the Sea Adopted by the International Law Commission at Its Eight Session, UN Doc. A/CONF.13/4 (1958)*, in *United Nations Conference on the Law of the Sea, Volume 1: Preparatory Documents*, 64–74. 1958.

Permanent Court of International Justice. *S.S. Wimbledon (Britain et al. v. Germany)*, (1923).

Peters, Christian H. *Innere Gewässer im Neuen Seerecht: Aspekte der fortschreitenden Entwicklung im Staats-, Europa – und Völkerrecht*. Tubingen: Medien Verlag Köhler, 1999.

Pharand, Donat. *International Straits, The Law of the Sea (4th Session September 1976)*, 7 Thesaurus Acroasium (1977) 64–100.

Pharand, Donat, and Leonard H. Legault. *The Northwest Passage: Arctic Straits*. International Straits of the World; 7. Dordrecht: Martinus Nijhoff, 1984.

Pirtle, Charles E. *Military Uses of Ocean Space and the Law of the Sea in the New Millenium*, 31 Ocean Development & International Law (2000) 7–45.

Pirtle, Charles E. *Transit Rights and U.S. Security Interests in International Straits: The Straits Debate Revisited*, 5 Ocean Development & International Law (1978) 477–497.

Polvinen, Tuomo. *Suomi kansainvälisessä politiikassa [1941–1947]. Jaltasta Pariisin rauhaan / 3, 1945–1947*. Porvoo; WSOY, 1981.

Potter, P.B. *The Doctrine of Servitudes in International Law*, 9 American Journal of International Law (1915): 627–641.

Prescott, J.R.V. *Political Frontiers and Boundaries*. London; Allen & Unwin, 1987.

Pufendorf, Samuel. *De Jure Naturae et Gentium, Libri Octo, 1688, English Translation by C. H. and W. A. Oldfather, Classics of International Law, No. 17*, edited by James Brown Scott. 1934.

Rauch, Elmar. *The Protocol Additional to the Geneva Conventions for the Protection of Victims of International Armed Conflicts and the United Nations Convention on the Law of the Sea: Repercussions of Naval Warfare*. 1984.

Regulations Governing the Visits of Men-of-War to Foreign Ports, 10 American Journal of International Law no. 3, Supplement: Official Documents (1916) 121–178.

Reisman, W. Michael. *The Regime of Straits and National Security: An Appraisal of International Law-Making*, 74 American Journal of International Law (1980) 48–76.

Reports of International Arbitral Awards. *Island of Palmas Case (or Miangas) (United States of America v. the Netherlands), Volume II* (1928).

Roach, J. Ashley. *Enforcement of International Rules and Standards of Navigational Safety in the Malacca and Singapore Straits*, 3 Singapore Journal of International and Comparative Law (1999) 323–336.

Roach, J. Ashley. *The Law of Naval Warfare at the Turn of Two Centuries*, 94 American Journal of International Law (2000) 64–77.

Roach, J. Ashley, and Robert W. Smith. *Excessive Maritime Claims*. Publications on Ocean Development; Vol. 73. Martinus Nijhoff, 2012.

Robertson Jr, Horace B. *Passage Through International Straits: A Right Preserved in the Third United Nations Conference on the Law of the Sea*, 20 Virginia Journal of International Law (1980) 801–857.

Robins, Graham. *Bomarsund: Imperiumin etuvartio*. Maarianhamina: Ahvenanmaan maakuntahallituksen museovirasto. 2004.

Robins, Graham. *Bomarsund och fredsavtalet i Paris. Fred som Provokation, Åland – fredens öar? Seminarium 19 Oktober 2006, Ålands Landskapsregering*. Mariehamn, 2007.

Ronzitti, Natalino. *The Law of Naval Warfare: A Collection of Agreements and Documents with Commentaries*. Dordrecht; Nijhoff, 1988.

Rosas, Allan. *The Åland Islands as a Demilitarised and Neutralised Zone,* in *Autonomy and Demilitarisation in International Law: The Åland Islands in a Changing Europe*, edited by Lauri; Hannikainen and Frank Horn, 23–40. The Hague: Kluwer Law International, 1997.

Rosenne, Shabtai. *Conference for the Codification of International Law (1930)*. Oceana Publications, INC/Dobbs Ferry, 1975.

Rothwell, Donald R. *International Straits*, in *The Oxford Handbook of the Law of the Sea*, edited by Donald Rothwell, Alex G Oude Elferink, Karen N Scott, and Tim Stephens, 114–133. Oxford University Press, 2015.

Rothwell, Donald R., and Tim Stephens. *The International Law of the Sea*. Oxford, 2010.

Rotkirch, Holger. *A Peace Institute on the War-Path: The Appilication of the Treaty on Open Skies to the Neutralized and Demilitarized Åland Islands and the Powers of the Åland Autonomy*, in *Nordic Cosmopolitanism – Essays in International Law for Martti Koskenniemi*, edited by Jarna Petman and Jan Klabbers, 61–88. Martinus Nijhoff Publishers, 2003.

Rotkirch, Holger. *The Demilitarization and Neutralization of the Aland Islands: A Regime "in European Interests" Withstanding Changing Circumstances*, 23 Journal of Peace Research, no. 4 (1986) 357–376.

Rozakis, Christos L., and Petros N. Stagos. *The Turkish Straits*. International Straits of the World; Vol. 9. Dordrecht: Martinus Nijhoff, 1987.

San Remo Manual on International Law Applicable to Armed Conflicts at Sea, 12 June 1994. 1994.

Schachte, William. L. Jr., and J. Peter A. Bernhardt. *International Straits and Navigational Freedoms*, 33 Virginia Journal of International Law (1993) 527–556.

Schüking, W. *Die Verwendung von Minen im Seekrieg*, Zeitschrift für Internationales Privat – und Öffentliches Recht (1906) 121–152.

Simonen, Katariina. *Suomi, Ahvenanmaa ja liittoutuminen*, 102 Lakimies (2004): 664–678.

Sjöstedt, Erik. *La Question des Iles d'Aland*. Paris, 1919.

Slonim, S. *The Right of Innocent Passage and the 1958 Geneva Conference on the Law of the Sea*, 5 Columbia Journal of Transnational Law (1966) 96–127.

Société des Nations, Secrétariat permanent. *Conference relative a la non-fortification et a la neutralisation des Iles d'Aland, tenue a Geneve, du 10 au 20 Octobre 1921: actes de la conference*. Geneve: Société des Nations, 1921.

Somers, Eddy. *The Legal Regime of the Danish Straits*, in *The Proceedings of the Symposium on the Straits Used for International Navigation, 16–17 November 2002, Ataköy Marina, Istanbul – Turkey*, edited by Bayram Öztürk and Reşat Özkan, 12–20. 2002.

Spiliopoulou Åkermark, Sia. *Åland's Demilitarisation and Neutralisation: Continuity and Change*, in *The Åland Example and Its Components – Relevance for International Conflict Resolution*, edited by Sia Spiliopoulou Åkermark, 50–71. 2011.

Spiliopoulou, Åkermark, Saila Heinikoski Sia, and Pirjo Kleemola-Juntunen. *Demilitarisation and International Law in Context: The Åland Islands*. Routledge, 2018.

Staël von Holstein, Lage. *Sverige och Åland*. Lund: C. W. K. Gleerups Förlag, 1916.

Stevenson, John R., and Bernard H. Oxman. *The Third United Nations Conference on the Law of the Sea: The 1974 Caracas Session*, 69 American Journal of International Law (1975) 1–30.

Stjernfelt, Bertil. *Ålands hav och öar – brygga eller barriär? Svensk-finsk försvarsfråga 1915–1945*. Marinlitteraturföreningen, 1991.

Suksi, Markku. *Ålands konstitution: en sammanställning av material och tolkningar i anslutning till självstyrelselag för Åland*. Åbo: Åbo Akademis förlag, 2005.

Suomen laivasto 1. Helsinki, 1968.

Suontausta, Tauno. *La situation juridique des îles d'Aland*, 13 Zeitschrift für ausländisches öffentliches Recht und Völkerrecht (1951) 741–742.

Säämänen, Juuso. *Operaatio "Kilpapurjehdus" Ahvenanmaan miehitysoperaatio kesällä 1941*, no. 12 (2005) 60–65.

Söderhjelm, J.O. *Démilitarisation et neutralisation des Iles d'Aland en 1856 et 1921.* Helsingfors, 1928.

'The First World War 1914–1918', in 'Most Dangerous Service': A Century of Royal Navy Submarines. http://www.lutonmodelboat.co.uk/history_submarines.html.

The Report of the Commission of Jurists, League of Nations Official Journal, no. 3 Supplement special (1920) 3–19.

Third United Nations Conference on the Law of the Sea, Volume I: Summary Records (Plenary and General Committee). http://legal.un.org/diplomaticconferences/1973_los/vol1.shtml.

Third United Nations Conference on the Law of the Sea, Volume II: Summary Records (1st, 2nd and 3rd Committee). http://legal.un.org/diplomaticconferences/1973_los/vol2.shtml.

Third United Nations Conference on the Law of the Sea, Volume III: Documents. http://legal.un.org/diplomaticconferences/1973_los/vol3.shtml.

Third United Nations Conference on the Law of the Sea, Volume IV: Third Session. http://legal.un.org/diplomaticconferences/1973_los/vol4.shtml.

Third United Nations Conference on the Law of the Sea, Volume VIII: Informal Composite Negotiating Tex. http://legal.un.org/diplomaticconferences/1973_los/vol8.shtml.

Third United Nations Conference on the Law of the Sea, Volume XVI: Eleventh Session. http://legal.un.org/diplomaticconferences/1973_los/vol16.shtml.

Treaty between Argentine Republic and Chile, Establishing the Neutrality of Straits of Magellan, 3 American Journal of International Law, Supplement: Official Documents, no. 2 (1903) 121–122.

Turtola, Martti. *Torniojoelta rajajoelle: Suomen ja Ruotsin salainen yhteistoiminta Neuvostoliiton hyökkäyksen varalle vuosina 1923–1940: puolustuspoliittinen vaihtoehto.* Porvoo: WSOY, 1984.

Ulkoasiainministeriö. *Ahvenanmaa Euroopan Unionissa, 176/2005.* 2005.

UN. Committee on the Peaceful Uses of the Seabed and the Ocean Floor beyond the Limits of National Jurisdiction. *Report of the Committee on the Peaceful Uses of the Sea-Bed and the Ocean Floor beyond the Limits of National Jurisdiction, Official Records, 26th Session Supplement No. 21 (A/8421).* 1971.

UN. Committee on the Peaceful Uses of the Seabed and the Ocean Floor beyond the Limits of National Jurisdiction. *Report of the Committee on the Peaceful Uses of the Sea-Bed Committee and the Ocean Floor Beyond the Limits of National Jurisdiction, Official Records, 28th Session, Supplement No. 21 (A/9021), Volume I.* 1973.

UN. Committee on the Peaceful Uses of the Seabed and the Ocean Floor beyond the Limits of National Jurisdiction. *Report of the Committee on the Peaceful Uses of the Sea-Bed Committee and the Ocean Floor Beyond the Limits of National Jurisdiction, Official Records, 28th Session, Supplement No. 21 (A/9021), Volume V.* 1973.

United Nations. *Yearbook of the International Law Commission 1952 Volume I, Summary Records of the Fourth Session 4 June–8 August 1952*. New York, 1958.

United Nations. *Yearbook of the International Law Commission 1955 Volume I, Summary Records of the Seventh Session 2 May—8 July 1955*. New York, 1960.

United Nations. *Yearbook of the International Law Commission 1956 Volume II, Documents of the Eighth Session Including the Report of the Commission to the General Assembly*. New York, 1957.

United Nations. *Yearbook of the International Law Commission 1949 Summary Records and Documents of the First Session Including the Report of the Commission to the General Assembly*. New York, 1956.

United Nations. *Yearbook of the International Law Commisson 1964 Volume II, Documents of the Sixteenth Session Including the Report of the Commission to the General Assembly*. New York, 1965.

United Nations (First) Conference on the Law of the Sea, Volume III: First Committee (Territorial Sea and Contiguous Zone).

Ünlü, Nihan. *The Legal Regime of the Turkish Straits*. International Straits of the World; 13. The Hague: Martinus Nijhoff Publishers, 2002.

US Department of State. *Papers Relating to the Foreign Relation of the United States, 1918. Russia. Volume II*. 1918. http://digital.library.wisc.edu/1711.dl/FRUS.FRUS1918Russiav02.

US Department of State. *Limits in the Seas No. 112, United States Responses to Excessive Maritime Claims*. 1992.

Vattel, Emmerich de. *Le droit des gens*. Leiden, 1758.

Visscher, C. de. *Le droit international des communications: cours professe a l'institut des hautes etudesi internationales de Paris (1921 et 1923)*. Gand, 1924.

Wahlbäck, Krister, Maija-Liisa Vuorjoki, Asko Vuorjoki. *Veljeys veitsenterällä*. 1968.

Westlake, J. *International Law, Part I, Peace*. 2nd ed. Cambridge University Press, 1910.

Wihtol, Erik, and Ohto Manninen. *Pohjois-Itämeren lukot: Ahvenanmaa ja Gotlanti, Neuvostolaivaston toiminta-alueen laajentuminen Itämerellä 1939–1941*, Sotilasaikakauslehti, no. 6–7 (1994) 61–65.

Wolfrum, Rüdiger. *Freedom of Navigation: New Challenges*, in *Freedom of Seas, Passage Rights and the 1982 Law of the Sea Convention*, edited by Myron H. Nordquist, Tommy T.B. Koh, and John Norton Moore, 79–102. 2009.

Yang, Haijiang. *Jurisdiction of the Coastal State over Foreign Merchant Ships in Internal Waters and the Territorial Sea*. Springer, 2006.

Yturriaga, Jose A. de. *Straits Used for International Navigation: A Spanish Perspective*. Publications on Ocean Development; 17. Dordrecht: Nijhoff, 1991.

Index